The behaviour of the labour market is widely seen as the cause of the UK's poor macroeconomic performance over the last thirty years. In this book, the functioning of the labour market is addressed by an international group of economists. They assemble micro- and macroeconomic evidence on the UK, and US, France and Germany, and discuss whether the UK labour market is different, and also if it has changed over time.

The microeconomic evidence is assessed by Blanchflower and Freeman and by Gregg and Machin. The Thatcher reforms to industrial relations, surveyed by Metcalf, appear to have increased inequality without producing a more flexible labour market. Gregory and Sandoval suggest that minimum wages might have helped alleviate the rise in inequality in the UK. The effects of the reforms of the 1980s are unclear. Minford and Riley suggest that they have had an impact, whilst Barrell, Pain and Young present evidence that little has changed. The micro- and macroeconomic approaches are complemented by Grubb's detailed survey of the effects of active labour market policies as well as by the overview paper by Anderton and Mayhew.

The UK labour market

The UK labour market

Comparative aspects and institutional developments

Edited by

RAY BARRELL
National Institute of Economic and Social Resarch

CAMBRIDGE
UNIVERSITY PRESS

Published by the Press Syndicate of the University of Cambridge
The Pitt Building, Trumpington Street, Cambridge CB2 1RP
40 West 20th Street, New York, NY 10011-4211, USA
10 Stamford Road, Oakleigh, Melbourne 3166, Australia

The National Institute of Economic and Social Research 1994

First published 1994

Printed in Great Britain by Bell and Bain Ltd., Glasgow

A catalogue record for this book is available from the British Library

Library of Congress cataloguing in publication data

The UK labour market: comparative aspects and institutional
developments / edited by Ray Barrell: [contributors, Bob Anderson
... et al.].
    p.   cm.
ISBN 0 521 46160 X
1. Labor market – Great Britain. I. Barrell, Ray. II. Anderton,
Bob.
HD5765.A6U378 1994
331.12′0941 – cc20 93-36552 CIP

ISBN 0 521 46160 X hardback
ISBN 0 521 46825 6 paperback

UP

Contents

Contents

Contributors

Bob Anderton *National Institute of Economic and Social Research, London*
Ray Barrell *National Institute of Economic and Social Research, London*
Professor David G Blanchflower *Dartmouth College, New Hampshire*
Professor Richard Freeman *National Bureau of Economic Research, Inc., Massachusetts*
Paul Gregg *National Institute of Economic and Social Research, London*
Dr Mary Gregory *St Hilda's College, Oxford*
David Grubb *OECD, Paris*
Dr Steve Machin *University College London and London School of Economics*
Ken Mayhew *Pembroke College, Oxford*
Professor David Metcalf *London School of Economics*
Professor Patrick Minford *University of Liverpool, Cardiff Business School and CEPR*
Nigel Pain *National Institute of Economic and Social Research, London*
Jonathan Riley *Cardiff Business School*
Véronique Sandoval *Centre d'Etude des Revenus et des Coûts, Paris*
Garry Young *National Institute of Economic and Social Research, London*

Introduction

RAY BARRELL

It is widely perceived that the macroeconomic performance of the United Kingdom over the last three decades has been poor. The UK experienced more than average increases in consumer price inflation in each of the three cycles which affected the advanced economies between 1970 and 1993. Inflation in the UK peaked at 24 per cent in 1975, well above the European average. There was a similar pattern in 1980 and 1990 when inflation rose to 18 and 8 per cent respectively. The average rate of output growth in the UK has also been rather poor and unemployment has risen relative to the rest of the advanced world. There are numerous competing explanations for this poor performance, but most concentrate on the functioning of the labour market.

The labour market in the UK was, by the end of the 1970s, characterised as inflexible, constrained by the behaviour of unions, and affected by the lethargy induced by high unemployment benefits. The 1980s saw a series of reforms that were designed to improve the functioning of the labour market. Benefits were reduced relative to income, and a sequence of labour market legislation gradually curtailed the power of trade unions. By the end of the decade the Secretary of State for Employment felt able to say: 'There can be no doubt about the transformation which has taken place in British industrial relations in the past decade.'[1] There is truth in this statement, but the consequences of the changes for economic performance are less easy to assess and are crucial to evaluation of the labour market reforms.

This book asks the question 'Is the UK labour market different?' There are three dimensions to this question. The transformation of industrial relations during the 1980s could have led to a better functioning labour market. We therefore have to ask the question. 'Has the UK labour market changed its behaviour over the last twenty years?' Similar events have afflicted (or benefited) similar countries in Europe, and it is of value to ask 'Is the UK labour market similar to those in Europe?' Similar ideologies and institutions have developed on both sides of the Atlantic, and outcomes may be similar in the UK and the US, and we must ask 'Is the UK labour market different from that in the US?' The chapters in this volume address all these issues, and allow us to draw some tentative conclusions.

This book contains the papers presented at a conference organised by the National Institute and the Centre for Economic Performance (CEP) at the Royal Society in London on 1 April, 1993. The initial impetus for the conference came from the Chancellor of the Exchequer and the National Economic Development Office (NEDO) in the Spring of 1992. NEDO wished to persuade a number of academics to join in the debate on the labour market. The UK was in the midst of a deep recession and it appeared that the labour market was still functioning badly. In June 1992 the government decided to abolish NEDO, a body that could be seen as the last vestige of the corporatist state built up under both Conservative and Labour governments in the 1960s and 1970s.

Some of the participants in the NEDO project decided that it was worth carrying on with a conference on labour markets even after the demise of the originating body. The National Institute and the CEP decided that they would keep the idea of the conference alive and the Department of Employment provided most of the funding. The initial organisers, Richard Jackman and Alex Bowen, had to step down, but they took an active role in the build-up to the conference. Five of the planned papers (those by Freeman, Grubb, Metcalf, Minford and Barrell) were retained. It was decided to give the conference a more microeconomic slant, and to address more directly the issues of poverty and low wages. To this end the papers by Gregg and Machin and Gregory were included. We also decided to include an overview paper which was jointly authored by Ken Mayhew, a former economics director of NEDO. The conference was chaired by John Fleming, then chief economist at the European Bank for Reconstruction and Development.

This book is organised into four sections. The first contains the overview paper by Anderton and Mayhew and reflects work undertaken at the National Institute, NEDO and Oxford. The second section is avowedly microeconomic in approach and contains papers by Blanchflower and Freeman, Gregg and Machin, and Metcalf. They are all concerned with the consequences of the reforms of the 1980s and especially with their effects on economic efficiency and inequality. In the third section, Gregory and Sandoval outline the differences in the scope and impact of minimum wages throughout Europe, whilst David Grubb casts a sceptical eye over the effectiveness of active labour market policies in reducing unemployment. The final section returns to the macroeconomic themes discussed in the overview. The paper by Barrell, Pain and Young suggests that there are both significant differences *and* similarities between the UK, France and West Germany, especially with respect to factor demands and wage formation. In the final chapter Minford and Riley put the view that, by 1986, the labour market reforms of the 1980s had cut sustainable unemployment to under one million in the UK. They then go on to explain why actual unemployment has been so high for the last eight years.

A comparative analysis of the UK labour market

The chapter by Anderton and Mayhew considers the differences between the UK and a representative selection of other countries. They have chosen what are often considered to be the two extremes: the US, which has evolved towards a free market, and Sweden, with a distinct corporatist structure. Both have experienced relatively low inflation and low unemployment throughout the 1970s and 1980s. The same cannot be said of the other comparator groups, France and Italy on the one hand and Germany and the Netherlands on the other. The former two countries experienced high inflation in the early 1980s and they have managed to reduce it, but at the cost of historically high unemployment. Germany and the Netherlands suffered less from inflation, but both experienced high unemployment in the early 1980s. Anderton and Mayhew present evidence to suggest that major economic indicators, such as inflation and GDP growth, have behaved in a more volatile fashion in the UK than in the other countries they study.

The UK labour market has clearly changed over the last twenty-five years. The drift away from manufacturing has been faster than elsewhere and, partly as a result, there has been a particularly marked movement into part-time and self-employment. All of the changes in legislation in the 1980s pushed the economy towards a labour market more like that in the US, and towards more decentralised bargaining, but without increasing product and labour market flexibility. However, Anderton and Mayhew show that labour market transitions are very different in the US, where rates of inflow into, and outflows from, unemployment are much higher than in the other countries in their comparator group. The move towards part-time and female employment in the UK should in some ways enhance the flexibility of the labour market because it should increase the ability of employers to vary hours. However, these influences may be relatively unimportant as both German and Italian employers have had much more ability to vary the hours of full-time employees than we observe in the UK, and the movement to both more flexible and more idiosyncratic working practices has been a common one in this group of countries.

Sustainable unemployment can be analysed in many ways and Anderton and Mayhew argue that we should look at both institutional detail and empirical evidence on the NAIRU. They discuss the work of Soskice (1990) and Calmfors and Driffill (1988). The latter authors argue that both centralised and decentralised labour markets work better than the intermediate cases. Soskice puts forward a case for the primacy of coordinated over uncoordinated wage setting and argues that the successful countries in Anderton and Mayhews' group, that is Germany, the Netherlands and Sweden, all display considerable centralisation. Anderton and Mayhew support these conclusions and go on to pull together disparate evidence on the NAIRU and on the speed of adjustment to equilibrium in differing economies. All the evidence points to a stubbornly high level of sustainable unemployment throughout much of Europe. It also suggests that real wages remain less flexible in the UK than elsewhere and that as a consequence it is likely to take longer for the mechanisms of the market to reduce unemployment in the UK than elsewhere. Anderton and Mayhew conclude that the UK labour market has remained less flexible than labour markets elsewhere. The chapters in the remainder of the volume attempt to assess and extend this conclusion.

Microeconomic evidence on the labour market

The second section of the book contains two chapters containing fresh insights into the UK, and a third by Metcalf that is a wide-ranging survey of the effects of the transformation of British industrial relations in the 1980s. All three rely heavily on microeconometric data sets either for their original work or for their comparative analysis. This style of statistical analysis has become more popular as computing power has developed, allowing a number of new insights into the functioning of the labour market. Work based in this area must inevitably rely on large cross-section and panel data sets. Such data are more freely available for the US and the UK (and to an extent for France) than elsewhere and hence the comparator group in these three chapters is sometimes limited. However, the Labour Force Surveys and other cross-sections have been available on a consistent basis for some time now in the UK and hence it is possible to build up a sequence of pictures of a changing labour market.

Blanchflower and Freeman analyse the changing pattern of labour market transitions in order to detect improvements in the micro-functioning of the labour market. A well functioning labour market should have a rapid transition from unemployment to employment. The authors construct a set of matrices of labour market transitions from the Labour Force Surveys for 1979 and 1990 for both men and women, allowing them to undertake a 'before' and 'after' comparison. They are able to show that for men transition probabilities from unemployment to work have fallen, suggesting a decline in the efficiency of the labour market and an increase in steady state unemployment from 5 to 7 per cent. The labour market reforms do appear to have improved the labour market position of women, with a more rapid transition out of unemployment and a higher steady state participation level.

Changes in the role and power of unions, the reduction in the costs of dismissing labour associated with redundancy legislation and increased privatisations were meant to help make employment more responsive to changes in demand. An analysis of employment data from the Workplace Industrial Relations Surveys (WIRS) of 1980 and 1990 provides only weak evidence of such a change. The micro-evidence gives little support to the belief that the labour market is functioning better now than in 1979. A more freely functioning labour market should produce smaller rent-related differentials in pay, and hence the importance of skills, education and training should be enhanced as explanations of the dispersion of earnings. Blanchflower and Freeman use the General Household Survey for 1979 and 1990/91 to analyse changes in the pattern of earnings and they find that the dispersion has increased. This is in part because of increased regional and industrial dispersion, but it also reflects a large increase in the unexplained dispersion of income, which cannot be attributed to the better functioning of the labour market.

Blanchflower and Freeman conclude that the Thatcher reforms may have slightly improved the functioning of the labour market and increased the responsiveness of wages and employment to changes in demand, but that these effects can only be described as a glimmer of light, not a powerful midsummer sunrise. The reforms have been accompanied by a considerable increase in the dispersion of earnings and have produced 'the worst of two possible worlds: the massive wage inequality of the decentralised US labour market together with high and lengthy spells of unemployment, European style'.

The rise in inequality in the distribution of earnings in the UK is addressed, from a comparative perspective, by Gregg and Machin. As far as can be ascertained, inequality in the UK is still less pronounced than in the US, Canada or Australia, but during the 1980s its has moved past the other European countries and is now closer to the majority of the English-speaking world.

Gregg and Machin undertake an analysis of the evolution of inequality in the UK, using a variety of microeconomic data sets. They use a combination of the Census of Production, the New Earnings Survey and the Labour Force Survey in order to analyse the factors affecting the change in the distribution of earnings in the 1980s. The residual dispersion of earnings not explained by structural factors is found to have increased and this is particularly true for non-manual workers. There have also been changes in the relative demand for different types of labour in manufacturing, with a shift to non-manual workers where the residual dispersion has risen most. This reflects a shift away from uneducated labour, with the returns to education rising. Skill upgrading has taken place mainly within industries and hence industry-level shocks are not particularly important in providing an explanation for the rise in income dispersion. As in the US, this reflects the effects of skill-biased technical progress. Neither changes in the microeconomic structure of demand for goods, nor macroeconomic factors, such as import penetration, appear to have had much impact on the distribution of earnings.

The institutional structure of unions, labour market legislation and minimum wages has also changed in the 1980s and Gregg and Machin suggest that this has increased the dispersion of earnings. They report on work undertaken by Gosling and Machin (1993) using the Workplace Industrial Relations Survey (WIRS) supporting the widely held belief that trade unions compress wage structures. Indeed the decline in unionisation in the 1980s appears to explain one fifth of the rise in inequality amongst the semi-skilled.

The effects on the dispersion of earnings of the gradual dismantling of Wages Councils appear to be clear. Minimum wages amongst the low-paid help support the incomes of those at the bottom end of the earnings distribution. Gregg and Machin report on Manning and Machin's (1992) finding that the removal of wage protection accounts for up to a fifth of the increase in the dispersion of income amongst the low-paid. This might not have had an effect on the distribution of incomes if employment had increased significantly as a result of the fall in relative real wages, but it is not clear that it has done so. Manning (1993b) argues that there is evidence of monopsony elements in the labour market, with many firms facing upward-sloping supply curves of labour. This is particularly so for female workers who are considerably less geographically mobile (and less skilled) than men. Equal pay legislation appears to have raised the earnings of women relative to men, without reducing employment levels.

International comparisons allow Gregg and Machin to evaluate the relative importance of the factors affecting the UK. Inequality started to rise earlier in the US than in the UK. Skill-biased technical progress appears to have been a major factor in the relative decline in wages for the unskilled, even though the unskilled proportion of the workforce has been declining. Trade union density has fallen markedly in the US and minimum wages have been frozen in nominal terms for some years. All these factors appear to have led to more inequality. In contrast, earnings inequality has hardly changed in France and has actually fallen in Italy. Both countries have effective minimum wage schemes.

British industrial relations changed in the 1980s, and David Metcalf in chapter 4 details the reasons and surveys a number of studies based on the WIRS in 1980, 1984 and 1990. No consensus exists concerning the extent and consequences of change in British industrial relations. A number of factors conspired to reduce union membership to around 40 per cent of all employees in 1990 compared with 53 per cent in 1979. The fall in density does not fully measure the decline in union influence: between 1984 and 1990 the proportion of establishments recognising unions for collective bargaining fell from two thirds to one half, and new recognitions declined. Closed shops covered a fifth of all workers in 1979, but by 1990 they had all but withered away. All of these changes can be seen as being driven in part by the Thatcher Revolution and the associated legislation. Decentralisation of bargaining has resulted, and it can be argued that this has given managers back the right to manage. Collective bargains now cover only 47 per cent of employees, compared with over 60 per cent for most of the previous thirty years. National agreements have collapsed or have been greatly reduced in influence since 1986, whilst multi-union agreements within plants have also declined.

Not all bargainers are members of unions and individuals may have some bargaining power if their firm-specific human capital is large enough. This may give 'insiders' some bargaining power and they will be able to capture some of the rent earned by the firm. Evidence from the 1990 WIRS suggests that many individuals do have some bargaining power and the growth of performance- related pay, or profit sharing, may reflect this.

There is a considerable amount of evidence that suggests that unionised workplaces pay higher wages than comparable non-union ones. On average in 1984 collective bargaining raised the earnings of semi-skilled workers by around 8 per cent. This mark-up, however, was largely confined to firms with high union density or pre-entry closed shops. The rent to be bargained over will itself depend upon product market conditions. Stewart (1990) was able to show that, in the vast majority of establishments facing competitive market conditions, the union mark-up was very low, and that international competition constrains unions[2] because rents are more limited.

The mark-up may have also been declining over time, although only slightly. Analysis of the 1984 and 1990 WIRS suggests that the union mark-up has fallen from 8.8 per cent to 6.2 per cent. This finding is supported by Gregg and Machin (1992) using a different data set.

The reduction in the power of unions should have helped the economy move down its demand curve for labour to a higher level of sustainable employment and a lower level of sustainable unemployment. However, there is very little evidence that this has happened. Unemployment has stayed stubbornly high in the UK and inflation began to rise in 1989/90 as soon as unemployment fell below two million. It appears that the assault on unions has done little to improve macroeconomic performance. The authors of the three chapters in this section all agree that the government has achieved virtually all that it set out to do in terms of changing institutions, but that the consequences have not always been those intended. 'Either the government got it wrong concerning the link between pay-setting institutions and the employment outcome ... or ... its macroeconomic policy must be a shambles' (Metcalf). Of course it could be argued that the government has not gone far enough or that we have not waited long enough. Blanchflower and Freeman regard this as implausible. They argue that labour market reforms cannot be expected to work in isolation 'The Thatcher reforms might have done wonders in the [tight labour markets of the] 1950s–1960s, but could not deliver in the 1980s-1990s because of the high rate of unemployment'. What have we gained then? Gregg and Machin conclude 'that if [we wish] to go further down 'flexibility' road then we are likely to induce further inequities in the distribution of earnings and incomes'. The UK has experienced major labour market reforms and an increase in inequality, but has failed to offset the resulting costs by moving to a more flexible US-style labour market in which rapid transitions between employment states would relieve much of the penury of the newly unemployed.

Labour market institutions

Labour market institutions and active government policies affect both the functioning of the labour market and the level of unemployment. David Grubb analyses the effects of active labour market policies. He concentrates on five areas of policy activity: administration and public employment service work, training, youth measures, job creation and measures to place the disabled. These policies can be structured so that their combined effect is to attenuate the rise in unemployment during a recession and ensure rapid transition through the state of unemployment.

Unfortunately not all active policies reduce the incentive to stay in unemployment. For instance the guarantee of a 'relief' job in the public sector at the end of the benefit entitlement period may reduce the incentive to search for work whilst on benefit. It is also possible to design active policies that produce an incentive for their managers to raise unemployment. This is particularly common where there are wage subsidies for taking on the long-term unemployed for short periods. Grubb points out many problems with active labour market policies and it is clear that their effects are not always beneficial.

Grubb claims that in its heyday active labour market policy in Scandinavia came close to the ideal. It was an essential component of a set of policies which came close to eliminating unemployment whilst simultaneously providing a safety net against poverty. The policy worked well over the two oil shocks, but growing political pressure has meant that it has begun to break down. Increasing numbers of the placements became passive jobs in the public sector causing the share of government expenditure in output to rise significantly. Of course, this may still have been a much better way of dealing with the effects of the three recessions than that adopted in the countries that allowed what appear to be irreversible steps up in the number of long-term unemployed. However, the slow expansion of the public sector and the concomitant rise in the tax burden has gradually lost popular support, and unemployment has risen to 6 per cent in Norway, 7 per cent in Sweden and 17 per cent in Finland in mid-1993.

The European Commission has been taking steps to change labour market institutions and the provisions of the Social Chapter of the Maastricht Treaty would harmonise and extend workers' rights throughout Europe. The provision for minimum wage regulations is at the heart of the Chapter, and Gregory and Sandoval discuss the structure of minimum wages and their effects on low pay throughout Europe. The incidence of low pay varies considerably across Europe and governments have adopted different approaches to it. Seven countries have instituted national minimum wages. In France, the Netherlands, Luxembourg, Spain and Portugal these are set by the government and have the force of law, whilst in Belgium and Greece they are set by national collective accord. Minimum wages can also be set through sectoral minima. These can either be negotiated, as in Denmark, Germany and Italy, or set by the government as in the UK and Ireland. The negotiated minima in Germany and Italy are virtually universal and are effectively enforced. Regulation in the UK was always patchy and a decision has been taken to follow the third way and abandon all attempts to set minima.

There is little evidence that minimum wages raise unemployment, except where they fail to discriminate between sectors, regions and age groups. In France the coverage of the SMIC has been increased in the 1980s and there has been an increase in the complexity of permitted departures that are designed to deal with local labour market pressures. In Italy nationally negotiated minima apply. The effects on employment differ between these two countries. The complex and well administered SMIC appears to have little effect on employment but does raise wages, whilst the Italian system is rather undiscriminating and probably raises both youth unemployment and unemployment in the South. Gregory and Sandoval present a convincing case in favour of minimum wages as a means of reducing the incidence of low pay with few offsetting costs.

The macroeconomic determination of unemployment

The sustainable level of unemployment in the UK appears to be high. In the final section of the book Minford and Riley claim that this is an illusion, and that labour market reforms and the decline in union power have changed behaviour, whilst Barrell, Pain and Young present some evidence to support the alternative proposition that little has changed. The microeconomic evidence discussed in section two does help throw some light on these issues. Blanchflower and Freeman use evidence on labour market transitions to estimate that in equilibrium male unemployment would settle down to around 7 per cent. This provides a useful benchmark against which macroeconomic estimates can be judged. Metcalf presents evidence that the union wage mark-up has fallen from 8.8 to 6.2 per cent in the 1980s, and that coverage has fallen by 10 per cent or more of the workforce. The decline in union power will therefore have reduced average real wages by 0.5–1 per cent. This will of course influence the sustainable level of unemployment, but the scale of the effect is likely to be very limited. A fall in real wages of this magnitude is likely to have reduced sustainable unemployment by 0.5–1.5 per cent, according to Britton (1993) and Barrell, Caporale and Sefton (1993).

We can look at the aggregate labour market by analysing the determination of wages, by investigating the demand for labour or by studying the supply of labour (or do any two of these). Barrell, Pain and Young look at both the demand for labour and the determination of wages in a European context. They find that there are significant similarities as well as differences in the demand for labour in the UK, France and Germany. German labour demand reacts more rapidly to changes in factor prices, reflecting the ability of German producers to rely on a more stable macroeconomic environment. German producers also seem to take a price leadership role in their markets. Changes in international competitiveness have a greater impact on employment in the UK and France.

The results for the process of wage formation and the associated determination of the level of sustainable unemployment produced by Barrell, Pain and Young are obtained using the approaches to the analysis of wage determination advocated by Layard *et al.* (1991) and Manning (1993a). All three countries display significant, long-run negative effects from unemployment onto real wages. The more commonly used specification advocated by Layard *et al.* (1991) suggests that real wages in Germany are considerably more flexible than those in the UK. This may reflect the adaptation of institutions and customs to a more stable economic environment, or it may be the result of a different and more cooperative bargaining structure. More flexible real wages, along with a more rapid response to changes in factor prices, suggest that the problem of macroeconomic management in Germany has been somewhat easier than in the rest of Europe. There does appear to be a role for supply-side factors such as the relative level of benefits and the influence of trade unions. However, the evidence is somewhat mixed, and pooling information across countries provides little support for a strong role for either factor.

Barrell, Pain and Young suggest that the equilibrium level of unemployment is between 7 and 8 per cent for the UK, 5.5–7 per cent for Germany and probably in the same range for France. These levels are well below the current rate of unemployment in these three countries but they are well above that experienced in the US. The research reported in this volume suggests that this is because technical progress appears to be skill-biased. This has led to falling real wages for the unskilled in the US, where unemployment benefits do not last for long periods, whilst in Europe it has led to high unemployment rates for the unskilled.

Barrell, Pain and Young conclude that the 'supply side' policies adopted in the 1980s seem to have had little effect on the macroeconomic functioning of the labour market. The reduction in benefits in the UK cut the replacement ratio from 43 per cent to 25 per cent of average earnings between the late 1970s and the early 1990s. This is clearly a major factor in the increase in poverty in the UK and it will have been one of the reasons why the relative pay of the bottom decile of the workforce has deteriorated so much (see Blanchflower and Freeman, and Gregg and Machin, in this volume). Barrell, Pain and Young estimate that this significant reduction in the relative incomes of the unemployed has produced a fall of less than 0.5 per cent in sustainable unemployment. They also suggest that the significant reduction of union density in the UK between the late 1970s and the early 1990s has probably reduced sustainable unemployment by 1.5 points at most.

The union reforms of the 1980s are the major factor behind Minford and Riley's claim that equilibrium unemployment has fallen to around 600,000 in the UK. They base this claim on the 'reduced form' equation for unemployment implied by their structural model of the wage-price system embedded in the Liverpool model of the UK. They have estimated a supply curve for labour containing both benefits and unionisation effects. A 1 per cent rise in benefits causes the real wage to rise by 1 per cent in the long run, whilst a rise in labour supply has a small negative effect on wages. They find an effect from unionisation, and changes in union density in the 1980s are the major force driving their estimated 2½ million fall in equilibrium unemployment between 1982 and 1992, contributing about 60-70 per cent of the explanation.

As Minford and Riley comment, their explanation could not be more different from either the generality of belief in the UK or the general view expressed in this collection. They contend that the microeconomic rigidities of the early 1980s have disappeared, and that the supply side is working well, and it is unfortunate that we have not yet seen the rewards in terms of low inflation *and* low unemployment. The macroeconomic policies adopted in the late 1980s did not help the economy move smoothly towards equilibrium. Financial liberalisation and tax cuts helped propel the economy towards equilibrium rather too rapidly. It takes time for new (and existing unused) capacity to come on stream and a rapid expansion of demand could bring the economy up against a temporary capacity constant. This would cause inflation to rise even though the economy was not at full employment. The boom of the late 1980s would have been more successful if it had been slower to take off and had been associated with a significant increase in investment that would have created the required capacity.

Actual unemployment can 'temporarily' diverge from equilibrium for long periods of time because there is considerable nominal inertia in the economic system. Minford and Riley suggest that it can take up to three years before the full effects of a change in equilibrium unemployment are fully reflected in actual unemployment. There are also shocks to demand whose effects can prove very persistent. In particular the high long-term real interest rates that were experienced whilst the UK was in the ERM may have had a significant effect on the temporary equilibrium level of unemployment. A combination of a looser monetary policy and a slower expansion of demand should allow the UK to approach equilibrium unemployment without a significant increase in inflation. Minford and Riley contend that the recovery that started in 1992/3 could last for some years and, if managed well, unemployment in the UK could fall slowly to below one million.

Conclusion

The generality of views in this volume is that the changes to the UK labour market in the 1980s have not had much impact on macroeconomic performance. Most authors agree that the Thatcher reforms have had very little effect on unemployment or wage formation. There are also strong similarities with developments elsewhere, especially those in the US where there has been a comparable increase in the degree of inequality. Reductions in benefits and union power have changed the distribution of earnings but they do not appear to have produced the desired goal of being able to achieve low inflation with low unemployment.

Notes

1 *Hansard* 166(39), 29 January 1990, col 38.
2 We should, however, be careful in extending this result and basing policy on it. The wholesale removal of trade barriers may not reduce rents. Freer competition may increase international specialisation and hence lower the (absolute) elasticity of demand for the products produced in any one country. This would give scope for higher rents and more room for bargaining.

References

Barrell, R., Caporale, G. and Sefton, J. (1993), 'Prospects for European unemployment' in Grieve-Smith, J. and Michie, J., *Unemployment in Europe: Policies for Growth*, Academic Press.

Britton, A. (1993), 'Two routes to full employment', *National Institute Economic Review*, 144, May 1993.

Calmfors, L. and Driffill, J. (1988), 'Centralisation of wage bargaining and macroeconomic performance', *Economic Policy*, 6.

Gosling, A. and Machin, S. (1993), 'Trade unions and the dispersion of earnings in UK establishments, 1980-1990', Centre for Economic Performance, London School of Economics, Discussion Paper no. 140.

Gregg, P. and Machin, S. (1992), 'Unions, the demise of the closed shop and wage growth in the 1980s', *Oxford Bulletin of Economics and Statistics*, 54(1), February, 53–72.

Layard, P., Nickell, S. and Jackman, R. (1991), *Unemployment: Macroeconomic Performance and the Labour Market*, Oxford University Press.

Manning, A. (1993a), 'Wage bargaining and the Phillips Curve: the identification and specification of aggregate wage equations', *Economic Journal*, 103, 98–118.

Manning, A. (1993b), 'The Equal Pay Act as an experiment to test theories of the labour market', mimeo, London School of Economics, February 1993.

Manning, A. and Machin, S. (1992), 'Minimum wages, wage dispersion and employment: evidence from the UK wages councils', Centre for Economic Performance, London School of Economics, Discussion Paper no. 80.

Soskice, D. (1990), 'Wage determination: the changing role of institutions in advanced industrialised countries', *Oxford Review of Economic Policy*, 6, 4.

Stewart, M. (1990), 'Union wage differentials, product market influences and the division of rents', *Economic Journal*, 100, December.

1 A comparative analysis of the UK labour market

BOB ANDERTON AND KEN MAYHEW[1]

Introduction

This chapter considers the major differences between the UK labour market institutions and those elsewhere. We analyse the differences in policies that may have produced these divergences. We also discuss whether these policies and institutions affect macroeconomic outcomes. The UK is compared to the US, Germany, France, Italy, the Netherlands and Sweden. The sample of countries represents a broad spectrum of labour markets which diverge in terms of performance and policy approach. The US represents the closest approximation to a free market economy. Its achievement of both low inflation and low unemployment over the last twenty years provides an interesting contrast to the European experience. Sweden, whose distinct corporatist structure is often cited as the major reason for its good performance, has also achieved very low unemployment and inflation in the last two decades. The EC countries — Germany, France, Italy and the Netherlands — represent some of the UK's major trading partners with whom an economic and monetary union may be formed. Comparisons with this group of countries will inform us about the extent of UK labour market convergence.[2] Throughout this chapter particular attention is given to how developments in the last decade have affected such comparisons.

We first compare key macroeconomic and labour market statistics and follow this with a discussion of the structure and nature of the workforce, disaggregating unemployment into age and gender and looking at employment by sector. We then compare institutional and legal characteristics with particular attention devoted to the structure of bargaining systems, trade union density, employment protection and minimum wages. We go on to consider more fundamental indicators of labour market performance such as sustainable unemployment, real wage flexibility and the persistence of unemployment.

Comparison of macroeconomic and labour market statistics

Over the past century unemployment rates have reached high levels in particular periods, such as the slump of the 1930s, but they have not trended upwards over the very long run. Figures 1.1 and 1.2 show that the last dozen years have been associated with unusually high unemployment rates in some countries in our sample but that experience has been diverse. Unemployment for the US and Sweden shows no discernible trend, whilst the number of people without jobs in most of the EC countries has been in-

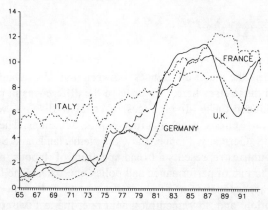

Figure 1.1 Unemployment rates for the UK, Germany, France and Italy
Source: OECD *Labour Force Statistics*

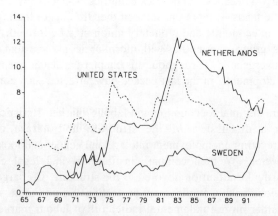

Figure 1.2 Unemployment rates for the US, Sweden and the Netherlands
Source: OECD *Labour Force Statistics*

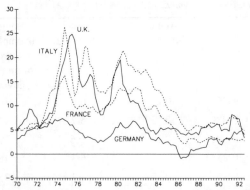

Figure 1.3 Annual growth rate of consumers' expenditure deflator for the UK, Germany, France and Italy
Source: OECD *Quarterly National Accounts*

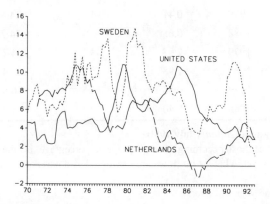

Figure 1.4 Annual growth rate of consumers' expenditure deflator for the US, Sweden and the Netherlands
Source: OECD *Quarterly National Accounts*

creasing since the mid-1970s. In some countries unemployment rose in two distinct steps around the time of the two oil price shocks of 1973–4 and 1979–80. These two episodes were associated with the implementation of deflationary policies designed to neutralise the inflationary effects of the oil price hikes.

The relatively higher unemployment rates of the EC countries in the 1980s might suggest that the level of activity was low relative to equilibrium unemployment. Figures 1.3 and 1.4 show a fall in inflation in the first half of the 1980s which is consistent with this analysis. However, in the sec-

Table 1.1   *The structure of unemployment*

		Annual inflows(a)	Annual outflows(a)	Long-term unemployment as a proportion of total unemployment(b)
France	1979	0.27	6.6	30.3
	1988	0.33	5.7	44.8
Germany	1979	0.18	19.6	19.9
	1988	0.26	6.3	46.7
Italy	1979	0.17	8.3	35.8
	1988	0.18	2.3	69.0
Netherlands	1979	0.29	-	27.1
	1988	0.23	-	50.0
UK	1979	0.41	14.3	24.8
	1988	0.68	9.5	44.7
US	1979	2.07	43.5	4.2
	1988	1.98	45.7	7.4
Sweden	1979	0.58	34.5	6.8
	1988	0.40	30.4	8.2

Source: OECD *Employment Outlook,* July 1990.
(a) Inflows are defined as those becoming unemployed as a percentage of the working age population (15–64), whereas outflows are expressed as a percentage of total unemployment.
(b) Unemployed for one year and over.

ond half of the decade inflation stopped falling even though unemployment remained high. Furthermore, inflation in the US followed a similar profile even though the unemployment rate returned to previous levels.

The stubborn persistence of unemployment separates the EC countries from the US and Sweden. Table 1.1 demonstrates that this is reflected in different structures of unemployment between these two groups of countries. Apart from the US, the rates of inflow into unemployment are similar in our various countries. However, the rate of outflow from unemployment is far higher in Sweden and the US. Furthermore, not only is the absolute probability of leaving unemployment relatively low in the EC countries, it has actually fallen in the late 1980s relative to the 1970s. Higher unemployment in the EC countries is not so much the result of people frequently los-

Table 1.2 *Volatility of inflation, GDP growth and the unemployment rate*

	Inflation	GDP growth	Unemployment rate
UK	0.57	1.39	0.49
Germany	0.52	0.88	0.47
France	0.51	0.59	0.42
Netherlands	0.65	-	0.42
Sweden	0.35	-	0.35
Italy	0.48	0.95	0.26
US	0.38	0.97	0.20

Source: GDP: OECD *Quarterly National Accounts.*
Notes: We have used the coefficient of variation as our measure of volatility. Sample period 1971Q1–1992Q4. Inflation as charts 1.3–1.4. Unemployment as charts 1.1–1.2. GDP growth: percentage change over previous quarter.

ing jobs, it is more to do with a lower probability of finding a job having once become unemployed. Table 1.1 shows that this is associated with much longer unemployment duration in the EC countries. Those unemployed for more than twelve months represent about 50 per cent of total unemployment in the EC countries compared to below 10 per cent in the US and Sweden.

Thus far we have described the UK labour market as having similar characteristics to the EC countries, whilst the US and Sweden appear to be outliers. But the UK is different in several important respects. First, the UK's inflation performance has been relatively poor. Second, UK unemployment has been relatively more volatile around an upward trend. Table 1.2 shows attempts to calibrate the volatility of inflation, GDP and the unemployment rate for the countries in our sample. According to this measure the UK is evidently a relatively volatile economy.

The UK exhibited strong manufacturing productivity growth in the 1980s. This is reflected in the low growth of UK trend unit labour costs in the middle of the last decade. Figures 1.5 and 1.6 show that even though growth in prices in the UK was faster than in Germany in the mid-1980s, manufacturing unit labour costs grew less rapidly. However, as strong output growth came to an end around 1989, growth in UK unit labour costs began to accelerate. Furthermore, German unit labour costs experienced greater stability even under the strain of reunification. French unit labour costs grew

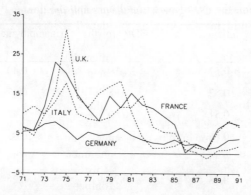

Figure 1.5 Annual growth rate of normalised unit labour costs in national currencies for the UK, Germany, France and Italy
Source: *Monthly Review of External Trade Statistics*

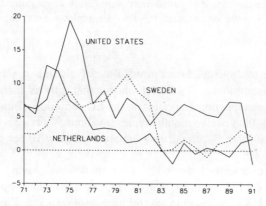

Figure 1.6 Annual growth rate of normalised unit labour costs in national currencies for the US, Sweden and the Netherlands
Source: *Monthly Review of External Trade Statistics*

much more slowly than the UK's from 1986 onwards and, in contrast to the UK, this was achieved through a low (and steady) rate of inflation rather than via strong productivity growth.

Structure of the workforce, employment and unemployment

In this section we concentrate on the relationship between labour market flexibility and the structure of the workforce, employment and unemployment. We compare participation rates by age and gender, the sectoral composition of employment, the use of part-time hours and the degree of self-employment and unemployment by age and gender. The increased participation of women over the last twenty years has several implications. It has been associated with increased part-time employment in service sector jobs and will affect the flexibility and skills of the labour force. More part-time workers may allow employers to vary hours rather than employment and hence reduce the volatility of unemployment. On the other hand, the general trend away from male manufacturing full-time employment to female service sector part-time employment may require a less skilled labour force. Hence labour hoarding may decline and unemployment may become more volatile. Flexibility of hours may imply a better productivity performance and improve international competitiveness but product quality may not be enhanced by using a less educated workforce. Conversely, labour flexibility may be decreased by increased female participation as increased dependence of households upon two incomes, combined with a high degree of home ownership in countries such as the UK, may discourage the geographical mobility of labour.

The composition of unemployment also provides insights about the performance of the labour market. A high male–female unemployment ratio may indicate stronger downward pressure on wages when employment falls, suggesting a lower level of sustainable unemployment than would otherwise be the case. A relatively high incidence of youth unemployment may indicate structural deficiencies as problems of insufficient aggregate demand should spread unemployment evenly across all age categories. For example, minimum wage legislation may impede flexibility of young persons' relative wages (see Hamermesh, 1985, for a useful survey).

Participation

Many factors can affect the decision to participate in the labour force. The major choice facing youths is either to enter the labour force or to further their education. High youth unemployment or high real returns to education will encourage them to choose the latter. Female participation may be particularly affected by the high unemployment rates of the past two decades, with women either being 'discouraged' by the low probability of finding a job or finding that they have to be 'added' to the workforce to supplement family income. Greenhalgh (1977), Corry and Roberts (1974) and McNabb (1977) all show that discouraged worker effects are significant determinants of female participation. Other obvious influences on female participation are the trend towards smaller families and increased opportunities for part-time work. Male participation rates have generally responded to opportunities to shorten working lives via early retirement and longer

Table 1.3 *Participation rates*

		Males			Females			Total partici-pation
		Youth	Adults	Total	Youth	Adults	Total	
US	1972	73.4	93.9	89.3	53.0	50.7	51.6	70.1
	1991	70.5	92.3	87.1	62.0	74.0	69.6	78.2
UK	1972	78.0	95.6	93.6	62.3	56.9	56.2	74.8
	1991	80.8	93.4	88.4	72.0	72.9	68.2	78.3
Germany	1972	71.4	96.0	90.1	63.2	49.6	49.3	69.1
	1989	63.1	92.1	81.4	58.2	62.6	55.9	68.8
France	1972	57.9	97.0	86.5	46.0	52.5	50.5	68.5
	1991	38.6	95.3	75.7	31.6	73.7	58.1	66.8
Italy	1972	50.1	93.7	80.2	33.4	28.5	28.2	53.7
	1991	45.3	90.7	75.5	39.1	49.9	44.3	59.8
Netherlands	1972	62.6	94.9	85.3	52.4	24.3	30.8	58.3
	1991	63.0	93.6	80.3	61.3	60.8	54.5	67.6
Sweden	1972	67.1	94.2	89.9	60.8	67.7	63.2	76.7
	1991	65.3	94.6	88.1	64.4	90.5	82.6	85.4

Source: OECD *Labour Force Statistics*.
(a) The participation rate for a given age group is defined as the ratio of the total labour force for the age group divided by the total population for the age group.

periods spent in education. The former has been influenced by higher real wages allowing substitution towards leisure and the latter has been helped by improved access to education.

Over the last twenty years the trend in our sample of countries has been towards increased female participation accompanied by a decline in male participation. This has generally been true for both youths and adults although female youth participation (16–24-year-olds) has grown less rapidly than female adult participation (25–54-year-olds).[3] Female youth participation has in fact fallen or remained fairly static in Germany, France and Sweden.

The UK has the third highest female participation rate of the countries considered here. Sweden has by far the highest and Italy has the lowest. However, the UK is an outlier in terms of male and female youth participation rates, both of which are higher than in any other country. UK

Table 1.4 *Size and composition of part-time employment, 1979-90*

		Total employ- ment (a)	Male employ- ment (a)	Female employ- ment (a)	Women's share in part-time employment
France	1979	8.2	2.5	16.7	82.2
	1983	9.7	2.6	20.0	84.4
	1990	12.0	3.5	23.8	83.1
Germany	1979	11.4	1.5	27.6	91.6
	1983	12.6	1.7	30.0	91.9
	1990	13.2	2.1	30.6	90.5
Italy	1979	5.3	3.0	10.6	61.4
	1983	4.6	2.4	9.4	64.8
	1990	5.7	3.1	10.9	64.7
Netherlands (b)	1979	16.6	5.5	44.0	76.4
	1983	21.4	7.2	50.1	77.3
	1990	33.2	15.8	61.7	70.4
Sweden	1979	23.6	5.4	46.0	87.5
	1983	24.8	6.3	45.9	86.6
	1990	23.2	7.3	40.5	83.7
UK	1979	16.4	1.9	39.0	92.8
	1983	19.4	3.3	42.4	89.6
	1990	21.8	5.0	43.8	87.0
US	1979	16.4	9.0	26.7	67.8
	1983	18.4	10.8	28.1	66.8
	1990	16.9	10.0	25.2	67.6

Sources: France, Germany, Italy, the United Kingdom: Eurostat, Labour Force Sample Survey. Netherlands: data provided by the Central Bureau of Statistics. Sweden: National Central Bureau of Statistics, The Labour Force Survey. United States: US Department of Labor, Bureau of Labor Statistics, Employment and Earnings.
(a) Part-time employment expressed as a percentage of the employment category.
(b) The series for the Netherlands has a break in 1985.

youth participation, particularly among males, has grown over the past twenty years, whereas it has fallen in most of the other countries. For example, male (female) youth participation was 81 per cent (72 per cent) in

1991 in the UK compared with 39 per cent (32 per cent) in France. Furthermore, the UK female youth participation rate is about the same as that for adults whereas in the other countries it is usually lower. These higher youth participation rates reflect the fact that fewer young people in the UK remain in full-time education beyond compulsory school-leaving age in the UK.

Sweden, the UK and the US have the highest total participation rates. Although this reflects both higher male and female participation rates these countries do have a particularly high proportion of total employment accounted for by females. In 1991 women accounted for about 45 per cent of total employment in the UK and the US and 48 per cent in Sweden, whereas in Italy women make up only 35 per cent of the workforce.

Hours

Increased female participation has been associated with a large increase in the number of part-time workers, particularly in the UK and the Netherlands. The UK accounts for about one third of female part-time employment in the EC as a whole. Many companies have a policy of employing female part-time workers, particularly in the service sector. This may be for reason of cost. Employers' social security contributions are waived for employees working below a certain number of hours in the UK and, in addition, extra hours can be worked without paying overtime premia. It is also the case that hiring and firing constraints and costs are generally lower for part-time workers. Additionally, flexibility and the control of working time is easier with part-time workers. Hence part-timers can be used as a buffer against cyclical downturns, which may be particularly important in unstable economies such as the UK.

The UK seems an outlier concerning the extent to which part-time female employment seems a matter of choice rather than necessity. For example, in 1987 the proportion of women in the UK who worked part-time due to the inability to find a full-time job was 32 per cent, whereas it was above 50 per cent in Sweden, Germany and the Netherlands (see OECD *Employment Outlook*, July 1990, table 7.2).

Table 1.4 gives details of part-time employment in our sample of countries. It is evident that it is high as a proportion of total employment in the UK compared to Germany, France and Italy, but it is similar to Sweden, the Netherlands and the US (that is, around 20 per cent). However, for the UK, this reflects the high proportion of part-time female employment since there are relatively few male workers in this category. In 1990 the Netherlands had the highest proportion of female part-time employment (62 per

Table 1.5 *Sectoral employment shares*[a]

		Agriculture	Services	Industry
US	1967	5.3	58.9	35.8
	1991	2.9	71.8	25.3
UK	1967	3.6	50.8	45.6
	1991	2.2	70.0	27.8
Germany	1967	10.4	42.8	46.9
	1991	3.4	57.4	39.2
France	1967	16.3	44.8	38.9
	1991	5.8	64.7	29.5
Italy	1967	24.4	38.3	37.3
	1991	8.5	59.2	32.3
Netherlands	1967	7.1	53.4	39.5
	1991	4.6	69.1	26.3
Sweden	1967	9.9	48.8	41.3
	1991	3.3	68.4	28.2

Source: OECD *Labour Force Statistics*.
(a) Employment by sector expressed as a percentage of total employment.

cent) in our sample of countries. The UK had the second highest (44 per cent). Similar figures for Sweden indicate that if female participation in the UK continues to rise towards Swedish levels, the result will not necessarily be a further increase in the proportion of female part-time employment.

Part-time working also varies across sectors of activity. For example, 80 per cent of all part-time workers in the EC are currently employed in the service sector. In most countries they are concentrated in the distributive trades, other services and finance, insurance and real estate.[4]

Flexibility has also been achieved by increasing overtime hours and/ or employing workers on a temporary basis. Flanagan (1988) argues that many European employers increased overtime hours to avoid the high hiring and firing costs of additional permanent workers. However, only a small proportion of the workforce is hired on a temporary basis. In 1985 in the UK only 5 per cent of wage and salary employment was temporary and this was concentrated primarily in the distributive trades and other services sector. This was not untypical of the countries considered in our sample. Most temporary work is also concentrated amongst young people.

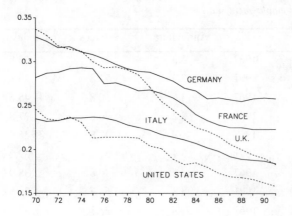

Figure 1.7 Employment in manufacturing as a percentage of total employment for the UK, US, Germany, France and Italy
Source: OECD *Main Economic Indicators*

Employment by sector

The sectoral composition of employment has implications for the flexibility of the aggregate labour market. Table 1.5 reports some details for our sample. A general feature is the shift away from industrial to services employment. For example, employment in services in the UK increased its share of the total by around 19 percentage points between 1967 and 1991. This reflected a decline in industrial employment of a similar magnitude. This may be a consequence of an increase in the demand for services relative to physical goods as people become wealthier. It may also reflect the apparent tendency of labour productivity to grow more rapidly in manufacturing. The growing share of services employment, which employs a much higher proportion of females, has been associated with strong growth in both female participation and female part-time employment. In addition, the share of youth employment in services has been falling over time, and this has exacerbated the decline in youth participation and the rise in youth unemployment.

Among our sample countries the UK is not an outlier in terms of the proportion of employees in industry. In fact, the US has the lowest proportion at around 25 per cent. However, the UK has a higher percentage of workers in services (approximately 70 per cent in 1991) than France (65 per cent), Italy (59 per cent) and Germany (57 per cent). This primarily reflects the lower share of employment in agriculture in the UK compared with France and Italy but it also reflects a much smaller industrial base in the UK relative to

Table 1.6   *Unemployment rates by age and gender*

		Males			Females			Total unempl-oyment rate
		Youth	Adults	Total	Youth	Adults	Total	
US	1972	10.6	3.0	4.8	12.3	4.9	6.6	5.5
	1991	13.4	5.8	6.9	12.3	5.4	6.3	6.6
UK	1972	6.4	3.2	4.3	3.3	0.7	1.3	3.2
	1991	16.5	10.0	10.9	8.6	3.7	4.7	8.2
Germany	1972	0.6	0.5	0.8	1.1	1.1	1.1	0.9
	1989	6.0	5.4	6.0	6.8	7.9	8.1	6.8
France	1972	3.1	1.1	1.7	5.5	3.0	3.6	2.4
	1991	15.8	6.0	7.0	24.0	10.4	11.7	9.0
Italy	1972	13.4	1.7	3.4	12.6	1.6	4.5	3.7
	1991	26.2	4.5	7.8	37.8	12.2	17.6	11.4
Netherlands	1972	3.8	2.2	2.5	1.4	1.3	1.4	2.2
	1991	10.1	4.3	5.3	10.9	9.3	9.3	6.9
Sweden	1972	5.4	1.8	2.5	6.2	2.2	3.0	2.7
	1991	6.7	2.4	2.9	5.4	1.8	2.3	2.6

Source: OECD *Labour Force Statistics*.

Germany.   The share of industrial employment in Germany is, however, an outlier — it was approximately ten percentage points higher than in the other countries in 1991. It is interesting to note that shares of industrial employment in the UK and Germany were similar and much higher than in the other countries in 1967. The different histories may well reflect the effects of the undervaluation of the Deutschmark during the 1980s, as well as the effects of the overvaluation of sterling during the same period. Figure 1.7 shows manufacturing employment as a percentage of total employment. It is clear that the UK has experienced a particularly rapid fall in manufacturing employment compared to the other sample countries.

The UK does not have a relatively high ratio of females to males in the service sector. Both sexes are more or less equally represented in this sector in the UK, the US and Germany. Sweden had the highest female–male employment ratio (60 per cent) in services in 1990, whereas Italy had the lowest at 41 per cent. Industrial employment is obviously dominated by males, with females only accounting for about 25 per cent of the total in

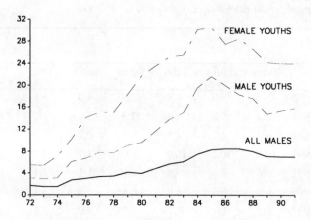

Figure 1.8 French unemployment for all males, male youths and female youths
Source: OECD *Labour Force Statistics*

this sector. In the UK, the US and Sweden, however, services account for about 84 per cent of female employment. This is an increase of 10 percentage points since 1970 in the US and Sweden but represents a 15 percentage point rise in the UK.

The general decline in agricultural employment may have substantially contributed to unemployment in France and Italy where the share of agricultural employment in the total fell from 16.3 to 5.8 per cent and from 24.4 to 8.5 per cent respectively between 1967 and 1991. This may have put upward pressure on the total number of jobs that needed to be created by the private corporate sector.

Unemployment

There are significant differences between countries in the age and gender composition of unemployment. As table 1.6 shows, youth unemployment rates in 1991 varied from 26 per cent in Italy to 6 per cent in Germany for males and from 38 per cent in Italy to 5.5 per cent in Sweden for females. Countries with the highest peak over the last twenty years for youth unemployment are the UK and Italy. Sweden has low youth unemployment rates, reflecting a generally lower aggregate unemployment rate. In general, youth unemployment is particularly affected by minimum wages policy, education and training policies, participation rates of adult females and by demographic factors.

For many countries the participation rates of adult females has had profound effects upon youth unemployment, since adult female labour is often

Figure 1.9 UK unemployment rate for females relative to males
Source: Department of Employment *Gazette*

used as a substitute for youth (particularly male) labour. The effect is to drive down the relative wages of youths. If this results in slower growth in youth wages relative to unemployment benefits, then equilibrium unemployment for this category may rise. In the UK high female participation, combined with high male youth participation, may partly explain high male youth unemployment.

French and Italian youth unemployment has been growing relative to adult unemployment (see figure 1.8).[5] This may be due to minimum wage policy contributing to relative wage rigidity between adult females and male youths, particularly in France. France and Italy have relatively high youth unemployment rates which implies they have, for a given unemployment rate, relatively lower prime age male unemployment rates. In 1991, total unemployment rates for the UK, France and Italy were 8.2, 9.0 and 11.4 per cent respectively whilst male adult unemployment rates were 10 per cent in the UK but only 6 per cent in France and 4.5 per cent in Italy.

The UK is exceptional in that female unemployment rates are lower than male rates for all age groups, whereas for the other countries the opposite is usually found. In 1991 Sweden and the US also had relatively low female unemployment rates but this is not as striking as in the UK where total female unemployment was 5 per cent in 1991 as compared with 11 per cent for males. However, these figures are distorted by systematic differences between countries in procedures for recording female unemployment. In the UK the ratio of the female unemployment rate to that for males, which is plotted in figure 1.9, is particularly low and it also declines during recessions. One possible explanation is that females are more likely to be 'discouraged workers' in comparison to males. In times of high unemployment females may be discouraged from entering the labour force or may withdraw from it. Alternatively the changing ratio may be related to benefit entitlement rules for part-time married females (see Gregg, 1992), or it could indicate that employers have a tendency to put women employees, particularly part-timers, on shorter working hours rather than lay them off.

Long-term unemployment (that is, those unemployed for over twelve months) has been a major European problem in the 1980s, frequently accounting for more than 50 per cent of the unemployed. In early 1993 the UK had over one million long-term unemployed, accounting for about 34 per cent of total unemployment. This compares favourably with higher percentages in France and Italy. Sweden and the US have much lower proportions of long-term unemployment, reflecting their lower total unemployment rates, and generally shorter unemployment duration. Sweden in particular spends more on training programmes for the unemployed.

Throughout the 1980s most of the long-term unemployed throughout Europe were prime age males rather than youths or females (see table 2.13, OECD *Employment Outlook*, July 1992). France was the exception, with a higher proportion of the long-term unemployed accounted for by females (58 per cent) than by males (42 per cent). In the UK a relatively high proportion of long-term unemployed are male, averaging around 74 per cent over the last decade. As in the rest of Europe, former manufacturing employees comprise a fairly high proportion of the long-term unemployed in the UK.

Most countries have introduced specific policies aimed at reducing long-term unemployment. For example, the UK has 'Restart' (1986) and 'Claimant Adviser Service', the French have 'Assessment of the 13th month' of unemployment (1983), and the Netherlands has 'Restart' interviews (1988). More recently France has introduced a major programme to deal with the problem (*'Neuf Cent Mille'* — 900 000, the number of long-term unemployed). In this programme each person is interviewed and a solution will be offered either in terms of job training (six-month courses for 350 000), a part-time employment contract in the public sector (covering 400 000) or employment in the private sector of at least six months duration (the state gives firms a grant and covers the employers' social security contribution).

Among OECD countries active supply-side policies to decrease unemployment involve either institutional training in specific centres or a set of training programmes which subsidise employers to train the unemployed (usually 'on- the-job' training). Here again the UK is an exception as it provides virtually no institutional training for the unemployed, concentrating instead on employer-based subsidised training.

Table 1.7   *Non-agricultural self-employment, 1973-90*

			As proportion of civilian employment	
	1973	1979	1985	1990
France	11.4	10.6	10.5	10.3
Germany	9.1	8.2	7.6	7.7
Italy	23.1	18.9	21.3	22.3
Netherlands		8.8	8.4	7.8
Sweden	4.8	4.5	4.5	7.0
UK	7.3	6.6	9.9	11.6
US	6.7	7.1	7.5	7.6

Source: OECD *Labour Force Statistics.*

Self-employment

Table 1.7 shows that, in 1990, the UK had the second highest proportion of self-employment (11.6 per cent) in our sample of countries. Generally, within the OECD, it is the less industrialised countries which have high proportions of self-employment, such as Spain (17.1 per cent), Turkey (27.6 per cent) and Portugal (18.5 per cent). The rapid growth of self-employment in the UK from 6.6 per cent in 1979 to 11.6 per cent in 1990 is also striking. In the other countries in our sample the share of self-employment either remained stable or declined. Most of the growth in the UK occurred in the services and building industry. Policies towards public sector contracting out and the removal of the insurance cover requirement in the building industry in 1980 were significant factors. Other influences are relatively low barriers to entry combined with government policy to encourage this form of economic activity. For example, Meager *et al.* (1992) argue that the qualifications necessary to start a business in the UK are relatively minimal compared with those prevailing in western Germany (specifically in the *Handwerk*, or crafts sector, which accounts for 20 per cent of self-employment in western Germany). Entry into this field in Germany requires apprenticeship and admission to the status of *Meister*, whereas there are no such requirements in the UK in similar areas of production. Government policy encouraged self-employment through the UK Enterprise Allowance Scheme (EAS) which was set up in 1983 to help unemployed people start their own business. Over half a million people have used the EAS and in 1987/8, for example, the scheme accounted for 25 per cent of the newly self-employed in the UK.

Table 1.8 *Economy-wide coordination in mid-to-late 1980s*

US	Zero employer and union coordination (0).
UK	Zero employer and union coordination (0).
France	Tacit government coordination via public services and large nationalised industry sector (1.5).
Italy	Informal employer coordination via big employers, especially Fiat, IRI and some regional employer associations; some help from union confederations, CGIL and CISL (2).
Netherlands	Strong employer organisations and informal coordination between giant companies; occasional differences between giants and industry organisations; medium union coordination (3).
Germany	Strong employer organisations, with considerable coordination across industries; medium-strong coordination (3.5).
Sweden	Powerful centralised employers' organisation; generally strong coordination across industries, with some divergence of interests; centralised union confederations with some internal conflicts (4).

Source: Soskice (1990).
Note: Numbers in parentheses are Soskice's measure of the degree of economy-wide coordination. A value of 4 represents the highest and zero the lowest.

Institutional and legal characteristics

Industrial relations arrangements

Calmfors and Driffill (1988) popularised the notion that the level at which collective bargaining takes place matters. They claimed to show a 'hump-shaped' relationship between the degree of centralisation and unemployment. Countries with heavily centralised systems (for example, Sweden and Austria) did well, as did countries with heavily decentralised systems (for example, Japan). By contrast mixed systems, such as that which used to typify the UK, worked badly. Highly centralised systems avoid 'prisoner's dilemma' problems whereby the various agents could all do better for themselves if they were allowed to 'collude'. For instance if individual bargaining units acted sequentially to attempt to each obtain real and relative pay increases, they might achieve neither of these, but aggregate pay and price inflation could rise, with consequential implications for the real money supply and employment. Centralised bargaining might allow unions to avoid pointless competitive behaviour and to maintain full

Table 1.9　Constructing an index of local pushfulness

| | | Plant-level union strength | |
		Strong	Weak
	Long-term consensual	2 Germany Netherlands Norway Sweden Austria	1 Japan Switzerland
Worker incentive structure	Long-term hierarchic		3 France
	Short-term	4 UK	1 US

Source: Soskice (1990).
Notes: Local pushfulness is defined as the extent to which plant or local level activity is potentially disruptive (and therefore capable of 'pushing' for higher real wages). This partly depends upon union strength but is also dependent upon the worker incentive structure. The former is measured along the top and the latter is indicated along the side. The numbers represent the degree of local pushfulness from the highest (4) to the lowest (1). The UK has the worst of both worlds in terms of union strength and incentive structure. The institutional structures conducive to wage moderation are therefore weakest in the UK.

employment. If centralised bargaining cannot be achieved, it is posited that full decentralisation is to be preferred in industry-wide bargaining. This is because the elasticity of product demand is higher for the individual firm than for the industry as a whole. Unions will be aware of this and therefore be more inclined to be moderate.

The Calmfors and Driffill hypothesis has received heavy criticism from, amongst others, David Soskice (1990). His most powerful criticism is that they incorrectly classify countries. He argues that what is relevant is not the extent of formal institutional centralisation, but the amount of actual coordination. Wage setting in Japan, for instance, is very coordinated. Germany and the Netherlands are more coordinated than would be simply implied by their mixed systems. At the same time failure to take account of international trade performance gives an unduly unfavourable picture of 'minimum equilibrium unemployment' in these two countries.

When countries are correctly classified, unemployment performance emerges as strongly positively correlated with the degree of coordination. Soskice also makes the important point that the elasticity of demand argument in favour of company as opposed to industry bargaining is tempered by a further consideration. This is the likelihood that pay increases awarded by profitable companies may feed through to employers less able to afford them. This danger is likely to be less in industry wage setting. Thus if there is any significant impact on macro performance from the 'level of bargaining', the balance of the argument seems to rest with the virtues of coordination.

The 1980s saw decentralisation of wage setting in most countries. Soskice lists a number of reasons for this: a trend towards more 'idiosyncratic' production; the reduced significance of manufacturing; the increased exposure of companies to international competition; a shift to the right in the governments of many countries, with an associated suspicion of unions and a stress on 'free markets' and deregulation. However, though coordination may have effectively disappeared in the UK, this is not the case in most other European countries. Soskice attempts to classify countries according to the substantive degree of coordination. His results are given in table 1.8. He stresses that for any given degree of coordination, two important additional factors influencing macro performance are 'plant-level union strength and the attitudes of unions' — particularly the extent to which they are primarily concerned with obtaining short-term pay increases. His categorisation is given in table 1.9.

However, to argue from the above that greater coordination would necessarily be achievable in Britain is to beg a number of questions. Prominent among these are whether successful coordination depends on a whole series of country-specific cultural and institutional features which, by their nature, are not capable of being replicated elsewhere; and whether the will exists among employers (who would be the critical players) to achieve it. For good or ill, Britain may well be committed to the route of decentralisation for a good many years to come.

Trade union strength

It is ironic that the 1980s saw a major research achievement that provided a more rigorous incorporation of unions into macro models of wage and employment behaviour, precisely at the time when unions were starting to become a much less significant force. Table 1.10a shows the percentage of workers unionised across time for non agricultural employees. It is clear that during the 1980s union density declined in many countries. In the US

Table 1.10a *Percentage of workers unionised*

	1970	1979	1986/7	1970-9	1979-86
				Percentage point change	
France	22	28	-	+ 6	-
Germany	37	42	43	+ 5	+ 1
Italy	39	51	45	+12	- 6
Netherlands	39	43	35	+ 4	- 8
UK	51	58	50	+ 7	- 8
US	31	25	17	- 6	- 8
Sweden	79	89	96	+10	+ 7

Source: Blanchflower and Freeman (1990).
Note: Non-agricultural employees only.

Table 1.10b *Union density in 1989*

	All sectors	Private	Public	Manu-facturing	Finance	Others
Sweden	81	81	81	99	72	87
UK	39	28	55	41	25	52
Italy	34	32	54	47	22	31
Netherlands	24	20	51	25	9	32
US	15	13	37	22	2	19
France	10	8	26	5	-	-
Germany	32	30	45	48	17	28

Source: Visser (1992).
Notes: All sectors = employed and unemployed wage and salary earners; Private = Private sector; Public = Public and semi-public sector (except nationalised firms); Finance = Financial services (banking, insurance, business services and real estate); Others = Community, social and personal services.

union membership declined dramatically in both the 1970s and 1980s. A less dramatic decline was registered in Italy, the Netherlands and the UK. In contrast Germany showed fairly stable union membership into the second half of the 1980s whereas in Sweden, which has by far the highest union density, it actually increased until 1986/7. More recent figures for all workers giving a sectoral breakdown are shown in table 1.10B. It is apparent that the public and manufacturing sectors are relatively more unionised. For example, in 1989 overall union density in the UK was 39 per cent, but only 28 per cent in the private sector as opposed to 55 per cent in the public sector (excluding nationalised industries). Furthermore, 41 per cent were unionised in the declining manufacturing sector and only 25 per cent in the growing financial sector.

Many factors account for the general decline in union density. Historically unions have found it more difficult to recruit members among female, non-manual and/or part-time workers in small non-manufacturing organisations. Trends in the composition of employment in most countries, particularly in the UK, have, therefore, been unfavourable to unionisation. New types of workers may also result in a discarding of both entrenched attitudes and adversarial relations between workers and management.

In addition, legislation and high unemployment rates have diminished the power and profile of unions. Ideologies shifted towards the rights of the individual rather than the collective. But the general trend of union density hides the diversity of experience between countries. Countries such as Sweden with centralised bargaining structures tend to have higher levels of union density. This arises partly because centralisation provides a clear link between trades unions and influence in national bargaining.

The decline in union density, in the UK at least, is not the only indication of a decline in the power of organised labour. The range of issues over which bargaining takes place has diminished, whilst in some establishments and firms (though so far in only a small minority) the annual pay bargain has receded into insignificance. The virtual disappearance of strikes in the UK from the mid-1980s onwards — there were only 240 officially recorded strikes in 1992 compared to ten times that number fifteen years earlier — gives a misleading picture of a new era of harmonious industrial relations. The ability to strike has been constrained by changes in the law, but the number of grievances has not declined. ACAS reports show the number of conciliation cases have remained stable compared to the late 1970s (see Milner, 1993). Employees now resort to action such as overtime bans as relatively low cost forms of industrial action.

Employment protection

Comparisons of employment protection across countries are extremely difficult to make. What is certain is that such protection has diminished faster in the UK than in other European countries. The provision of special protection for women and youths has effectively disappeared. Unfair dismissals and redundancy provisions have been considerably reduced in scope. It is probably easier and less expensive to sack a worker in Britain than in any other major European country. Wage protection used to be greater in Britain than the absence of a national minimum wage appeared to imply. This protection was given by the Fair Wages Resolution, Schedule 11 of the 1975 Employment Protection Act and by Wages Councils. The first two are long gone. Wages Councils will shortly disappear. In contrast, most countries in our study have wage protection in the form of minimum wages but there is great variation in practice. France and the Netherlands have a statutory minimum imposed by government whereas Germany and Italy have minimum rates established by industry-level agreements. The US also has a statutory minimum wage and the UK currently has some minimum wages limited to certain sectors covered by wages councils. It is difficult to gauge the effectiveness of minimum pay but it is useful to measure the minimum as a proportion of median earnings. Expressed in this fashion, statutory minimum wages are high in the Netherlands and France at 72 and 61 per cent respectively but only 25 per cent in the US.[6]

In the 1980s minimum wages have generally been frozen in nominal terms and actually reduced in real terms (see Chan Lee et al., 1987). In the Netherlands minimum wages have not been increased since 1980. Reductions in minimum wages for youths also became popular. In the Netherlands the minimum wage for workers under 23 was decreased by 10 per cent in 1983 and in the mid-1980s the UK excluded employees under 21 from the coverage of wage councils which (at that time) set minimum wages for about 11 per cent of workers.

In contrast, France increased real minimum wages throughout the 1980s, which partly explains why the proportion of the workforce covered by the *Salaire Minimum Interprofessional de Croissance* (SMIC) increased until the late 1980s.[7] The SMIC affects a much higher proportion of females than of males. Although, in a similar fashion to other countries, France has lower minimum rates for young workers, 40 per cent of workers covered by the SMIC are under 26 years old. In a comprehensive study of French minimum wages, Bazen and Martin (1991) find that there is a small negative relationship between the SMIC and the employment of young people.

Realisation that job security rights may be partly responsible for the decreased outflow rate from unemployment in Europe in the 1980s encouraged many countries to implement labour market reforms. These included easing of regulations covering temporary contracts, reducing hiring and firing costs and removing trade union recognition rights. For example, in France in 1986 the requirement of firms to gain official permission for any dismissal was abandoned. In Germany legislation in 1985 made it easier to terminate employment contracts of limited duration. In 1985 in the UK the qualifying period for unfair dismissal cases increased from 52 to 104 weeks of continuous service.[8]

Sustainable unemployment

The concept of sustainable unemployment has been analysed in many ways in the literature on macroeconomics and on the labour market. If there are no forces at work that will change the level of unemployment then we may say that this level is sustainable. This does not mean to say that the sustainable level of unemployment is either acceptable, immutable or unique. External shocks to the economy may change the sustainable level of unemployment and it may be difficult to design policies to reverse such shocks. It is, however, possible to design policies that may return the economy to sustainable unemployment more quickly than the market mechanism left to itself. It is also possible, albeit more difficult, to design policies that might shift the sustainable level of unemployment. Both Britton (1993) and Barrell, Caporale and Sefton (1993) discuss policies that might affect the equilibrium of the economy.

One of the most commonly used approaches to the analysis of sustainable unemployment is that developed by, amongst others, Richard Layard and Stephen Nickell. The volume by Layard, Nickell and Jackman (1991) [hereafter LNJ] sets out their analysis of the Non-Accelerating Inflation Rate of Unemployment, or the NAIRU. The NAIRU is defined as the level of unemployment consistent with stable inflation. Stable inflation requires that the real wage desired by both wage and price setters is the same. The variable which adjusts in order to equalise these is the unemployment rate.

This can be illustrated by equations (1) and (2) below which are simple long-run wage and price setting relationships which depend on the capital–labour ratio (k-l). Wages (w) are assumed to be set as a mark-up on prices (p) with the mark-up falling as unemployment (U) rises. In turn, prices are set as a mark-up on wages with the mark-up again rising as activity increases. A rise in productivity is assumed to increase real wages and decrease prices. Other structural factors which affect real wages are captured by the term z_w. When the real wage desired by wage and price setters is equalised we are left with equation (3) which gives us an expression for sustainable unemployment.

$$wages \qquad w - p = \beta_0 - \beta_1 U + z_w + \beta_3(k - l) \qquad\qquad (1)$$

$$prices \quad p - w = \gamma_0 - \gamma_1 U - \beta_3(k - l) \tag{2}$$

$$NAIRU \quad U^* = \frac{\beta_0 + \gamma_0 + z_w}{\beta_1 + \gamma_1} \tag{3}$$

Table 1.11 is taken from Cromb (1993) and shows the range of different estimates for the UK NAIRU. Most of the above NAIRU calculations depend on the structural factors included in z_w in equation (1).

In the LNJ model wage determination is assumed to be the outcome of a bargaining process between employers and unions. It is assumed that the union's utility depends positively upon the difference between the insider and outsider wage (the latter may be unemployment benefit). LNJ derive an expression for the mark-up of the insider wage over the outsider wage:

$$M = (1 - \alpha K) / (\varepsilon_{SN} + \alpha K / \beta) \tag{4}$$

where M is the mark-up, α is the Cobb Douglas production parameter reflecting the labour intensity of production, K is the indicator of product market competitiveness that depends upon the elasticity of demand for products produced by the unionised sector, β is an indicator of union power and ε_{SN} the elasticity of the probability of remaining an insider with respect to the level of employment. All of these factors could be included in z_w in the real wage equation (1). In addition, some measure of unemployment benefit is usually included to capture the outsider wage. Other variables such as a labour mismatch measure and taxation and the real exchange rate are often added to (1). The next section outlines the major structural factors which have been found to be significant in real wage equations.

Table 1.11 *NAIRU Estimates for the UK (claimant definition)*

| | Period within which the estimates fall | | | |
	1969-73	1974-80	1981-87	1988-90
NAIRU range	1.6-5.6%	4.5-7.3%	5.2-9.9%	3.5-8.1%
Actual U rate	2.5%	3.8%	10.1%	6.8%
Number of estimates	11	13	15	5

Source: Cromb (1993), first published in the *Journal of Economic Studies*, vol.20, no.1/2, 1993.

Table 1.12   *Unemployment benefit replacement ratios*

Per cent

	Aggregate ratios (a)			Memorandum item:
	1965-70	1971-79	1980-85	Hypothetical rate (b)
US	11	13	10	48
France	28	25	37	72-71
Germany	59	52	36	70-72
Italy	6	8	10	90-80
UK	29	29	23	74-76
Netherlands (c)	56	41	37	88-82
Sweden (c)	23	26	39	92-40

Sources: OECD (1989) and table 2 in Chan-Lee *et al.* (1987).
Notes:
(a) Ratio of unemployment benefits per unemployed person, divided by compensation per employee.
(b) Numerator is unemployment benefits plus social transfers, net of tax; denominator is after-tax income for a married unemployed person on average earnings with two children and non-working spouse in first full year of unemployment. Figures refer to 1982-3, but to 1981 for the US, Canada and Australia, and to 1980 for Sweden. When there is a range, the first rate is after one month of unemployment, the second after thirteen months. For Sweden, they refer to two different insurance schemes.
(c) The first column refers to the year 1970.

Replacement ratio

The replacement ratio is a measure of income while unemployed relative to income while employed, and is influenced by, among other things, the relative generosity of the benefits system. It is hypothesised that this can affect the probability that the unemployed will accept job offers and hence it will change the search intensity of the unemployed and the bargaining power of workers. But the influential LNJ study calculates that, of the 6.2 percentage point rise in the UK NAIRU between 1960–68 and 1981–7, only 0.8 percentage points were caused by changes in the replacement ratio.

Table 1.12 gives details of replacement ratios for our sample of countries. Replacement ratios are generally high in Sweden, the Netherlands, France and Germany and particularly low in the US. About three quarters of the unemployed receive benefit in Europe and only about a third in the US. The duration of unemployment benefit is shorter in the US and Sweden. Replacement ratios have generally been on a downward trend in the 1980s and stricter rules regarding eligibility for benefit have been applied almost everywhere. From 1986 onwards the unemployed in Britain have been interviewed every six months under the Restart Programme and put under more pressure to find work. Stricter tests of availability for work are now applied in the UK.

Mismatch

Mismatch increases when the unemployed become less suited to the available vacancies. The degree of mismatch can be affected by three factors; first, changes in the composition of production which will require different types of labour, skills and perhaps location of production. Second, mobility, flexibility and adaptability of the labour force and third, the efficiency of the matching process, that is, employment agencies, screening devices and so on.

A common, but crude, proxy for mismatch is the 'industrial turbulence index' which measures the absolute change in the proportion of employees in production industries'. Bean and Gavosto (1989) estimate that, on the basis of this measure, mismatch added 3.75 percentage points to the UK NAIRU over the period 1967–87. Similarly, LNJ estimate the effect of mismatch to be 2.5 percentage points over the period 1960–68 to 1981–7.

It is often claimed that mismatch has not changed sufficiently to explain the trend in UK and European unemployment.[9] However, as we saw earlier, there has been a substantial trend movement away from industrial to services employment throughout Europe and particularly in the UK over the past twenty-five years. This itself would provide a substantial mismatch in terms of skills and geographical location.

Bargaining and unions

Union bargaining influences the extent to which workers gain higher wages at the expense of lower employment. Bargaining outcomes are primarily influenced by union objectives, union power and the degree of coordination and synchronisation in wage setting. Trade union power is usually proxied by union density or the union mark-up over the competitive wage. Estimates of the effect of trade union power upon the UK NAIRU are quite diverse and range from 1 to 6 percentage points over the 1960s to the 1980s.

As we have seen, trade union density has been falling rapidly in most of our sample countries in the 1980s and this should exert a downward influence on the NAIRU. Sweden is the only country where trade union density has increased in the 1980s and this has been accompanied by low unemployment relative to the other countries. This supports the notion that a high degree of coordination causes wage negotiators to be more aware of the unemployment consequences of high wage settlements.

Tax and real exchange rate wedge

The tax and exchange rate wedges capture the real wage desires of workers relative to the firms' ability to meet them. The wedge is usually represented by the ratio of the real consumption wage to the real producer wage. Although many studies for the UK find permanent effects from tax and exchange rate wedges, the LNJ study is based on a theoretical structure which implies that real wages are only temporarily affected by the wedge. However, the empirical results of the latter study still retain a long-run effect from the real exchange rate wedge.[10] However, even if the wedge only has temporary effects it can still be an important determinant of the NAIRU in the short run. In particular, by belonging to a semi-fixed exchange rate regime, the ERM member countries have experienced upward pressure on their real exchange rates vis-à-vis Germany. This should have put downward pressure on the NAIRU as lower import prices resulting from a high exchange rate should have increased the consumption real wage. This seems counter to the claim that ERM-related policies have increased unemployment.

Other factors

The degree of product market competition can also affect the NAIRU via the relationship between price setting, labour demand and the mark-up. If the degree of openness increases this reduces the rents from product market power as competition has increased. Therefore, the mark-up of union wages over those of the competitive sector should decline, and the NAIRU should fall. The liberalisation of trade within the EC has greatly increased the openness of European economies. If we proxy openness by the ratio of imports and exports of goods and services relative to total GDP, it seems that that openness has trended upwards over the past twenty years. However, the US tends to be less 'open' according to this measure than the other countries but the greater degree of product market competitiveness, at least when compared with Europe, will put downward pressure on sustainable unemployment.

There are many possible effects on the NAIRU of the compositional changes discussed earlier. First, the movement from manufacturing to service employment has reduced trade union density and should decrease the

NAIRU. Second, discouraged worker effects should reduce the NAIRU, at least in terms of the claimant unemployed, in recessions but increase it in booms. Third, the extent to which total unemployment has to rise in order to equate the 'feasible' and 'target' real wage partly depends upon the composition of unemployment. Unemployed adult males probably exert the most downward pressure on real wages. For a given unemployment rate the UK seems to have the highest adult male unemployment rate. However, offsetting this is the fact that a substantial number of these males in the UK are long-term unemployed. Fourth, the general movement from manufacturing to services employment may have resulted in a mismatch of skills. The rapid decline of manufacturing employment may make this particularly relevant for the UK. Finally, increased flexibility in terms of working hours should decrease the NAIRU.

Estimates of the NAIRU are usually concerned with internal but not external equilibrium and as such it must be seen as medium-term in nature. The analysis of the equilibrium level of unemployment must also take into account external balance and the associated asset stock equilibrium. For this reason, the equilibrium unemployment rate is that which delivers both stable inflation and a sustainable balance on trade in goods and non-factor services. Therefore, the expression for the NAIRU in (3) can be extended by adding competitiveness and trade balance terms in order to calculate the equilibrium level of unemployment. This extension is important in the analysis of recent history and, if either the wage or the price equation above has real exchange rate wedges, then the real exchange rate will influence the sustainable level of unemployment.

Unemployment persistence and real wage flexibility

The structural factors mentioned above relate to long-term sustainable unemployment but the actual unemployment rate can diverge from this for considerable periods of time. The extent to which a temporary shock to unemployment tends to cause unemployment to deviate from equilibrium is called the persistence of unemployment. One reason why deviations away from equilibrium may persist is nominal wage and price inertia. The role of overlapping contracts in creating nominal inertia and hence persistence of unemployment is described in Taylor (1979, 1980). Structural factors which may affect unemployment persistence such as insider power, inertia in labour demand, real wage flexibility and the degree of co-ordination in bargaining structure are some of the factors examined by Lindbeck and Snower (1986), Blanchard and Summers (1986), Layard and Bean (1988), Barro (1988) and Alogoskoufis and Manning (1988a, 1988b).

Table 1.13   *Factors affecting unemployment persistence*

	Unemploy-ment persistence (a)	Real wage flexibility (b)	Duration of unemploy-ment benefit (yrs) 1985 (c)	Expenditure on 'active' labour market progs per unemploy-ed person (as % of output per persons 1987) (c)	Bertola 'job security positions' ranking (d)
France	1.04	-0.014	3.75	3.9	3
W Germany	0.94	-0.026	Indef	10.4	5
Italy	0.95	-0.001	0.5	0.8	1
Netherlands	0.94	-0.007	Indef	2.7	8
UK	0.91	-0.004	Indef	4.6	7
US	0.48	-0.012	0.5	2.4	10
Sweden	0.52	-0.008	1.2	34.6	4

Notes:
(a) The figures represent the sum of the lagged coefficients of the unemploy-ment rate in simple vector auto regressions. Unemployment persistence increases as the coefficient tends towards unity. Figures are from Alogoskoufis and Man-ning (1988a).
(b) Percentage change in real wages in response to one percentage point change in unemployment. Figures for Sweden and the Netherlands are from Bean, Layard and Nickell (1986), the remainder are from Anderton, Barrell, in't Veld and Pittas (1992).
(c) Source: Layard, Nickell and Jackman (1991).
(d) Source: Bertola (1990).

The degree of persistence of unemployment is sometimes estimated by re-gressing the unemployment rate on its own lagged value. Column 1 of table 1.13 gives some estimates of unemployment persistence using this method.[11] Unemployment persistence is presumed to increase as the coef-ficient on the lagged dependent variable tends towards unity. It is clear that shocks to unemployment persist for longer in the EC countries relative to Sweden and the US.

Blanchard and Summers (1986) argue that a higher degree of insider power in Europe explains the higher persistence of unemployment. If the degree of insider power is high then a temporary increase in unemployment may result in a smaller group of insiders who then set the wage so as to

Figure 1.10 UK: average hours of overtime worked per operative in manufacturing per week and unemployment rate
Source: Department of Employment *Gazette*
Note: Overtime hours shown on left-hand side

maintain a permanently lower level of employment. If the unemployed have no insider status then unemployment exhibits hysteresis. The extreme version of the insider–outsider analysis predicts that the level of unemployment puts no downward pressure on real wages. However, table 1.13 indicates that all countries in our sample show some negative relationship between unemployment and real wages.

Unemployment may also persist if individuals reduce their search effort after being unemployed for a prolonged period. In addition, the long-term unemployed may become less attractive to employers. This may be through erosion of skills or simply because potential employers use duration of unemployment as a 'negative' screening device. Reduced search effort would result in the long-term unemployed exerting only minimal downward pressure on wage inflation relative to the short-term unemployed. Layard and Nickell (1986), Nickell (1987) and Nickell and Wadhwani (1990) provide evidence to support this hypothesis. Our measures of real wage flexibility are consistent with these results in the case of Sweden but less so for the US. The duration of unemployment given in table 1.13 shows that countries with a higher proportion of long-term unemployed exhibit higher unemployment persistence.

Layard and Bean (1989) show that unemployment persistence is positively correlated with benefit duration and negatively related to corporat-

ism and active labour market policies. Table 1.13 shows that benefit duration is particularly short for Sweden and the US whereas benefits are
usually of indefinite duration in the high persistence countries. Sweden's low persistence also seems to arise from its degree of coordination
in wage bargaining combined with large expenditure on training and
employment programmes for the unemployed.

Alogoskoufis and Manning (1988a) claim that unemployment persistence
is also positively related to the degree of inertia in labour demand. This
seems to be the case in the UK where employers appear to prefer increasing
overtime hours rather than hiring new employees. Figure 1.10 shows
that even at high unemployment, when labour supply is plentiful, paying
overtime premia appears less costly than increasing the workforce. This
may be due to hiring and firing costs but may also reflect uncertainty
about future demand given the volatility of the UK economy (see Flanagan,
1988). Obstacles to firing make labour particularly unattractive to firms as
a factor of production if the economic environment is unstable. Bertola
(1990) uses the results of Emerson (1988) to rank countries according to job
security provisions. The ranking is given in table 1.13 where 1 indicates the
most restrictive and 10 the least. The ranking suggests that the relative
job security of the UK is not particularly high, but unemployment persistence is generally higher when job security provisions are more restrictive.

Conclusions

This chapter has surveyed the comparative evidence on the structure of
employment and unemployment. This has allowed us to put the performance of the UK economy over the last two decades into perspective.
Changes to the UK labour market — in terms of a greater degree of part-
time and self-employment, trade union reform, redundancy legislation and
tighter unemployment benefit regulations — should have enhanced flexibility. However, the intended improvements in flexibility have been partly
neutralised by the move towards decentralised bargaining which appears to
have reduced the degree of labour market coordination. Furthermore, the
adaptability and flexibility of the workforce has not been enhanced by the
absence of substantial measures to improve skills and training, particularly
during a period of rapid structural change away from manufacturing towards
services.

The UK labour market appears to have remained less flexible than the rest
of our sample. Real wages remain hard to change. The sustainable level
of unemployment has, it appears, remained stubbornly high and consid-

erable amounts of excess unemployment are required to put downward pressure on wage inflation. The Thatcher reforms may have made participants in the labour market tremble, but the reforms do not appear to have persuaded them to change their behaviour in the required direction. In addition, changes on the micro side may have been frustrated by volatility at the macro level. However, aggregate volatility may be due not only to unsuccessful policies such as ERM membership but may also be related to the labour market reforms themselves. The result of shifting the costs of flexibility away from the firm onto the workforce may be greater insecurity and uncertainty for the consumer and hence a less stable demand side.

Notes

1 We would like to thank R. Barrell, A. Britton, Z. Hornstein, S. Soteri and D. Worswick for helpful comments.
2 For a detailed analysis of European economic convergence see Anderton, Barrell and in't Veld (1992).
3 Definitions of youth and adult are not the same for all countries. The general definition for youths is 16–24-year-olds and 25–54-year-olds for prime age adults. The exceptions are Germany (15–24), France (15–24), Italy (14–24) and (55–59) and Netherlands (15–24).
4 See OECD *Employment Outlook*, July 1989.
5 Italy imposes a legal obligation on large firms to select job applicants in numerical order from waiting lists of job seekers at public employment offices. The waiting lists rank individuals by age, family circumstances and unemployment duration, which effectively discriminates against young people entering the labour force.
6 The figures for France and the Netherlands apply to all sectors in 1987 and 1988 respectively whereas for the US the data relate to the manufacturing sector in 1985 (see Chan Lee *et al.*, 1987).
7 The SMIC was revalued substantially in 1981 after the socialists' election victory and again in 1986.
8 See OECD (1986), tables III-1 and III-2 for a summary of redundancy notice and individual dismissal legislation up to 1986.
9 OECD *Employment Outlook*, July 1992, table 2.12 shows two measures of skills mismatch: the dispersion of relative and absolute occupational unemployment rates. Neither measure shows a discernible difference between 1979 and 1989.
10 LNJ justify this by arguing that their sample period is not large enough to distinguish between long-run effects and highly persistent effects.
11 This method of calculating unemployment persistence is a crude approximation as changes in the NAIRU are not adequately taken into account.

References

Alogoskoufis, G. and Manning, A. (1988a), 'On the persistence of unemployment', *Economic Policy*, 7, 427–69.

Alogoskoufis, G. and Manning, A. (1988b), 'Wage setting and unemployment persistence in Europe, Japan and USA', *European Economic Review*, 32, 213, 698–706.

Anderton, R., Barrell, R. and in't Veld, J.W. (1992), 'Macroeconomic convergence in Europe: achievements and prospects', in Barrell, R. (ed.), *Economic Convergence and Monetary Union in Europe,* London, Sage Publications.

Anderton, R., Barrell, R., in't Veld, J.W. and Pittas, N. (1992), 'Forward-looking wages and nominal inertia in the ERM', *National Institute Economic Review*, no. 141, August.

Barrell, R., Caporale, G. and Sefton, J. (1993), 'Prospects for European unemployment' in Grieve-Smith, J. and Michie, J. (eds), *Unemployment in Europe: Policies for Growth*, Academic Press.

Barro, R.J. (1988), 'The persistence of unemployment', *American Economic Review*, 78, 5, 32–7.

Bazen, S. and Martin, J. (1991), 'The effect of the minimum wage on the employment and earnings in France, 1963–85', *OECD Economic Studies*, no. 16.

Bean, C. (1992), 'European unemployment: a survey', Centre for Economic Performance, Discussion Paper no. 71.

Bean, C. and Gavosto, A. (1989), 'Outsiders, capacity shortages and unemployment in the UK', Centre for Labour Economics, Discussion Paper no. 332.

Bean, C. and Holden, K, (1992), 'Cross-national differences in trade union membership in OECD countries', *Industrial Relations Journal,* 23(1), Spring.

Bean, C., Layard, R. and Nickell, S. (1986), 'The rise in unemployment: a multi-country study', *Economica* (Supplement), 53, S1–S22.

Bertola, G. (1990), 'Job security, employment and wages', *European Economic Review*, 34, 851–86.

Blanchard, O. and Summers, L. (1986), 'Hysteresis and the European unemployment problem' in Fischer, S. (ed.), *NBER Macroeconomics Annual*, Cambridge, Mass., MIT Press.

Blanchflower, D. and Freeman, R. (1990), 'Unionism in the United States and other advanced OECD countries', *Industrial Relations*, 31, 11, 56–80.

Britton, A.J.C. (1993), 'Two routes to full employment', *National Institute Economic Review*, 144, May.

Calmfors, L. and Driffill, J. (1988), 'Centralisation of wage bargaining and macroeconomic performance', *Economic Policy*, 6, 13–61.

Chan-Lee, J.H., Coe, D.T. and Prywes, M. (1987), 'Microeconomic changes and macroeconomic wage disinflation in the 1980s', *OECD Economic Studies*, 8, Spring, 121–57.

Coe, D. (1985), 'Nominal wages, the NAIRU and wage flexibility', *OECD Economic Studies*, 5, Autumn, 87–126.

Corry, B. and Roberts, J. (1974), 'Activity rates and unemployment. The UK experience: some further results', *Applied Economics*, 1974, 6, 1–21.

Cromb, R. (1993), 'A survey of recent econometric work on the NAIRU', *Journal of Economic Studies*, 20, 1/2.

Emerson, M. (1988), 'Regulation or deregulation of the labour market', *European Economic Review*, 32, 775–817.

Flanagan, R.J. (1988), 'Unemployment as a hiring problem', *OECD Economic Studies*, 11, Autumn.

Greenhalgh, C. (1977), 'A labour supply function for married women in Great Britain', *Economica*, 44, 249–65.

Gregg, P. (1992), 'Out for the count again: a social scientist's analysis of unemployment statistics in the UK', National Institute Discussion Paper no. 25.

Grubb, D., Jackman, R. and Layard, R. (1983), 'Wage rigidity and unemployment in OECD countries, *European Economic Review*, 21, (1/2), 11–39.

Hamermesh, D. (1985), 'Substitution between different categories of labour, relative wages and youth unemployment', *OECD Economic Studies*, 5, Autumn.

Layard, R. and Bean, C. (1988), 'Why does unemployment persist?' LSE Centre for Economics Discussion Paper no. 321.

Layard, R. and Nickell, S. (1986), 'Unemployment in Britain', *Economica*, 53, supplement.

Layard, R., Nickell, S. and Jackman, R. (1991), *Unemployment: Macroeconomic Performance and the Labour Market*, Oxford University Press.

Lindbeck, A. and Snower, D.J. (1986), 'Wage setting, unemployment and insider-outsider relations', *American Economic Review*, Papers and Proceedings.

McNabb, R. (1977), 'The labour force participation of married women', *The Manchester School*, 3, 221–35.

Manning, A. (1993), 'Wage bargaining and the Phillips Curve: the identification and specification of aggregate wage equations', *Economic Journal*, 103, 98–118.

Meager, N., Kaiser, M. and Dietrich, H. (1992), 'Self employment in the United Kingdom and Germany', Anglo-German Foundation, London (forthcoming).

Milner, S. (1993), 'Strike and non-strike action: evidence on relative incidence', Discussion Paper no. 136, Centre for Economic Performance, London School of Economics.

Nickell, S. (1987), 'Why is wage inflation in the UK so high?' *Oxford Bulletin of Economics and Statistics*, 49, 103–128.

Nickell, S. and Wadhwani, S. (1990), 'Insider forces and wage determination', *Economic Journal*, 100, 496–509.

OECD (1986), 'Flexibility in the labour market: the current debate', Paris.

OECD (1989a), 'Economics in transition: structural adjustment in OECD countries'.

OECD (1989b), *Employment Outlook*, July.

OECD (1990), *Employment Outlook*, July.

OECD (1992), *Employment Outlook*, July.

OECD *Labour Force Statistics*, various issues.

OECD *Main Economic Indicators*, various issues.

OECD *Quarterly National Accounts*, various issues.

Soskice, D. (1990), 'Wage determination: the changing role of institutions in advanced industrialised countries', *Oxford Review of Economic Policy*, 6, 4.

Taylor, J.B. (1979), 'Staggered wage setting in a macro-model', *American Economic Review*, Papers and Proceedings, 69, May, 108–113.

Taylor, J.B. (1980), 'Aggregate dynamics and staggered contracts', *Journal of Political Economy*, 88(1), 1–23.

Visser, J. (1992), 'Union organisation: why countries differ', in *Proceedings of the International Industrial Relations Association 9th World Congress* (forthcoming).

2 Did the Thatcher reforms change British labour market performance?

DAVID G BLANCHFLOWER AND RICHARD B FREEMAN[1]

'They used ... to talk about us in terms of the British disease. Now, they talk about us and say, "Look Britain has the cure. Come to Britain and see how Britain has done it." M. Thatcher in 1988 (as quoted by Gilmour, 1992, p.76).

In the 1980s the United Kingdom led the West in altering economic policies and institutions in ways designed to produce a better-functioning market system. The Thatcher and Major governments sought to limit institutional interventions in the free market and to unleash the powers of entrepreneurship and untrammelled competition. Many reforms focused directly on the labour market, or were expected to improve the economy by changing the labour market: industrial relations laws that weakened union power; measures to enhance self-employment; privatisation of government-run or owned businesses; reduction in the value of unemployment benefits and other social receipts relative to wages; new training initiatives; tax incentives to increase use of private pensions; lower marginal taxes on individuals; and the elimination of wage councils that set minimum wages.

In the price-theorists' ideal world, these changes would reduce market rigidities, increase mobility, and raise incentives. In the price-theorists' ideal world, they would create the micro-institutional base for a more effective market economy with higher productivity, lower unemployment, improved living standards, and possibly a higher permanent rate of economic growth as well.

Did the Thatcher reforms alter the British labour market in the desired direction? From the vantage point of the 1990s were they the right medicine for the 'British disease'? In what areas do the changes seem to have succeeded and in what areas do they seem to have failed?

This chapter is a first assay at these questions. It is a first assay because the analysis consists largely of comparisons of reduced form labour market outcomes before and after the reforms, rather than of a set of detailed investigations of specific reforms in the context of a structural labour market model. In addition, while we analyse several data sets, we have not validated each finding on all available bodies of data nor, where the data is weak, developed our own survey to determine the 'facts'. Still, if 'The achievement of Mrs Thatcher is that she succeeded in changing Britain, probably permanently, by a cumulative series of half-measures or even quarter-measures' (Matthews and Minford, 1987, p.92), looking at the labour market before and after the Thatcher reforms, as we do, may be an appropriate research strategy. Such a broad-based analysis is more likely to capture the overall effects of the changes in economic policies than a more in-depth analysis of a particular reform measure.

Our primary conclusion is that the Thatcherite reforms succeeded in their goals of weakening union power and they may have marginally increased employment and wage responsiveness to market conditions and may have increased self-employment. They were accompanied by a substantial improvement in the labour market position of women. But the reforms failed to improve the responsiveness of real wages to unemployment. They were associated with a slower transition from non-employment to employment for men. There was a devastating loss in full-time jobs for male workers and they produced substantial increases in wage inequality that are hard to justify on the grounds of improved competitiveness. While we cannot rule out the possibility that the reforms created the preconditions for an economic 'miracle' in the mid-1990s there is little in the data to support such a sanguine reading of the British experience. Higher inequality and poverty and lower full-time employment are not normally viewed as ideal preconditions for economic success. We offer some speculations as to why the reforms seemingly failed to fulfil their promise.

Why reform the labour market?

Call it the British disease or what you wish, but prior to Mrs Thatcher, there was a general perception and some evidence that the British labour market operated less efficiently than those in other countries.

— The rate of unionisation was high for a non-corporatist economy, and unions often acted irresponsibly, as in the 1978–9 Winter of Discontent and the 1983 miners' strike. Britain had a poor strike record.

— In contrast to the US, where high union wages were accompanied by high productivity compared to non-union workplaces, productivity in the UK was no better in union than in non-union settings despite a 10 per cent or so union wage effect.

— Growth of labour productivity and output was slower in the United Kingdom than in other OECD countries. Real GDP per person employed rose by 2.7 per cent, 3.2 per cent, and 1.3 per cent in the UK over the periods 1960–68, 1968–73, and 1973–9 compared to 4.6 per cent, 4.3 per cent, and 2.4 per cent in the EC in total (OECD, 1991).

— British employees were relatively less skilled and educated than in other highly developed economies. The proportion of British 17–year-olds in education and training fell far below that of other advanced OECD countries and of development successes like Korea.

— The country had large nominal wage increases even when unemployment rose in the 1970s. Low productivity growth and high nominal wage increases produced unit labour cost increases and inflation faster than EC averages from 1968–79.

— Compared with the US, Britain (like other European countries) had long durations of unemployment. In 1979 25 per cent of British spells of unemployment exceeded twelve months compared to 4 per cent of US spells (OECD, *Employment Outlook*, 1985, p.126).

— Still, Britain had a relatively modest rate of unemployment: in 1979 unemployment was 5.3 per cent, below US and OECD–Europe rates; and the British employment population rate was 71 per cent, higher than the 63 per cent in OECD Europe (OECD, *Employment Outlook*, 1985, pp.42 and 25). Britain's youth unemployment problem did not approach the employment crisis of youths in the US (Layard, 1982 and OECD, 1978, 1981).

To obtain a more detailed picture of how economic outcomes differed between the UK and other OECD countries we estimated pooled time-series cross-country regression equations of the following form:

$$Y_{it} = T_t + D_{uk} \qquad (1)$$

where Y_{it} is the dependent variable for country i in year t; T_t is a vector of year dummies; and D_{uk} is a dummy variable for the UK. We estimate (1) separately for 1950–59, 1960–69, 1970–79 and 1980–88. The coefficients on the UK dummy variable in each period measures the difference between outcomes in the UK and outcomes in the other OECD countries.

Columns 1–3 of table 2.1 record the estimated coefficients on the UK dummy variable for 1950–59, 1960–69 and 1970–79. The estimates show that the UK did poorly in most periods relative to other OECD countries on the growth of GDP and productivity, inflation, growth of unit labour costs (in the 1970s) but did well in providing employment for the population. Poor aggregate performance in these outcomes and high employment rates do not mean

Table 2.1 *Regression estimates for the difference between outcomes in the UK and other OECD countries*

	1950-59	1960-69	1970-79	1980-89	Δ1970-79 to 1980-89
Unemployment rate	-0.022 (0.088)	-0.006 (0.006)	-0.000 (0.007)	0.025 (0.016)	0.025
Male unemployment rate	-0.024 (0.008)	-0.004 (0.005)	0.013 (0.007)	0.049 (0.017)	0.036
Female unemployment rate	-0.028 (0.014)	-0.016 (0.008)	-0.023 (0.010)	-0.013 (0.020)	-0.010
Employment-population rate	0.040 (0.019)	0.048 (0.020)	0.051 (0.022)	0.020 (0.032)	-0.031
Price inflation	0.005 (0.011)	-0.002 (0.006)	0.034 (0.011)	0.004 (0.011)	-0.030
Growth of GDP	-0.016 (0.009)	-0.021 (0.007)	-0.011 (0.007)	-0.002 (0.005)	0.009
Growth of productivity	-0.014 (0.007)	-0.017 (0.008)	-0.004 (0.007)	0.005 (0.008)	0.009
Growth of unit labour costs (ULC)	0.010 (0.014)	0.004 (0.010)	0.024 (0.017)	0.003 (0.020)	-0.021

Sources: Calculated from CEP-OECD Data Set, with Iceland, Portugal and Luxembourg omitted. See Bagliano, Brandolini and Dalmazzo (1991).
Notes: Price inflation is the increase in consumer prices. Gross domestic product is in constant dollars. Productivity is GDP divided by employment. Unit labour costs are defined as manufacturing wage divided by productivity. Standard errors in parenthesis.

that the British labour market failed to function properly. Analysts have offered diverse hypotheses that go beyond labour market troubles to explain why Britain's growth fell short of that of other capitalist countries in the post-World War II period (see Caves, 1968, for one assessment). Still, most agree that the country's labour market performance was below par and some have put great stress on the adverse economic effects of rigidities in the labour market. Minford, for example, identified: 'two major distortions in the UK labour market which prevent[ed] real wages and productivity from adjusting naturally to shifts in technology, demand, and industrial structure, and relocating those freed from one sector into other sectors ... the unemployment benefit system ... [and] the power of unions to raise wages relative

to non-union wages' (Minford, 1983, pp.2–3). His solution was to limit union power and enact policies to enhance the rewards of work over joblessness. Others (Layard, 1986, for instance) favoured more corporatist
Swedish-style arrangements.

One does not have to buy any particular policy cure to accept as plausible the view that improving the British economy required reforms in labour
market institutions and policies. The question is whether the reforms the
government adopted in the 1980s succeeded in improving the labour market
and curing the 'disease'.

The reform programme

The Thatcher government enacted a wide range of laws and programmes to
alter labour market performance. While no single document lays out the
goals of these laws and programmes, most observers would agree that they
were designed to weaken the power of unions, to enhance the rewards of
work relative to unemployment and other non-work-related benefits
(meeting Minford's two criticisms given above), to reduce govern-
ment/institutional influence on market outcomes, and to expand self-employment. The vision guiding the reforms was that of a more flexible labour market, where wages depended more on company performance than on
the 'going rate' (Oswald, 1992) and where labour was highly mobile and
firms responded rapidly to market signals — a labour market resembling the
decentralised US labour market rather than the regulated and institutionally
structured labour markets of EC–Europe.

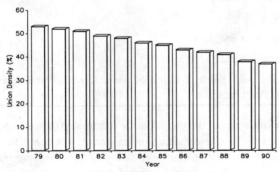

Figure 2.1 Union densities in the UK, 1979-90
Source: Beatson and Butcher (1993)
Note: Union membership expressed as a percentage of the civilian workforce in em-
ployment

Table 2.2 *British reforms with labour markets impacts, by goal of reform*

---

1) Reduce union power

a) Employment Act of 1980 abolishes statutory recognition procedures; extends grounds to refuse to join a union; limits picketing.

b) Employment Act of 1982 prohibits actions that force contracts with union employers; weakens closed shop; removes some union immunities.

c) Employment Act of 1984 weakens union immunities, requires pre-strike ballots, strengthens employer power to get injunctions.

d) Employment Act of 1988 removes further union immunities; extends individual rights to work against a union.

2) Change welfare state to increase work incentives

a) Diverse acts that reduce replacement ratio for unemployment benefits; eliminate benefits for young people.

b) Restart Programme introduced in 1986 required all unemployed to be interviewed about job search every six months.

c) Many administrative changes to make it more difficult to obtain benefits.

d) Diverse acts that maintain real value of other non-work benefits but lower the value relative to wages.

3) Reduce governmental role in market

a) Private pensions.

b) Abolish wages councils.

c) Lower tax rates.

d) Reduce government employment.

e) Privatisation.

4) Enhance self-employment and skills

a) Enterprise Allowance Scheme.

b) New training initiatives; Youth Training Scheme; Community Programme; Employment Training Programme.

Table 2.2 summarises some of the major policy changes, grouped along the four dimensions listed above. New trade union legislation was one of the most important policies to revamp the institutional structure of the labour market. Thatcher critic Ian Gilmour regards 'successful trade union reform [as] Margaret Thatcher's most important achievement' (1992, p.79). Freeman and Pelletier (1990) indicate that the new laws were the primary factor in the huge fall in British union density (see figure 2.1). While there is some disagree-

Table 2.3 *Estimates of the effect of unemployment on income, 1979 and 1990*

	1979	1990/91	Change
1. All	-0.80	-1.20	-0.40
2. Male	-0.74	-1.18	-0.44
3. Female	-0.93	-1.26	-0.33
4. Under 26	-0.74	-1.09	-0.34
5. 26-49	-0.83	-1.26	-0.44
6. 50-60	-0.94	-1.30	-0.37

Sources: General Household Surveys, 1979 and 1990.
Notes: Base = individuals aged 16-60 ($n = 12\ 181$ in 1979 and $n = 8\ 620$ in 1990/91). All equations include fifteen highest qualification dummies, four age dummies, four marital status dummies, ten regional dummies, eleven month-of-interview dummies, a self-employment dummy plus gender and race dummies. In 1990/91 a dummy for being on a government scheme was also included. Dependent variable is the log of gross weekly income from all sources.

ment about the role of government policy in reducing density (Disney, 1990) no one gainsays that the union movement lost power in the 1980s. The closed shop was outlawed, so that an increasing number of workplaces did not have complete union coverage; many firms chose not to recognise unions at workplaces; and those that did often signed single plant-single union agreements (Millward *et al.*, 1992). Strikes per worker fell more rapidly than in other countries in the 1980s, in part because of the drop in unionisation and in part because of the rise in unemployment (McCormick, 1993). Note, however, that strikes per worker in the UK were already dropping towards the OECD average prior to the 1980s and that the British strike record even in the 1970s was not excessive relative to past history (Elgar and Simpson, 1992, McConnell and Takla, 1993, Milner and Metcalf, 1993).[2] There is no indication that the legislation reduced strikes by lowering union propensity to strike at a given unemployment rate.

Concomitant with these changes was a pattern of faster productivity growth in union than in non-union firms, suggesting that unions reduced restrictive work practices and took a more positive attitude towards productivity. Overall, the union wage differential appears roughly constant throughout the 1980s (Blanchflower, 1991, Stewart, 1991, Lanot and Walker, 1992),[3] though in some sectors and for some sub-groups, union wages increased less than non-union wages (Gregg and Machin, 1992, Ingram, 1991, our table 2.7), reducing union differentials moderately. Even with a constant differential, however, the fall in density and strikes meant that British unions did

not dominate the job market in the 1980s as they did in the 1970s. The industrial relations reforms thus met one of Minford's two criteria for a better
functioning labour market: less union influence on outcomes.

On the welfare state front, the Thatcher government altered unemployment
benefits in several ways, as described in detail in Atkinson and
Micklewright (1989) and summarised in our appendix A. The result was
that a smaller proportion of the unemployed were eligible for benefits and
that the value of benefits, while roughly constant in real terms, fell relative
to average earnings. In 1978/9 the replacement rate of unemployment benefits relative to average male earnings was 16.3 per cent for a single person
and 26.2 per cent for a married couple on a husband's insurance; in 1991/2, the
replacement rates were 12.4 per cent and 20.1 per cent — declines of roughly
one quarter.[4]

To see how this change affected actual income received by those with jobs
and those without jobs, we turn to micro data from the General Household
Survey for 1979 and 1990/91. We regressed the logarithm of gross weekly
income from all sources on a dummy variable for unemployment status and a
host of standard controls in both years. The results of our calculations,
given in table 2.3, show that the incentive to work versus staying unemployed
increased by about 0.40 logarithm points for virtually every demographic
group. The changes in unemployment benefits thus increased the advantage of working over being unemployed, which — all else being equal —
should have reduced unemployment and shortened the duration of spells of
unemployment. Thus, the reforms met the second of Minford's criteria for a
better functioning labour market: an increase in the rewards to work relative to
unemployment.

Many of the other changes documented in table 2.2, and others that we
have not listed, could have also affected labour market performance. A full
evaluation of the 'Thatcher Programme' in the labour market requires detailed
analysis of each measure, its implementation, and its quantitative effect
on market outcomes or behaviour (presumably by comparing the sectors or
groups most affected by a given change with other sectors or groups). Such
an undertaking lies beyond the scope of this study. Instead, we examine the
effects of the reforms as a package, comparing a limited set of labour market
outcomes or relations 'before' and 'after' the reforms. We ask: did key labour market outcomes or relations change post-1979 in ways that indicate increased market flexibility? For our counterfactual of how the 1980s
might have looked in the absence of the reforms, we use outcomes or patterns
in other OECD countries in that period, or earlier British patterns.

The biggest problem our analysis faces is the poor macroeconomic
performance of the British economy, which could readily mask the success of

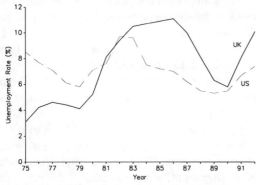

Figure 2.2 UK and US unemployment 1975-92

the microeconomic and structural reforms in which we are interested. The adverse effects of high or rising unemployment may dominate the positive effects of micro-institutional changes on labour market outcomes. We deal with this problem in two ways; in some calculations we take the year 1990, when unemployment was relatively low (see figure 2.2) as our indicator of the 'after' period, and we examine outcomes in the relatively low unemployment South East region as well.

Outcomes and adjustment patterns

Successful reform of the labour market ought to improve aggregate labour market outcomes such as unemployment rates, productivity growth and durations of unemployment, and ought to create more flexible disaggregate responses to market signals by individuals and enterprises.

Aggregate outcomes

To evaluate the impact of the reforms on aggregate outcomes, we contrast selected outcome variables in the UK with those variables in other OECD countries from 1980-88 relative to the analogous differences in outcomes pre-1980, using equation (1). Our estimated coefficients that measure British relative performance in the 1980s is given in column 4 of table 2.1. If the UK performed better in the 1980s relative to other OECD countries than in the 1970s (or earlier), the column 4 coefficients should show improvements compared with the coefficients in column 3 (or in columns 1 and 2 for earlier years).

The estimates show improvement in inflation and growth. The UK moved from doing worse to doing about the same as other countries. But on unemployment and employment-population rates, the difference between the UK and other OECD countries moved in the opposite direction. Despite numerous changes in definitions that reduced measured unemployment,[5] the rate of unemployment rose relative to unemployment in other OECD countries (see also figure 2.2, which contrasts the UK with the US). The relative worsening of the UK unemployment position was especially marked for male workers.

Despite the high unemployment during the 1980s, growth of real wages was high in the UK, indicating that the Thatcher reforms did not produce a better Phillips curve adjustment pattern. OECD data show that from 1979 to 1989 real hourly earnings in manufacturing increased by 2.6 per cent in the UK compared with 1.4 per cent in OECD–Europe despite the above-average rate of unemployment (9.5 per cent in the UK from 1980 to 1989 versus OECD–Europe 9.1 per cent, OECD, *Historical Statistics*, 1991).

Disaggregate adjustments: transitions

To try to detect improvements in the micro-functioning of the market, we turn to micro-data that measure worker or employer mobility or adjustments in transitions of workers among employment, unemployment, and other states, adjustments of employment to changing economic conditions and the response of earnings to differences in area unemployment and company performance.

A major goal of supply-side economic policies is to increase the rewards for work relative to non-work activity. As we saw in table 2.3, the Thatcher reforms accomplished this, raising the income gap between the employed and unemployed by roughly 0.40 ln points. All else being equal, the improved work/unemployment trade-off ought to have speeded the flow of labour from unemployment to employment. At the same time, the weakening of unions and privatisation of enterprises may have affected the flow of labour from employment to unemployment, potentially raising the rate of job loss. Formally, we examine labour market mobility in terms of a Markov matrix:

$$M = (P_{ij}) \tag{2}$$

where P_{ij} are the probabilities of moving from state i to state j. We identify the following states in the pre-Thatcher period: unemployment (u); working (w) as self-employed or as an employee; and not-in-the-labour force (n). In the post-reform period we identify one additional state: being on a government training scheme (y). By treating not-in-the-labour force and training as separate states, we avoid arbitrarily classifying them as part of a positive employment or negative unemployment outcome. By distinguishing employment and self-employment we can examine the effect of the government's effort to increase self-employment.

A flexible labour market should have high values of P_{uw}, with corresponding short durations of unemployment. It may also have high values of P_{wu} as well due to faster relocation of labour across sectors with intermediate spells of joblessness. The US job market, for instance, has high transition parameters compared with a typical European market, low durations of unemployment, moderately lower job tenure than some European countries, and substantial mobility of young workers. In 1988, for example, P_{wu} in the United States was 1.98 per cent a month, which was roughly three times the 0.68 per cent inflow from employment to unemployment in the UK; P_{uw} in the United States was 45.7 per cent, nearly five times the 9.5 per cent flow from unemployment to employment in the UK (OECD, *Economic Outlook*, 1990, p.13).

To see if transition matrices moved towards the more 'mobile' US pattern during the period of Thatcher reforms, we calculated transition frequencies for men and women 16-60 using retrospective Labour Force Survey questions that asked respondents 'about your situation twelve months ago — that is, in (month-of-interview, previous year)' and about their current state. For instance, we estimated the transition probability from unemployment to work (P_{uw}) as the proportion of people who said they were unemployed in the previous year but were currently working. The result are a set of recall-based transitions that relate what respondents said they were doing a year earlier to what they were doing in the survey week. Transition frequencies based on recall are, we recognise, subject to error that would not occur in a longitudinal file, but there is no reason to expect any trend in recall biases. Even perfectly estimated Markov transitions may not, moreover, be the best way to summarise transitions, as the actual hazard functions may reject the Markov assumption. Still, the transition matrices provide a way of assessing transitions before and after the labour market reforms.

We calculated transitions for the UK as a whole and for the 'low unemployment' South East region. To minimise the effect of cyclical factors on the transitions, we chose 1990 as our 'after year', though we have calculated Markov matrices for every year up to 1991 for which data exist. The transition probabilities and numbers used to calculate them for 1979 and 1990 are given in appendix B to this chapter. The steady state solutions to the Markov chains are shown in appendix C.

Table 2.4 gives transition matrices for men and women in 1979 and 1990. The top panel gives transitions with employment and self-employment lumped together as 'working'. The table reveals substantial changes in P_{uw}

Table 2.4 *Work transitions, 1979-90*

	w	u	y	n
Males 1979				
w	0.966	0.025		0.009
u	0.455	0.468		0.078
n	0.026	0.058		0.682
Males 1990				
w	0.959	0.031	0.003	0.010
u	0.318	0.568	0.084	0.113
y	0.313	0.229	0.407	0.051
n	0.219	0.087	0.050	0.693
Females 1979				
w	0.912	0.025		0.063
u	0.426	0.360		0.213
n	0.137	0.039		0.825
Females 1990				
w	0.926	0.048	0.002	0.027
u	0.433	0.346	0.049	0.221
y	0.319	0.169	0.380	0.132
n	0.166	0.062	0.015	0.772

Notes: Constructed from appendix table B3. Further details are available from the authors.

and P_{wu} (work-unemployment) in the direction of creating greater unemployment, with the (possibly desirable) increase in the P_{wu} transition from 0.025 to 0.031 accompanied by a decrease in the P_{uw} transition from 0.455 to 0.313. The steady state solution to the transition matrices for men shows a rise in male unemployment from 5 to 7 per cent and of male not-in-the-labour force from 4 to 5 per cent, and a predicted fall in the employment-population rate from 91-86 per cent. Data in the appendix show that even in the South-East region that did best in the 1980s, the increase in joblessness was associated with both a sizeable fall in the transition out of unemployment and an increase in the transition into unemployment. To make sure that our results do not hinge critically on the years we picked, we also took averages of different years and obtained the same qualitative story.[6] The changes in transition probabilities for men did not move the British Markov matrix very much in the direction of the more flexible United States.

The transition probabilities for women tell a different story. The rate of flow from employment to unemployment rose but that from employment to non-employment fell, with P_{ww} rising slightly from 1979 to 1990. At the same time the transition from unemployment to employment changed just modestly; while that from not-in-the-labour force to employment rose. The result was an increase in the predicted steady state employment-population rate for women. For the female part of the population, transitions moved in a way favourable to the reform programme. If the male transition matrix had changed in a similar manner to the female matrix, we would have judged the reforms (or something in the period) as a success in improving labour mobility.

However, overall, the transition from unemployment to employment worsened in the 1980s. This can be seen in the proportion of the jobless out of work over one year in the UK, which rose from 25 per cent in 1979 to 36 per cent in 1990 (OECD, *Employment Outlook*, 1985 and 1992). OECD data on durations of unemployment for other European countries show that the UK did not do better than other EC countries in altering the share of the unemployed who are long-term. The reforms that succeeded in making work more attractive relative to joblessness for men did not work in moving them into employment rapidly, though they may have done so for women.

Disaggregate adjustments: employment and wages

What about employment adjustments by firms? Given that UK employers were probably the most flexible in Europe prior to the 1980s, we do not expect great changes in employer responsiveness to economic shocks. But, recognising that the reductions in union strength, privatisation of firms, and the changed labour relations climate might have increased the speed of employment adjustments, we estimated employment adjustment equations for private sector establishments in the 1980 and 1990 Workplace Industrial Relations Surveys (WIRS) of the following form:

$$\ln E(t) = a + k(\text{signals to change}) + (1 - k)\ln E(t - 1) + \text{Controls} \quad (3)$$

where E = employment; and the major signals to change are whether the establishment reported that sales rose or fell in the preceding twelve months; *DUP*, a dummy = 1 if they reported a rise; *DDN*, a dummy = 1 if they reported a fall in sales. In a simple partial adjustment model, a large coefficient on lagged employment implies a more sluggish adjustment pattern — employment depends more on past employment than on the signal to change. The

Table 2.5 *WIRS employment regressions*

	(1)	(2)
	1980	1990
Log E_{t-1}	0.9903	0.9796
	(0.0044)	(0.0048)
Demand up	0.0268	0.0764
	(0.0093)	(0.0135)
Demand down	-0.0707	-0.0823
	(0.0257)	(0.0243)
Constant	0.0828	0.1412
	(0.0315)	(0.0355)
$\bar{R}^2$	0.9821	0.9783
N	1258	1236

Sources: Workplace Industrial Relations Surveys, 1980, 1984, 1990.
Notes: Base = private sector establishments with at least 25 employees (full or part-time) at the time the sample was drawn (usually 2-3 years earlier) as well as at the date of interview. Equations 1–2 include ten regional dummies, eight industry dummies and a union recognition dummy (any group of workers, manual or non-manual) and a dummy variable where the respondent reported that they did not know what had happened to demand (always insignificant). *DUP* = 1 if respondent reports the change in value of sales over the preceding twelve months was rising, zero otherwise. *DDN* = 1 if respondent reports the change in value of sales over the preceding twelve months was falling, zero otherwise. Specifications equalivalent to those reported in Blanchflower, Millward and Oswald (1991). Standard errors in parentheses.

coefficients on the sales-up or down variables also indicate firm responsiveness; if firms responded more to changes in sales post-1980 than in 1980, this would suggest more rapid short-term adjustments.

The regression results in table 2.5 provide only weak evidence of greater employment responsiveness in 1990 than in 1980. The coefficient on lagged employment fell from 0.99 in 1980 to 0.98 in 1990. But because the WIRS has no 'scale' variable for size of firm besides employment, the lagged employment coefficients are biased towards unity (a big firm will invariably be big the next year), making possible changes in adjustment behaviour hard to detect. Thus we put greater stress on the increase in the coefficients on sales up and (to a lesser extent) sales down dummy variables after 1980. The change in these coefficients suggests that firms adjusted employment more

Table 2.6 *UK wage responsiveness to regional unemployment, 1973-90*

	(1)	(2)	(3)	(4)
	1973-1980		1981-1990	
Log U_t	-0.0896	-0.0697	-0.1619	-0.0927
	(18.05)	(4.41)	(22.91)	(2.79)
Reg. dummies	No	Yes	No	Yes
Constant	1.9049	2.8946	3.4217	3.3408
	(84.72)	(90.46)	(104.70)	(51.19)
$\bar{R}^2$	0.7029	0.7076	0.6654	0.6720
F	4387.04	3240.78	2916.73	2534.60
DF	96352.0	96332.0	79108.0	79098.0
N	96405.0	96405.0	79163.0	79163.0

Sources: General Household Survey Series.
Notes: Unless stated otherwise the following control variables were included: ten industry dummies, four marital status dummies, fifteen highest qualification dummies, seventeen year dummies, a gender dummy, experience and its square, a part-time dummy, eleven month-of-interview dummies, a race dummy, eleven regional dummies interacted with dummy for years up to 1977. Dependent variable is real log of gross earnings. U_t is the regional unemployment rate. t-statistics in parentheses.

in 1990 than in 1980,[7] consistent with some increase in flexibility of employment, though the pattern is hardly overwhelming.

The Thatcher reforms might also be expected to make wages more responsive to labour market conditions. To see if this was the case, we examined the link between unemployment/other indicators of market imbalance or pressure at a disaggregate region and firm level and wages. For regional disaggregation we rely on Blanchflower and Oswald (1993), which gives 'Wage Curves' — the relation between regional unemployment and the log of gross earnings, with diverse other factors held fixed — for the periods 1973–90 and 1981–90. Their estimated coefficients on unemployment, presented in table 2.6, are consistent with the notion that reforms created greater wage responsiveness: the coefficients in the column 1 and 3 regressions are -0.09 in the 1973–80 and –0.17 in the 1981–90 periods; those which include regional dummies in columns 2 and 4 also show an increase in wage responsiveness to unemployment, though of a much more modest magnitude, from –0.07 to –0.09. There may be something in the data, but it is far from overwhelming.

Table 2.7 *Wage equation, 1980 and 1990 — skilled manual workers*

	(1) 1980	(2) 1990
Demand up	-0.0081	0.0441
	(0.45)	(1.94)
Demand down	-0.0217	-0.0316
	(1.30)	(0.77)
Union recognition	0.0329	0.0061
	(1.81)	(0.61)
50-99 employees	0.0385	0.0451
	(1.60)	(1.24)
100-199 employees	0.0276	0.1154
	(1.12)	(3.10)
200-499 employees	0.0524	0.1291
	(2.07)	(3.42)
500-999 employees	0.0889	0.1583
	(3.20)	(3.84)
1000-1999 employees	0.1409	0.2259
	(4.42)	(5.42)
2000+ employees	0.1593	0.2254
	(4.81)	(4.49)
Constant	4.4649	9.2001
	(109.92)	(138.14)
$\bar{R}^2$	0.2866	0.3445
F	14.76	14.47
DF	997	739
N	1028	770

Sources: Workplace Industrial Relations Survey 1980 and 1990.
Notes: Equations also include the following controls: per cent part-time, per cent manuals female, eight industry dummies, ten regional dummies, single establishment dummy. Base = private sector establishments. Specifications equivalent to those reported in Blanchflower (1984) and Blanchflower, Oswald and Garrett (1989). t-statistics in parentheses.

In order to analyse wage responsiveness at the establishment level, we estimated the effects of our demand-up and demand-down dummy variables and selected other variables on the earnings of skilled workers in the WIRS surveys. Because the WIRS does not provide wages in preceding years, however, the regression focuses on differences in wage levels rather than on changes in wages, which makes interpretation of coefficients on the change in sales variables as adjustment parameters problematic.[8] This said, the regression results in table 2.7 indicate that wages were more affected by changed market conditions in 1990 than in 1980. The coefficients on the demand-up and demand-down variables are insignificant in 1980 but are positive on the demand-up dummy and negative on the demand-down dummy in 1990. In addition, the table 2.7 regressions reveal two other potentially important changes in the effect of variables on earnings. First, there is a modest drop in the coefficient on union recognition, consistent with the presumed reduction in union power. Second, there is an increase in the effect of establishment size on earnings, consistent with the general widening of wage differentials over the period. If the former is interpreted as a (possibly desirable) reduction in non-competitive wage differentials, the latter should be interpreted as the opposite: an increase in non-competitive wage differentials (in the absence of some identifiable skill or supply-based cause for the change). From this perspective the greater size-of-firm effects on wages suggest that increasing the power of firms in wage-setting may have simply shifted the locus of 'insider' or rent-sharing pressures in wage setting from unions to firms.

Finally, in standard theory, markets with more limited institutional interventions should produce smaller rent-related differentials in pay than mar-

(Notes to table 2.7 continued)

Demand Up and Demand Down are dummy variables derived from the following questions: (a) 1980 ...'Over the past twelve months would you say that demand for the main products or services of this establishment have been (1) rising, (2) falling, (3) neither'. (b) 1990...As for 1980 but option (3) is now 'stable'. Demand Up is set to one if (1) above, zero otherwise and Demand Down set to one if (2) above, zero otherwise.

Dependent variable is log of gross weekly earnings. In 1980 the question asked was, 'Over the last month what has been the gross pay of the typical employee in each of these groups I am going to read out?'. In 1990 the question was, 'If all employees in this group were listed individually in order of their gross earnings (including any bonuses or overtime) which of the ranges on this card would apply to the employee in the middle of such a list?' For estimation purposes midpoints were allocated.

Table 2.8 *Standard deviation in ln hourly earnings and the effect of region and industry on ln hourly earnings, 1979–1990/91*

	1979	1990/91	Change
SD in Ln hourly earnings	0.526	0.611	0.085
SD in region coefficients	0.059	0.085	0.026
SD in industry coefficients	0.118	0.142	0.024
Residual S.E. from regression	0.377	0.455	0.078

Notes: Based on regressions in appendix B, based on GHS survey. The standard deviations in the second and third lines are standard deviations of the estimated coefficients on region and industry (including a zero for the omitted group).

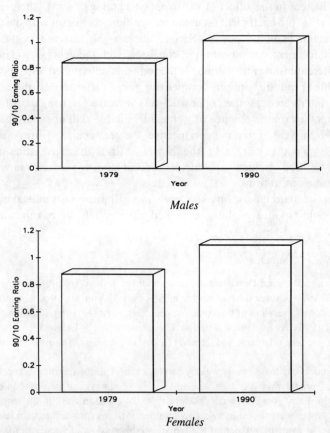

Males

Females

Figure 2.3 90/10 Log earnings ratios
Source: NES

kets where government or union interventions affect wages and ought to bring the unemployment rates of workers with differing skills closer together, as flexible wages respond to market imbalances and create employment for those who would in a less flexible world end up unemployed.

We examine the potential effect of the Thatcher reforms on wage relativities by multivariate regressions that link these outcomes to demographic characteristics of workers, and to region and industry dummy variables, among other factors. Table 2.8 summarises the wage differential results in terms of standard deviations of the estimated coefficients of region and industry on ln earnings and overall standard deviation of ln earnings (appendix B contains our regressions for 1979 and 1990/91). There are three findings. First is the massive increase in the raw standard deviation of ln earnings from 0.53 to 0.61. This growth of inequality is consistent with the evidence of a massive rise in earnings inequality shown by the decile incomes in the New Earnings Survey (figure 2.3). Second, the increased dispersion in the dummy variables for region and industry show that some of this rise took the form of greater regional and industrial earnings differentials for nominally similar workers. Third, however, the large increase in the standard deviation of the residual in the earnings equation tells us that in the UK (as in the US) most of the rise in earnings inequality occurred for workers with similar measured skills, which is not what we would expect from a better functioning labour market.

How should one interpret the increased inequalities in table 2.8.?

Shifts in demand and supply that raise returns to skill may account for some of the rise in earnings differentials or inequality. But we find it hard to explain the massive increase in inequality in terms of the operation of an ideal competitive market. Differentials by qualification fell in the early 1980s and rose in the latter part of the decade (Schmidt, 1993, Katz *et al.*, 1993), so that our regressions show roughly comparable education differentials in 1990/91 as in 1979 (see our appendix B tables). This pattern makes dubious any broadsweeping explanation of the increase in inequality in terms of market-driven rises in the returns to a single skill factor. While the table 2.6 regressions suggest that regional differentials may have widened in response to unemployment, the increased differential in unemployment rates among regions[9] implies that the labour market reforms did not create a sufficiently rapid adjustment process to offset the different demand shocks that affected the regions. We speculate that the pattern of rising inequality and unemployment differentials may reflect a tendency for decentralised labour markets to 'de-couple' in a period of high unemployment. Our sus-

Table 2.9a *Self-employment transitions, 1979-90, UK*

	se	e	u	y	n
Males 1979					
se	0.9285	0.0528	0.0132		0.0055
e	0.0200	0.9441	0.0262		0.0097
u	0.0390	0.4157	0.4676		0.0776
n	0.0058	0.2544	0.0577		0.6821
Males 1990					
se	0.9018	0.0597	0.0283	0.0018	0.0084
e	0.0199	0.9348	0.0310	0.0035	0.0109
u	0.0523	0.2392	0.5205	0.0840	0.1040
y	0.0255	0.2873	0.2291	0.4073	0.0509
n	0.0085	0.1958	0.0759	0.0503	0.6694
Females 1979					
se	0.8688	0.0679	0.0163		0.0471
e	0.0058	0.9053	0.0252		0.0637
u	0.0063	0.4198	0.3603		0.2135
n	0.0031	0.1335	0.0386		0.8248
Females 1990					
se	0.8129	0.1243	0.0142	0.0037	0.0449
e	0.0080	0.9140	0.0276	0.0022	0.0482
u	0.0365	0.3755	0.3294	0.0488	0.2098
y	0.0064	0.3131	0.1693	0.3802	0.1310
n	0.0103	0.1493	0.0596	0.0154	0.7654

Notes: *se*: self-employed, *e*: employee in employment, *u*: registered unemployed, *y*: government training scheme, *n*: not in workforce.

picion is that rent-sharing and insider pressures on wages are greater in loose than in tight labour markets: in the former low wage firms do not face market pressures to pay 'the going rate' as they do when unemployment is low. If this is correct, some of the lessening of institutional interventions that was meant to create a more perfect market may have perversely increased market segmentation and dispersion of earnings. For instance, if lower unemployment benefit replacement ratios increased the incentive to take a job quickly, they also would have reduced the pressure from search towards a

Table 2.9b *Self-employment transitions, 1979-90, South East including London*

	se	e	u	y	n
Males 1979					
se	0.9243	0.0500	0.0189		0.0068
e	0.0261	0.9472	0.0178		0.0088
u	0.0797	0.5319	0.3110		0.0771
n	0.0100	0.2781	0.0389		0.6729
Males 1990					
se	0.9020	0.0579	0.0301	0.0014	0.0087
e	0.0270	0.9335	0.0275	0.0016	0.0104
u	0.0639	0.3018	0.4783	0.0512	0.1049
y	0.1000	0.3400	0.1800	0.3600	0.0200
n	0.0080	0.2728	0.0833	0.0354	0.6005
Females 1979					
se	0.8397	0.0801	0.0289		0.0513
e	0.0062	0.9063	0.0216		0.0659
u	0.0154	0.4962	0.2500		0.2385
n	0.0025	0.1366	0.0317		0.8292
Females 1990					
se	0.8039	0.1382	0.0127	0.0042	0.0409
e	0.0104	0.9156	0.0260	0.0010	0.0471
u	0.0425	0.4286	0.2664	0.0193	0.2432
y	0.0256	0.3077	0.2051	0.4103	0.0513
n	0.0145	0.1742	0.0586	0.0088	0.7330

Note: definitions as table 2.9a.

convergence of wages among work sites. Whatever the causal factors for rising inequality, those factors evidently dominated the rent-squeezing effects of the reforms.

Self-employment and employment

The Thatcher government introduced measures to aid individuals, including the unemployed, to become self-employed business persons as part of its effort to create an entrepreneurial culture. Such policies included secured loans, advice centres, financial incentives such as the Enterprise Allowance Scheme, grants, training programmes, tax deductions, higher VAT thresholds, and various regional policies to encourage firm formation (Smeaton, 1992). By the simple measure of growth of the self-employed share of the workforce these policies seem to have succeeded. The proportion of the British workforce who were self-employed rose in the period (see Curran and Borrows, 1989, Daly, 1991, Campbell and Daly, 1992) more rapidly than in other OECD countries (OECD, 1992). *Employment Gazette* data show an increase in the self-employed share of the labour force from 7.2 per cent in 1979 to 10.7 per cent in 1992. But self-employment can be an unstable and poor paying option forced onto people unable to find work as wage or salary earners: there were many self-employed men selling apples on street corners in the great depression. Was the 1980s rise in self-employment a success (see OECD, 1992) or a form of disguised unemployment?

To answer this question, we turn to the transition matrices in table 2.9 that distinguish between flows into and out of self-employment. In appendix C we use these transition data to construct Markov transition matrices. While the Markov assumption is probably less adequate for self-employment than for other states, it still offers a useful benchmark for assessing changes. Among men the transitions from unemployment and non-labour force to self-employment increased from 1979 to 1990, consistent with government policy favouring self-employment. But there was also an increase in the flow from self-employment to unemployment or non-employment. We could find no evidence of any change in the flow from employment to self-employment for men;[10] it is hard to believe claims that an 'enterprise culture' has been established without some significant increase in this flow. Moreover, our calculations show that on balance there was no increase in the steady-state male self-employment rate due to changes in the transition matrices from 1979 to 1990. The steady-state proportion of men who were self-employed would have been 22 per cent with the 1979 matrix whereas with the 1990 transition matrix it would have been 18 per cent; the actual rate in 1990 was 14 per cent. Both matrices thus predict increased rates of male self-employment but both also overstate that rate of self-employment in 1990. That we get a greater predicted increase in the steady-state solution with the 1979 than the 1990 matrix suggests, moreover, that the increase in the P_{seu} transition dominated the increase in the P_{use} transition, which casts doubt on contribution of the reforms to the rise in self-employment. For females, the 1990 transitions predict a modestly higher self-employment rate than the 1979 transitions, though here both matrices give 'steady state' results comparable to the observed self-employment rates.[11]

Table 2.10 *Full-time and part-time work; Great Britain 1978–92, seasonally adjusted, thousands*

	Employees		Self-employed		All	
	Full-time	Part-time	Full-time	Part-time	Full-time	Part-time
All						
1978	17854	4392	1602	240	19456	4632
1981*	16726	4499	1724	347	18450	4846
1983	16030	4527	1767	393	17797	4920
1985	16141	4769	2050	500	18191	5269
1987	16049	5031	2229	571	18278	5602
1989	16750	5393	2673	509	19423	5902
1991	16018	5705	2499	567	18517	6272
1992	15450	5768	n.a.	n.a.	n.a.	n.a.
Male						
1978	12390	704	1385	93	13775	797
1981*	11439	718	1543	99	12982	817
1983	10908	766	1526	126	12434	892
1985	10827	810	1753	170	12580	980
1987	10559	878	1895	204	12454	1082
1989	10814	911	2258	170	13072	1081
1991	10265	1077	2118	215	12383	1292
1992	9868	1134	n.a.	n.a.	n.a.	n.a.
Female						
1978	5499	3653	217	147	5716	3800
1981*	5262	3806	181	248	5443	4054
1983	5122	3761	241	267	5363	4028
1985	5314	3958	297	331	5611	4289
1987	5490	4153	334	367	5824	4520
1989	5936	4481	415	339	6351	4820
1991	5753	4628	381	352	6134	4980
1992	5582	4634	n.a.	n.a.	n.a.	n.a.

Sources: *Employment Gazette* Historical Supplement no. 3, June 1992 and *Employment Gazette*, January 1993.
Note: Except where noted, all estimates are for June. * = September.

The evidence that a rise in self-employment for both sexes was predictable in terms of 1979 transition matrices raises the possibility that the trend in self-employment was due to factors other than government policies;[12] at the minimum it suggests the need for a more detailed investigation of the contribution of policy to the change than a simple 'before–after' comparison. An alternative way to probe the rise of self-employment is to estimate income differences between self-employed and other workers. If self-employment was largely disguised unemployment, we would expect rising income gaps between self-employed and other workers in the 1980s. If self-employment was a more positive outcome, we would expect constant or even declining income gaps. We estimated the effect of a 0–1 dummy variable for self-employment on reported gross weekly income in the General Household Surveys for 1979 and 1990. Our regression model contained many human capital controls, and a set of region dummy variables. The estimated coefficient on self-employment in 1979 was -0.77 ($t = 28.6$); the coefficient on self-employment in 1990 was -0.60 ($t = 22.6$).[13] The decrease in the gap between the two groups between 1979 and 1990 indicates that the increased flow into self-employment did not come at the expense of declines in their relative earnings.

Our bottom-line assessment is that the rise of self-employment, whether policy-induced or not, was a positive feature of the period. But the growth of self-employment must be placed in the context of extraordinary reductions in employment of full-time workers, particularly full-time men. Table 2.10 gives employment figures from 1978 to 1992 for four groups: full and part-time employed workers and full and part-time self-employed workers. The two things that stand out for men are the massive drop in full-time employment and the upward trend in self-employment. The latter, however, is by no means large enough to compensate for the former. Among women, by contrast, the situation looks much better, but increased self-employment is dwarfed by an increase in full-time employment. With greater employment, and improved earnings relative to men (see appendix B), women workers appear to be a major beneficiary of the reforms.

Conclusion

We conclude that the Thatcher reforms succeeded in reducing union power and increasing the incentive to work — and may have increased the responsiveness of wages and employment at the micro-level. But they did not improve the response of real wages to unemployment nor the transition for men out of unemployment, and were accompanied by rising wage inequalities that do not seem to reflect the working of an ideal market system.

While there are glimmers of improved market adjustments and responsiveness that may serve the British economy well in a prolonged boom, there is no strong evidence that the British labour market experienced a deep microeconomic change. Indeed, the observed outcomes raise the disheartening possibility that the reforms in fact brought the UK a mixture of the worst of two possible worlds: the massive wage inequality of the decentralised US labour market together with high and lengthy spells of unemployment, European-style.

Why did the reforms not succeed as their proponents hoped?

One interpretation is that they have not gone far enough nor had enough time to succeed; the road to Neo-Classical Nirvana is bumpy, as marketisation in East Europe or in Sweden indicate. Just wait until the mid-1990s, and we will all be praising the labour market reforms for setting the precondition for the British economic miracle. It took Chile, after all, some 10–15 years before its market reforms produced a vibrant economy. Given that Mrs Thatcher seemed to think that the reforms had cured the British Disease by 1988, this is a loose interpretation; with unspecified long and variable lags for successful outcomes, it is nearly impossible to reject the value of the reforms.

The other interpretation is that the reforms were premised on an incorrect understanding of how the labour market operates. In particular, the reform package failed to recognise the power of insider pressures for rent-sharing and related policies that segment decentralised labour markets in periods of less than full employment. From this perspective, reforms that 'free up markets' may require exceptionally tight labour markets to succeed. The Thatcher reforms might have done wonders in the 1950s-1960s but could not deliver their promise in the 1980s and 1990s because of the high rate of unemployment. This hypothesis suggests that the success of market-enhancing policy reforms does not depend solely on the reforms themselves but also on the broader economic environment and that in a world subject to business cycle and other fluctuations, placing all of one's eggs in the decentralised labour market of competitive theory may be far from ideal.

Appendix A Major reductions in benefits for the unemployed, 1979–88

Ending of earnings related supplement (ERS)
The Social Security Act (no. 2) 1980 abolished ERS. The 15 per cent rate of

ERS was reduced to 10 per cent in January 1981 and from January 1982 no new claims could be made for ERS. As a result no ERS was payable after June 1982. Britain is thus the only member of the EC with no element of unemployment benefits (UB) linked to past earnings.

Taxation of unemployment benefit

The income tax treatment of the unemployed was changed in two respects; tax refunds are no longer paid until after the resumption of work, or the end of the tax year if that is sooner and unemployment benefit and supplementary benefit both became taxable. Both of these measures were implemented in 1982.

Suspension of statutory indexation

The Social Security Act (no. 2), 1980, suspended the direct indexation of national insurance (NI) short-term benefits for three years, giving powers to increase them by up to 5 percentage points below inflation. Between 1980-83 there was a 5 per cent withholding of unemployment benefit. The Social Security Act of 1986 provides for the government to vary the amount of any increase in benefits more or less at will.

More stringent administration

The operation of Unemployment Review Officers (UROs), responsible for finding out what the claimant is doing to find a job, traditionally based on the supplementary benefit (SB) side, were extended to cover those receiving NI Unemployment Benefit supplemented by SB in 1980. The number of UROs was increased from 300 in 1978 to 880 in 1981. In 1983 the Department of Employment set up Regional Benefit Investigation teams. The total number of staff in the Department of Health and Social Security allocated to fraud work increased from 2044 in 1980–81 to 3674 in 1986–7.

In 1984 a major drive was started in fifty-nine areas to identify social security abuse. UROs questioned 18–25-year-olds about why they left jobs; the Social Security Policy Inspectorate interviewed young people not joining a Government scheme. The Restart programme was introduced in 1986 with a benefit monitoring function. A more stringent availability-to-work test was introduced in 1986 involving a new questionnaire for new claimants. A revised questionnaire for new claimants and those called for Restart interviews was introduced in 1988. All unemployed people were to be called to restart interviews every six months and all new claims were to be handled by more senior staff than before. In 1989 anyone who refused a 'reasonable' job offer would have benefit removed, even if this meant accepting lower pay than in the person's previous job.

Disqualification period increased

The Social Security Act of 1986 extended the maximum period of benefit disqualification from six to thirteen weeks. This applies where there is quitting without cause, or loss of job through industrial misconduct, or refusal to take suitable work or training offers. From April 1988 there was a further increase to twenty-six weeks. The Act also allows that days of disqualification count towards the entitlement to a total of 312 days of benefit.

Contribution conditions

The Social Security Act of 1988 tightened the contribution condition for NI benefit. The entitlement was altered to depend upon a contribution record for the two preceding tax years rather than one. Class 1 contributions on earnings of at least 50 times the lower weekly earnings limit must have been paid or credited in both years.

Student entitlements removed

From 1986 regulations were made to remove the entitlement by full-time students to UB and SB benefits during the 'grant-aided period', effectively ending entitlements for most students in the short vacations.

Mortgage interest deductions reduced

As from 1987 owner-occupiers aged under 60 were allowed to receive only 50 per cent of the mortgage interest eligible for SB during the first sixteen weeks on benefit. Claimants then have to make an appropriate application within four weeks of the end of the period or else start a new claim again.

16 and 17-year-olds' entitlements removed

The Social Security Act, 1988 and the Employment Act, 1988, made major changes in the income support for school-leavers aged under 18. The former removes the general entitlements to benefits, allowing Income Support (IS) — which replaced SB in 1988 — to be given only on a discretionary basis where 'severe hardship' might occur (this might include those with disabilities and single parents). The Act also allows parents to continue to receive child benefits for a period after their child leaves school. The Employment Act extends the circumstances in which benefit may be withdrawn or reduced for unemployed people leaving or refusing places on job training schemes. This has had the effect of removing all 16–17-year-olds from the official unemployment figures which is a count of unemployed claimants.

School-leavers' entitlements reduced

Prior to 1980 school-leavers could claim benefit as soon as they left school.

In 1980 the concept of a 'terminal date' was introduced, under which benefit could not be claimed until approximately the first Monday of the following term. Easter leavers entered for a summer examination were deemed to be ineligible for benefit until September.

Payment of rates and poll tax

The Social Security Act of 1986 introduced a common basis of assessment for Housing Benefit (HB) and IS. Where a person's income was below the IS level, then HB was paid in full, where this was 100 per cent of rents and 80 per cent of rates. Where the income was above IS level the rate rebate was reduced by 20 per cent of the excess, and the rent rebate is reduced by 65 per cent of the excess. Claimants had thus to meet a minimum of 20 per cent of the rates. Subsequently claimants would have to pay a portion, and subsequently all, of their poll/council tax.

Social Fund

In April 1988 the Social Fund replaced supplementary benefit single payments. This old system allowed one-off payments to be made for claimants facing exceptional needs. Major household items such as furniture and general maintenance could be financed in this way. Payments are at the discretion of Social Fund Officers; there is no legal right to appeal if help is refused. The payments are in most cases loans, not grants, the only exception, apart from maternity and funeral payments, being grants for certain types of community care. To repay loans a claimant's weekly benefit is reduced, normally by 15 per cent, for a maximum period of eighteen months. The loans are not available to families with savings in excess of £500.

Source: Atkinson and Micklewright (1989).

Appendix B

Table B1 *Unemployment level equations, 1979-91 (GHS) — ages 16-60*

	1979		1990-91	
Variable	Coefficient	t-statistic	Coefficient	t-statistic
Male	0.0107	2.67	0.0384	7.88
Black	0.0390	3.71	0.0557	4.71
Separated	0.0155	0.98	0.0295	1.53
Divorced	0.0316	2.50	0.0151	1.17
Widowed	-0.0039	0.27	-0.0436	2.05
Married	-0.0357	6.06	-0.0598	8.58
Age 20-24	-0.0244	2.86	-0.0964	8.99
Age 25-34	-0.0389	4.36	-0.1182	11.15
Age 35-44	-0.0564	6.02	-0.1395	12.33
Age 45-54	-0.0616	6.49	-0.1548	13.21
Age 55-60	-0.0610	5.94	-0.1316	9.94
Qualifications				
Higher degree	-0.0394	1.81	-0.0709	3.32
Degree	-0.0432	5.02	-0.0786	8.84
Teaching qual.	-0.0549	3.79	-0.0625	3.73
HNC/HND	-0.0545	5.70	-0.0892	9.07
Nurse	-0.0214	1.43	-0.0496	3.21
A-levels	-0.0511	6.49	-0.0810	9.94
≥5 O-levels	-0.0535	7.96	-0.0627	8.01
1-4 O + cler.	-0.0530	3.36	-0.0515	3.89
1-4 O-levels	-0.0496	5.95	-0.0387	4.39
Clerical/comm	-0.0150	1.45	-0.0330	2.51
CSE	-0.0314	2.72	-0.0114	0.97
Apprenticeship	-0.0235	2.91	-0.0459	3.29
Foreign	-0.0270	1.67	-0.0258	1.21
Other	-0.0110	0.89	-0.0278	1.49

(Table B1 continued)

| | 1979 | | 1990-91 | |
Variable	Coefficient	t-statistic	Coefficient	t-statistic
Regional dummies				
North	0.0292	3.35	0.0627	5.87
Yorks/Humber	0.0143	1.92	0.0499	5.45
NW	0.0329	4.81	0.0492	5.97
E Midlands	0.0114	1.40	0.0339	3.56
W Midlands	0.0195	2.71	0.0251	2.82
East Anglia	-0.0024	0.22	-0.0006	0.05
London	0.0010	0.14	0.0181	2.10
SW	0.0129	1.57	0.0420	4.49
Wales	0.0253	2.62	0.0482	4.42
Scotland	0.0361	4.90	0.0471	5.08
Constant	0.1160	11.07	0.2263	14.42
F	9.85		22.42	
$\bar{R}^2$	0.0305		0.0699	
DF	12897		13347	
N	12944		13395	

Source: General Household Surveys, 1979–90.
Notes: All equations also include year dummies and 11-month dummies. Estimation by OLS. Dummy variable set to one if unemployed on a government scheme, zero if employed. Excluded categories: December, no qualifications, single, age 16–20, South East.

Table B2 *Unemployment level equations (LFS) — UK total, 1979, 1990 and 1991*

Variable	1979 Coeff.	t-stat.	1990 Coeff.	t-stat.	1991 Coeff.	t-stat
Male	0.0077	4.87	0.0138	6.30	0.0254	10.83
Separated	0.0645	7.40	0.0334	3.56	0.0365	3.71
Divorced	0.0514	10.05	0.0443	7.18	0.0520	8.00
Widowed	0.0163	2.71	-0.0178	1.71	-0.0171	1.48
Married	-0.0103	4.55	-0.0438	13.76	-0.0492	14.37
Age 20-24	-0.0140	4.12	-0.1116	23.02	-0.0970	18.06
Age 25-34	-0.0308	8.69	-0.1238	25.59	-0.1273	23.86
Age 35-44	-0.0523	14.09	-0.1514	29.48	-0.1573	27.90
Age 45-54	-0.0597	15.90	-0.1608	30.18	-0.1717	29.34
Age 55-60	-0.0565	13.77	-0.1505	24.85	-0.1707	25.87
Race dummies						
Polish	0.0040	0.32	n.a.		n.a.	
Italian	0.0037	0.35	n.a.		n.a.	
Other European	0.0136	2.01	n.a.		n.a.	
W Indian	0.0474	6.20	0.0578	4.91	0.0719	5.77
Indian	0.0254	3.65	0.0442	4.77	0.0432	4.43
Pakistani	0.0657	5.29	0.1118	7.55	0.1748	11.73
Bangladeshi	0.0202	0.63	0.1336	3.57	0.1130	3.43
Chinese	-0.0415	2.18	0.0452	2.08	0.0256	1.02
African	0.0743	4.99	0.1240	5.36	0.1884	7.79
Arab	0.0566	1.79	0.1083	2.58	0.1731	4.33
Mixed origin	n.a.		0.0313	1.99	0.0470	2.80
Other origin	0.0238	2.37	0.0502	2.96	0.0470	2.62
Qualifications						
Higher degree	n.a.		-0.0827	9.53	-0.1001	11.38
Degree	-0.0417	8.52	-0.0908	19.92	-0.0932	19.09
Other deg.	-0.0497	8.31	-0.0817	9.10	-0.0942	9.65
HNC/HND	-0.0457	6.69	-0.0960	14.62	-0.0939	13.79
Teaching qual. - FE	n.a.		-0.0954	4.55	-0.0901	4.51

(Table B2 continued)

Variable	1979 Coeff.	t-stat.	1990 Coeff.	t-stat.	1991 Coeff.	t-stat
Teaching qual-second.	-0.0437	6.30	-0.0634	4.64	-0.0676	4.27
Teaching qual-primary	-0.0361	6.72	-0.0517	4.30	-0.0703	4.98
Nurse	-0.0356	15.06	-0.0767	10.42	-0.0903	11.23
App. complete	-0.0725	11.41	n.a.		n.a.	
App. incomplete	-0.0523	6.63	n.a.		n.a.	
ONC/OND	-0.0361	7.87	-0.0859	14.00	-0.0988	14.75
City & Guilds	-0.0385	10.69	-0.0703	18.26	-0.0581	13.70
A-levels	-0.0417	17.46	-0.0791	17.24	-0.0877	17.82
O-levels	-0.0248	6.33	-0.0663	21.24	-0.0678	20.45
CSE	-0.0100	2.68	-0.0305	5.78	-0.0326	5.61
YTS Cert	n.a.		0.0676	2.87	0.1222	4.32
Other prof/voc.	0.0031	0.02	-0.0366	9.13	-0.0304	6.92
Regional dummies						
North	0.0454	13.47	0.0785	15.79	0.0391	6.60
Yorks/Humber	0.0145	5.05	0.0336	7.99	-0.0006	0.11
NW	0.0235	8.82	0.0391	9.96	0.0148	3.43
E Midlands	0.0075	2.30	0.0263	5.95	-0.0067	1.26
W Midlands	0.0058	2.09	0.0221	5.36	0.0101	2.00
East Anglia	0.0020	0.46	0.0033	0.57	-0.0221	3.30
London	-0.0028	1.02	0.0123	3.10	-0.0174	4.04
SW	0.0091	2.95	0.0072	1.70	-0.0040	0.75
Wales	0.0297	8.18	0.0470	8.93	0.0184	2.97
Scotland	0.0388	13.37	0.0556	13.70	0.0175	3.43
Constant	0.0996	20.23	0.2567	50.96	0.2967	49.01
F	45.29		95.25		97.77	
$\overline{R}^2$	0.0226		0.0614		0.0613	
DF	91886		69079		68140	
N	91935		69128		68187	

Source: Labour Force Surveys 1979, 1990 and 1991.
Notes: All equations also include month dummies. Estimation by OLS. Dependent variable set to one if respondent was unemployed or on a government scheme in the survey week, zero if employed. Excluded categories: March, no qualifications, single, age 16–20, South East. In 1979 degree and higher degree included as a single category. In 1979 'other origin' includes 'mixed origin'.

Table B3 *Labour market transitions, 1979–91 (LFS)*

	16-25		Male		Female	
	P	F	P	F	P	F
UK 1979						
wn	0.048	899	0.009	514	0.063	2310
wu	0.043	805	0.025	1390	0.025	912
uw	0.512	660	0.455	990	0.426	537
un	0.130	168	0.078	169	0.213	269
nu	0.050	575	0.058	370	0.039	1077
nw	0.261	3002	0.260	1668	0.137	3810
ww	0.908	16853	0.966	53412	0.912	33333
uu	0.357	460	0.468	1018	0.360	454
nn	0.689	7914	0.682	4372	0.825	23013
nl	0.311	3577	0.318	2038	0.175	4887
ln	0.054	1067	0.012	683	0.068	2579
UK 1990						
wn	0.036	452	0.010	388	0.027	786
wu	0.053	672	0.031	1130	0.048	1410
uw	0.428	441	0.318	802	0.433	599
un	0.125	129	0.113	286	0.221	305
nu	0.080	543	0.087	438	0.062	993
nw	0.308	2092	0.219	1099	0.166	2652
ww	0.911	11521	0.959	35453	0.926	27324
uu	0.447	460	0.568	1432	0.346	479
nn	0.612	4148	0.693	3475	0.772	12365
nl	0.426	3077	0.342	1803	0.239	3890
ln	0.042	618	0.017	702	0.035	1756
wy	0.010	122	0.003	118	0.002	69
uy	0.105	121	0.084	231	0.049	71
ny	0.061	442	0.050	266	0.015	245
yy	0.484	310	0.407	224	0.380	119
yw	0.300	192	0.313	172	0.319	100
yu	0.159	102	0.229	126	0.169	53

Source: Labour Force Surveys (various)
Notes: P = probability F = frequency.

(Table B3 continued)

	16-25		Male		Female	
	P	F	P	F	P	F
South East 1979						
wn	0.042	124	0.008	76	0.068	425
wu	0.026	76	0.015	140	0.021	134
uw	0.720	90	0.685	146	0.539	76
un	0.104	13	0.056	12	0.227	32
nu	0.072	66	0.047	44	0.036	168
nw	0.534	488	0.283	266	0.139	652
ww	0.933	2769	0.978	9414	0.911	5719
uu	0.176	22	0.258	55	0.234	33
nn	0.394	360	0.671	631	0.825	3874
nl	0.885	2780	0.517	675	0.175	820
ln	0.044	660	0.009	88	0.071	457
South East 1990						
wn	0.031	73	0.008	55	0.045	254
wu	0.044	105	0.024	173	0.024	133
uw	0.620	44	0.393	68	0.536	67
un	0.070	5	0.121	21	0.224	28
nu	0.081	83	0.073	46	0.055	134
nw	0.373	381	0.299	187	0.206	503
ww	0.925	2183	0.968	6957	0.931	5235
uu	0.310	22	0.486	84	0.240	30
nn	0.546	557	0.628	393	0.739	1800
nl	0.479	513	0.401	263	0.269	661
ln	0.032	78	0.010	76	0.049	283
wy	0.003	6	0.002	12	0.001	7
uy	0.053	4	0.039	7	0.038	5
ny	0.046	49	0.046	30	0.010	24
yy	0.395	15	0.387	12	0.333	7
yw	0.447	17	0.484	15	0.381	8
yu	0.158	6	0.129	4	0.238	5

Source: Labour Force Surveys (various).
P: Probability, F: Frequency, *w*: employment, *u*: registered unemployed, l = w + u, i.e. labour force, *n*: not in labour force, *y*: government training scheme.

Table B4 *Hourly earnings equations, 1979–91 (GHS)*

Variable	1979		1990-91 (Q1)	
	Coeff.	t-stat.	Coeff.	t-stat.
Personal controls				
Male	0.3240	34.18	0.2805	24.61
Black	-0.0629	2.91	-0.1216	4.61
Separated	0.0551	1.73	0.0237	0.60
Divorced	0.0778	2.99	0.0432	1.63
Widowed	0.1073	3.75	0.0833	1.98
Married	0.0977	8.18	0.0884	6.17
Age 20-24	0.3203	18.81	0.3248	14.26
Age 25-34	0.4750	26.59	0.4976	21.97
Age 35-44	0.5277	27.97	0.5733	23.89
Age 45-54	0.5177	27.03	0.6048	24.23
Age 55-60	0.4516	21.80	0.5887	20.75
Part-time	-0.1685	15.08	-0.1729	13.39
Qualifications				
Higher degree	0.6665	15.63	0.6840	16.53
Degree	0.6130	34.40	0.6735	36.04
Teaching qual.	0.7648	27.25	0.6539	20.07
HNC/HND	0.3721	19.38	0.4268	21.00
Nurse	0.3314	11.39	0.5335	17.72
A-levels	0.2296	14.38	0.3284	19.10
$\geq$5 O-levels	0.2081	15.23	0.2824	16.99
1-4 O + cler.	0.2277	7.33	0.2462	9.59
1-4 O-levels	0.1817	10.88	0.2000	10.90
Clerical/comm	0.0899	4.37	0.1269	4.92
CSE	0.0980	4.27	0.1032	4.23
Apprenticeship	0.0959	5.79	0.1246	4.11
Foreign	0.2108	6.43	0.2640	5.67
Other	0.1490	6.06	0.1627	4.21
Regional dummies				
North	-0.0911	5.24	-0.1796	8.25
Yorks/Humber	-0.1078	7.19	-0.1267	6.83
NW	-0.0632	4.59	-0.1355	8.10
E Midlands	-0.0685	4.19	-0.1378	7.07

Source: General Household Surveys, 1979–91. Notes: All equations also include year dummies.

(Table B4 continued)

Variable	1979		1990-91 (Q1)	
	Coeff.	t-stat.	Coeff.	t-stat.
W Midlands	-0.0782	5.38	-0.1503	8.26
East Anglia	-0.0809	3.88	-0.0987	3.76
London	0.0982	7.14	0.1236	6.96
SW	-0.1140	7.06	-0.1409	7.32
Wales	-0.1106	5.57	-0.1697	7.56
Scotland	-0.0546	3.72	-0.1240	6.53
Month of interview				
January	-0.1638	9.12	-0.0857	3.65
February	-0.1453	8.11	-0.1022	4.31
March	-0.1378	7.65	-0.0861	3.58
April	-0.1354	5.98	-0.0464	1.80
May	-0.0768	4.27	-0.0585	2.24
June	-0.1021	5.62	-0.0126	0.47
July	-0.0525	2.92	-0.0331	1.30
August	-0.0445	2.52	-0.0334	1.30
September	-0.0455	2.52	-0.0406	1.51
October	-0.0518	2.95	-0.0204	0.78
November	-0.0218	1.21	-0.0208	0.81
Industry dummies				
Agric., forestry & fishing	-0.1767	5.27	-0.2787	5.71
Energy & water	0.1961	6.76	0.2670	8.60
Extraction	0.2331	12.79	0.1143	4.21
Metal manufacture	0.0997	8.18	0.0911	5.33
Other manufacturing	0.1027	8.06	0.0141	0.78
Construction	0.0542	3.12	-0.0138	0.59
Distribution	-0.0613	4.95	-0.1331	9.22
Transport & communication	0.1084	6.72	0.0496	2.35
Financial services	0.1729	9.77	0.1278	7.77
Constant	-0.1396	6.23	0.5318	17.18
F	181.12		140.83	
$\overline{R}^2$	0.4864		0.4460	
DF	10597		9844	
N	10654		9902	

Estimation by OLS. Excluded categories: December, no qualifications, single, age 16–20, South East and SIC Order 9. Sample is wage and salary workers.

Table B5 *Hourly earnings equation, 1979–91 (GHS) — South East (including London)*

Variable	1979		1990-91 (Q1)	
	Coeff.	t-stat.	Coeff.	t-stat.
Personal controls				
Male	0.2961	17.46	0.2868	14.19
Black	-0.1118	3.84	-0.1046	2.99
Separated	0.0025	0.05	0.0126	0.17
Divorced	0.0995	2.18	0.0382	0.08
Widowed	0.0552	1.08	-0.0039	0.08
Married	0.0737	3.50	0.0382	1.54
Age 20-24	0.2656	8.62	0.3282	7.93
Age 25-34	0.4431	13.84	0.5172	12.61
Age 35-44	0.5250	15.18	0.6143	14.16
Age 45-54	0.5631	16.10	0.6258	13.76
Age 55-60	0.4825	12.97	0.5878	11.41
Part-time	-0.1775	8.51	-0.1800	7.43
Qualifications				
Higher degree	0.6466	11.20	0.6863	10.10
Degree	0.6244	21.79	0.6304	19.70
Teaching qual.	0.6651	12.85	0.6213	9.81
HNC/HND	0.4171	12.43	0.4474	12.21
Nurse	0.2840	5.42	0.5866	10.63
A-levels	0.2758	9.42	0.3238	10.48
≥ 5 O-levels	0.2390	9.66	0.3532	11.11
1-4 O + cler.	0.2985	5.19	0.2511	5.43
1-4 O-levels	0.1962	6.66	0.2391	7.03
Cler/comm.	0.1088	2.82	0.1571	3.43
CSE	0.1373	3.40	0.1630	3.75
Apprenticeship	0.0975	2.40	0.1419	2.37
Foreign	0.2316	5.76	0.2804	4.63
Other	0.0782	1.64	0.1759	2.36

(Table B5 continued)

Variable	1979		1990-91 (Q1)	
	Coeff.	t-stat.	Coeff.	t-stat.
Month of interview				
January	-0.2172	6.64	-0.0702	1.70
February	-0.2502	7.63	-0.0883	2.11
March	-0.1932	5.87	-0.1291	3.07
April	-0.1689	3.69	-0.1015	2.14
May	-0.1740	5.20	-0.1005	2.19
June	-0.1811	5.31	-0.0089	0.19
July	-0.0806	2.43	-0.0747	1.68
August	-0.0775	2.41	-0.0526	1.18
September	-0.0934	2.79	-0.0569	1.17
October	-0.1396	4.40	-0.0451	0.98
November	-0.0811	2.48	-0.0434	0.96
Industry dummies				
Agric. for.& fishing	-0.2511	3.13	-0.2057	1.72
Energy & water	0.1416	2.71	0.2177	3.54
Extraction	0.1461	3.25	0.1664	2.89
Metal manufacture	0.0450	2.00	0.0944	3.00
Other manufacture	0.0873	3.44	0.1153	3.14
Construction	0.0860	2.72	0.0013	0.03
Distribution	-0.0870	3.90	-0.1409	5.35
Transp.& communic.	0.1107	6.66	0.0994	2.78
Financial services	0.1823	6.89	0.2034	7.70
Constant	-0.0377	0.97	0.8798	14.34
F	63.37		48.84	
$\bar{R}^2$	0.4712		0.4287	
DF	3243		3013	
N	3291		3062	

Source: General Household Surveys, 1979–91
Notes: All equations also include year dummies and a London dummy. Estimation by
OLS. Excluded categories: December, no qualifications, single, age 16–20, South East
and SIC Order 9. Sample is wage and salary workers.

Appendix C Steady state solutions to transitional matrices

	Male		Female	
	1979	1990	1979	1990
Working (w)	0.91	0.86	0.66	0.76
Unemployed (u)	0.05	0.07	0.04	0.07
Not in labour force (n)	0.04	0.05	0.29	0.15
Government training schemes (y)	-	0.02	-	0.01
Self-employed (se)	0.22	0.18	0.04	0.05
Employed (e)	0.70	0.69	0.63	0.69
Unemployed (u)	0.04	0.03	0.04	0.05
Not in labour force (n)	0.04	0.06	0.29	0.20
Government training schemes (y)	-	0.05	-	0.01

Source: Calculated from transitional matrices in Appendix B.

Notes

1 We would like to thank Mark Beatson, Andrew Oswald, Mark Stevens and Ian Walker for helpful comments and suggestions.

2 The issue in judging the effect of the Thatcher reforms in this and other situations related to the posited counterfactual; what would have happened in the absence of the new policies. Different interpretations are possible, depending on whether one assumes that the levels of variables (absolutely or relative to those in other countries) would have remained the same or if past trends would have continued. Unless otherwise noted we assume the former, though we will remark on how interpretations might change, assuming the latter.

3 We re-estimated the results in Blanchflower (1991) using data from the two more recent British Social Attitudes Surveys of 1990 and 1991 and found no evidence of any significant change in the differential.

4 These data are from HMSO, *Social Trends*, various editions.

5 There were a sizeable number of changes in definition, virtually all of which were in the direction of lowering the unemployment rate (see Johnes and Taylor, 1990, p.305). According to the 1991 Labour Force Survey (see Naylor and Purdie, 1992) unemployment in Great Britain was 2.08 million in the spring of 1991 according to the new claimant based count, compared with 2.3 million according to the ILO measure

(available for work and looked for work in the preceding four weeks). In addition there were 400 000 individuals on government schemes at that time who are also excluded from the unemployment count. Using the ILO definition of unemployment and counting individuals on schemes as unemployed gives an unemployment rate of 9.7 per cent compared with an official rate of 8 per cent (*Employment Gazette*, April 1992, table 2.2).

6　Had we used the transition matrix for 1991 the situation would have looked much worse post-reforms due to the recession.

7　We reject the possibility that these coefficients are bigger because the changes were larger in the latter period. From 1979 to 1980 British real GDP fell by 2.2 per cent, but GDP rose by 1 per cent in 1990. One might expect that establishments that had increases in sales responded to larger increases while those that had decreases faced bigger decreases in 1979-80 than in the other two years. If this were the only thing going on, the coefficient on the sales up variable would be smaller in the first period than later while the coefficient on the sales down would be larger, which it is not.

8　For these regressions to measure responsiveness, we must assume that previous wage levels are uncorrelated with indicators of market signals. Alternatively, if signals are positively correlated over time and affect past wages, we are implicitly comparing wages with those in some earlier period when the firm did not face the relevant changes.

9　Consider the standard deviation in the coefficients on region in our appendix unemployment regressions. In the GHS the standard deviation in the coefficients rises from 0.030 to 0.056. By this measure regional unemployment differentials widened. But because the overall rate of unemployment rose from 4.7 per cent to 7.8 per cent in the period, the coefficient of variation in unemployment fell. However, the coefficient of variation in employment probabilities rose. There is a basic problem in comparing the dispersion of unemployment/employment rates, due to differing potential metrics.

10　There was a small increase for women but this was extremely modest, particularly given its very low starting level (0.0058 to 0.008).

11　We also estimated Markov transition matrices for other years, for the South East and using the average of the labour market transitions across a number of years and the results were the same.

12　A similar conclusion was reached by Blanchflower and Oswald (1990) using data from a variety of other sources and somewhat different methods.

13　The equations included fifteen highest qualification dummies, four marital status dummies, a gender dummy, a race dummy, eleven month-of-interview dummies and ten region dummies. The sample sizes were 12 181 (1979) and 8194 (1990). The $\overline{R}^2$s were 0.29 in 1979 and 0.34 in 1990.

References

Atkinson, A.B. and Micklewright, J.W. (1989), 'Turning the screw: benefits for the unemployed 1979–1988', in Dilnot, A. and Walker, I. (eds), *The Economics of Social*

Security, Oxford University Press.

Bagliano, F.C., Brandolini, A. and Dalmazzo, A. (1991), 'The OECD–CEP data set (1950–1988)', London School of Economics, CEP Working Paper no. 118, June.

Beatson, M. and Butcher, S. (1993), 'Union density across the employed workforce', *Employment Gazette*, January, pp. 673-89.

Blanchflower, D.G. (1984), 'Union relative wage effects: a cross-section analysis using establishment data', *British Journal of Industrial Relations*, 22, pp. 311–32.

Blanchflower, D.G. (1991), 'Fear, unemployment and pay flexibility', *Economic Journal*, March, pp. 483–96.

Blanchflower, D.G., Millward, N. and Oswald, A.J. (1991), 'Unionism and employment behaviour', *Economic Journal*, July, pp. 815–34.

Blanchflower, D.G. and Oswald, A.J. (1990), 'Self-employment and the enterprise culture', in Jowell, R., Witherspoon, S. and Brook, L. (eds), *British Social Attitudes: the 1990 Report*, Gower.

Blanchflower, D.G. and Oswald, A.J. (1993), 'International wage curves', forthcoming in Katz, L. and Freeman, R. (eds), *Differences and Changes in Wage Structures*, University of Chicago Press and NBER.

Blanchflower, D.G., Oswald, A.J. and Garrett, M. (1989), 'Insider power and wage determination', *Economica*, 57, pp. 143–70.

Campbell, M. and Daly, M. (1992), 'Self-employment; into the 1990s', *Employment Gazette*, June, pp. 269-92.

Caves, R. (1968), *Britain's Economic Prospects*, Allen and Unwin.

Centre for Economic Performance (1991), The OECD–CEP Data Set (Bagliano, F.C., Brandolini, A. and Dalmazzo, A.), Working Paper no. 118, June.

Curran, J. and Burrows, R. (1989), 'National profiles of the self-employed', *Employment Gazette*, July, pp. 376–85.

Daly, M. (1991), 'The 1980s — a decade of growth in enterprise. Self-employment data from the Labour Force Survey', *Employment Gazette*, March, pp. 109–34.

Disney, R. (1990), 'Explanations of the decline in trade union density in Britain: an appraisal', *British Journal of Industrial Relations*, 28, July, pp. 165–78.

Elgar, J. and Simpson, R. (1992), 'The impact of the law on industrial disputes in the 1980s', Centre for Economic Performance, London School of Economics, Discussion Paper no. 104.

Freeman, R. and Pelletier, J. (1990), 'The impact of industrial relations legislation on British union density', *British Journal of Industrial Relations*, 28, July, pp. 141–64.

Gilmour, I. (1992), *Dancing with Dogma*, Simon and Schuster.

Gregg, P. and Machin, S. (1992), 'Unions, the demise of the closed shop and wage growth in the 1980s', *Oxford Bulletin of Economics and Statistics*, 54, February, pp. 53–72.

Heath, A. and McMahon, D. (1992), 'Changes in values' in Jowell, R., Brook, L., Prior, G. and Taylor, B. (eds), *British Social Attitudes: the 9th Report*.

Ingram, P. (1991), 'Ten years of wage settlements', *Oxford Review of Economic Policy*, 7, March, pp. 93-106.

Johnes, G. and Taylor, J. (1990), 'Labour' in Artis, M. (ed.), *The UK Economy, a Manual of Applied Economics,* 12th edition.

Katz, L., Loveman, G. and Blanchflower, D. (1993), 'A comparison of changes in the structure of wages in four OECD countries', forthcoming in Katz, L. and Freeman, R. (eds), *Differences and Changes in Wage Structures,* University of Chicago Press and NBER.

Lanot, G. and Walker, I. (1992), 'Alternative estimators of the union/non-union wage differential: UK pooled cross-section evidence', Keele University Department of Economics working paper no. 92–19.

Layard, R. (1982), 'Youth unemployment in Britain and the US compared' in Freeman, R. and Wise, D. (eds), *The Youth Labor Market Problem: its Nature, Causes, and Consequences,* University of Chicago Press and NBER.

Layard, R. (1986), *How to Beat Unemployment,* Oxford University Press.

McConnell, S. and Takla, L. (1993), 'Mrs Thatcher's trade union legislation: has it reduced strikes?' *Economic Journal* (forthcoming).

McCormick, A. (1993), PhD thesis in progress, Harvard University.

Matthews, K. and Minford, P. (1987), 'Mrs Thatcher's economic policies, 1979–1987', *Economic Policy,* 5, pp. 57-102.

Millward, N., Stevens, M., Smart, D. and Hawes, W. (1992), *Workplace Industrial Relations in Transition,* Dartmouth.

Milner, S. and Metcalf, D. (1993), 'A century of UK strike activity: an alternative perspective', Centre for Economic Performance, London School of Economics, Discussion Paper no. 22.

Minford, P. (1983), *Unemployment: Cause and Cure,* Martin Robertson.

Naylor, M. and Purdie, E. (1992), 'Results of the 1991 Labour Force Survey', *Employment Gazette,* April, pp. 153-72.

OECD (1978), *Youth Unemployment. A Report on the High-level Conference 15/16 December 1977,* vol. 1, OECD.

OECD (1981), *Youth Unemployment: Causes and Consequences,* OECD.

OECD (1991), Historical statistics, *OECD Economic Outlook.*

OECD (1992), *Employment Outlook,* OECD.

Oswald, A. (1992), 'Pay setting, self-employment and the unions: themes of the 1980s', *Oxford Review of Economic Policy.*

Schmidt, J. (1993), 'The changing structure of male earnings in Britain', forthcoming in Katz, L. and Freeman, R. (eds), *Differences and Changes in Wage Structures,* University of Chicago Press and NBER.

Smeaton, D. (1992), 'Self-employment — some preliminary findings', Centre for Economic Performance, London School of Economics, discussion paper no. 96.

Stewart, M. (1991), 'Union wage differentials in the face of changes in the economic and legal environment', *Economica,* 58, pp. 155–72.

3   Is the UK rise in inequality different?

PAUL GREGG AND STEPHEN MACHIN[1]

Introduction

The 1980s saw significant changes in the structure of income and earnings distributions in a number of industrialised countries. In some countries these distributions widened, increasing the gap between the best-off and worst-off individuals. Table 3.1 reports measures of income and earnings inequality for several countries in the early 1970s, in the late 1970s/early 1980s and in the late 1980s. The table makes apparent the different levels of inequality and the differing experiences in inequality trends across countries. It has been well documented that the US rise in inequality started as far back as the late 1960s and has continued to rise unabated through the 1970s and 1980s. On the other hand, inequality only started to rise in the UK from the late 1970s onwards, but the rate of growth in the 1980s appears to have been faster than that of other countries. As far as can be reasonably assessed, given problems of data comparability across countries, UK inequality still lies at a lower level than in the US, Canada or Australia, but the 1980s certainly saw the UK leapfrogging some European countries.

Focusing specifically on the UK experience, income and earnings inequality remained relatively constant for most of the postwar period up to the early 1970s. In the 1970s some relatively small moves towards equality occurred (with the Social Contract and the Equal Pay Act), but since 1979 inequality has risen dramatically. This is true of both income and earnings distributions. Figures 3.1 and 3.2 illustrate this by plotting Gini coefficients for income between 1957 and 1990 and measures of hourly earnings inequality (90–50 and 10–50 log wage differentials) for men and women between 1972 and 1991. Both point to an extremely large opening out of the distribution of income and earnings in the 1980s.

A number of structural changes in the UK labour market went hand-in-hand with this move towards greater inequality. Unemployment rose to

Table 3.1 *Changes in income and wage inequality in several industrialised countries in the 1970s and 1980s*

Country	Gini coefficient of income				Male 90-10 log wage differentials			
	Income measure	Early 1970s	Late 1970s/ early 1980s	Late 1980s	Wage measure	Early 1970s	Late 1970s/ early 1980s	Late 1980s/ early 1990s
UK	Post tax	27 (1977)	28 (1981)	35 (1988)	Hourly earnings	0.91 (1973)	0.88 (1979)	1.22 (1991)
US	Post tax	36 (1973)	37 (1979)	40 (1989)	Hourly earnings	1.55 (1975)	1.56 (1980)	1.72 (1989)
Canada	Pre tax	n.a. - slight fall	40 (1981)	40 (1988)	Hourly earnings	-	1.28 (1981)	1.37 (1990)
France	Pre tax	38 (1975)	36 (1979)	37 (1984)	Hourly earnings	1.17 (1973)	1.18 (1980)	1.23 (1991)
Australia	Pre tax	34 (1974)	37 (1983)	39 (1988)	Weekly earnings	0.69 (1975)	0.70 (1980)	0.82 (1991)
Sweden	Post tax	30 (1972)	29 (1981)	n.a. - slight rise	Hourly earnings	0.73 (1973)	0.68 (1981)	0.77 (1991)
Finland	Post tax	27 (1971)	21 (1981)	20 (1985)	-	-	-	-
Norway	-	-	-	-	Hourly wages	-	0.72 (1979)	0.68 (1991)
Denmark	-	-	-	-	Hourly earnings	-	0.76 (1980)	0.77 (1990)
Austria	-	-	-	-	Monthly earnings	-	0.96 (1980)	0.98 (1991)
Japan	-	-	-	-	Monthly earnings	-	0.95 (1979)	1.04 (1987)

Notes: Gini coefficients are defined consistently across years except for Sweden. Sources for Gini coefficients: Australia, Raskall (1992); Sweden, 1972 number from Stark (1977), 1981 number from Saunders *et al.* (1991); all others from Atkinson (1993). Sources for earnings differentials: OECD (1993), 'Earnings inequality: changes in the 1980s', *OECD Employment Outlook;* figures for Canada are from *Canadian Labor Force Survey*. Earnings figures for Norway and Denmark apply to both sexes. The Gini coefficient is defined as $c = 100. \int_0^1 (x - f(x))$ where $f(x)$ is the cumulated proportion of income earned by the poorest x per cent of the population. A larger coefficient implies more inequality.

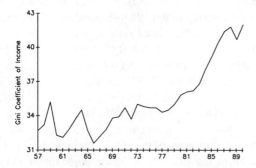

Figure 3.1 Gini coefficients for UK gross normal weekly income,1957–1990
Source: Stark (1992)

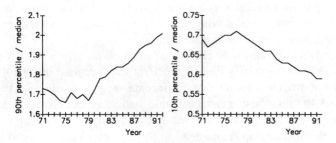

Figure 3.2a Trends in UK male hourly earnings inequality ratios of 90th percentile
and 10th percentile to median earnings

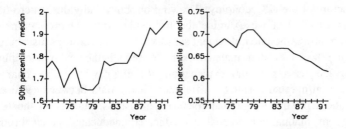

Figure 3.2b Trends in UK female hourly earnings inequality ratios of 90th percentile
and 10th percentile to median earnings
Source: Based on New Earnings Survey data

postwar record levels, reaching 3.1 million workers (or 11 per cent of the labour force) by 1986, and then falling in the 1987/88 boom and then increasing to three million again by early 1993. The extent of union activity in the economy fell dramatically: aggregate union density fell from a high of 58 per cent in 1979 to 38 per cent in 1991. There was an increase in the numbers of more highly educated workers: Schmitt (1993) documents that, whilst 52 per cent of male workers had no educational qualifications in 1974–6 this fell to 32 per cent by 1986–8; the proportion of males with a degree rose from 5 per cent in 1974–6 to 11 per cent in 1986–8. The 1980s also saw considerable changes in the nature of the employment relationship with shifts away from manufacturing towards service sector employment and a big shift towards the use of 'flexible' labour (that is, towards part-time work, usually done by women, and the increased use of sub-contracting and short-term labour contracts).

In this chapter we examine whether the 1980s rise in UK inequality can be explained by the same forces driving increases in inequality in other countries. The structure of the chapter is as follows.

The second section looks at the rise in inequality and poverty in the UK and we report evidence suggesting that an important shift occurred in the 1980s. On the basis of macroeconomic data on income inequality and poverty we find that, whilst observable macroeconomic indicators can provide a good explanation of the UK poverty and income inequality experience up to the mid-1980s, this relationship breaks down during the boom in the second half of the decade.

We then go on to examine the evolution of inequality in the labour market, using a variety of data sources to investigate potential (and potentially competing) explanations of the observed changes in the wage and employment structure of the UK economy. Drawing on both individual micro-data and on industrial data we examine the following issues: changes in the returns to schooling; the unemployment sensitivity of the earnings distribution of more and less educated male workers to see whether rising unemployment also acts as a potential explanation of rising pay inequality; changes in non-manual/manual earnings differences using data between 1980 and 1990 for about 100 three-digit manufacturing industries; changes in the relative usage of manual/non-manual and educated/uneducated labour through the 1980s; the respective importance of between and within industry changes to the overall change in the structure of employment; and the importance of labour market institutions. In particular, we look at evidence on the declining importance of trade unions and Wages Council minimum rates of pay.

In the fourth section we evaluate the results reported in the chapter and compare and contrast the UK experience with that of other countries, especially the United States where the bulk of the recent work on inequality has been carried out (see Katz and Murphy, 1992; Murphy and Welch, 1992; plus many other US papers cited in the survey by Levy and Murnane, 1992). We conclude that, although the magnitude of inequality and the date of onset of any increases differs considerably by country, the forces that seem to explain trends in increased inequality are quite similar across countries. A simple supply and demand framework augmented by a role for declining labour market institutions appears to be able to explain the trends observed in several countries.

It appears that the biggest rises in inequality in the 1980s have occurred in those countries which have experienced both an increased supply of more skilled workers coupled with an even higher demand for these workers and a decline in unions and/or minimum wages. It appears that one can form a 'league table' with the UK, the US, Australia and (recently) Sweden experiencing all of these trends. Next come some countries who may have experienced some of these trends but not all of them (for example, France, where the supply/demand shifts have occurred but minimum wages have not declined, or Canada, where returns to skill have not increased by as much as in the US). Finally, there are some countries (for example, Italy) which have not experienced any of these trends (or they have moved in the opposite direction) and where inequality has stayed constant or even fallen.

The rise in inequality: poverty and income inequality

Unlike the US, there is currently very little UK work (Nolan, 1986, is an exception) that systematically relates poverty or inequality to macroeconomic conditions over time.[2] US labour economists (Ellwood and Summers, 1986; Blank and Blinder, 1986; Blank, 1989; Cutler and Katz, 1991) have identified a strong link between the growth in living standards of the average family, median or mean family income, and declining absolute poverty.

It is certainly true that discussions of poverty in the UK are hampered by there being no official measure of poverty. Unlike the United States (where there is a consistent definition of the poverty line based on 1964 real incomes, see Blank and Hanratty, 1992) there is no published data for the UK on the number of families below a consistently defined poverty line. For example, defining a poverty line in terms of benefit levels (for example, 140 per cent of income support) can be sensitive to changes in the real value of benefits and changes to the benefit system. Having said that, articles describing the distribution of household income are regularly published in *Economic Trends*. It is

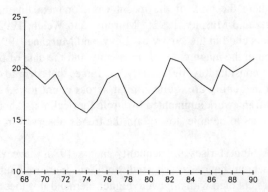

Figure 3.3 Percentage of households with below half the median of 1979 real expenditure
Source: Family Expenditure Survey data

evident that one can draw on income or expenditure data from the annual
Family Expenditure Surveys to compute absolute measures of poverty defined
as the proportion of the population below some absolute income line.

Figure 3.3 thus shows the percentage of adults in households with below half
of the median of 1979 real expenditure (excluding housing costs) based on
data drawn from the Family Expenditure Survey. The use of expenditure
rather than income is in line with many specialists in the field who argue it is
a more appropriate variable on which to base an inequality measure (see, for
instance, Slesnick, 1993, or Robert Hall's discussion of Cutler and Katz,
1991). However, the data suffers from some definition changes in the classifi-
cations of expenditure used which may distort the picture. Most notably the
sharp rise in 1987 is driven by such definitional changes. Hence this plot
should only be taken as indicative of broad patterns over time (see also
Jenkins, 1991a, who argues that one can draw 'relatively broad-brush conclusions' from these kind of data). In figure 3.3 a countercyclical pattern
emerges in that the downturns of 1971, 1975–7 and 1980–82 are associated
with marked rises in poverty. It is, however, important to notice that the late
1980s recovery (that is, the boom of 1988–9) did not see falling poverty.

Table 3.2 presents more systematic, regression based evidence on the role of
rising living standards and the economic cycle in shaping poverty. Column
(1) presents a regression of this measure of the poverty rate on a number of
contemporaneous macroeconomic indicators for quarterly data between
1968 and 1985. Over this period, a higher median real wage was associated
with lower poverty, whilst higher inflation or unemployment were linked to
higher poverty. However, macroeconomic indicators alone are not enough to

Table 3.2 *Poverty and macroeconomic performance 1968-90*

	(1)	(2)	(3)
	1968II-1985IV	1968II-1990IV	1968II-1990IV
Constant	0.3727	0.3621	0.2620
	(0.0272)	(0.0266)	(0.0405)
Median real wage	-0.0820	-0.0769	-0.0590
	(0.0120)	(0.0116)	(0.0124)
Inflation rate	0.0832	0.0792	0.0809
	(0.0400)	(0.0390)	(0.0371)
Unemployment rate	0.7327	0.6485	0.5814
	(0.0966)	(0.0798)	(0.0100)
Post-1985 trend	-	0.0041	0.0031
		(0.0005)	(0.0006)
Poverty rate (t - 1)	-	-	0.3068
			(0.0968)
R^2	0.565	0.542	0.590
Mean of dependent variable	0.184	0.187	0.187
Diagnostics			
Functional form:	0.434	2.261	0.088
$\chi^2(1)$ test (p-value)	(0.510)	(0.133)	(0.767)
Heteroskedasticity:	0.000	0.006	0.372
$\chi^2(1)$ test (p-value)	(1.00)	(0.939)	(0.542)
Normality:	0.890	4.938	3.294
$\chi^2(2)$ test (p-value)	(0.641)	(0.085)	(0.193)
Serial correlation:	6.425	10.044	1.424
$\chi^2(4)$ test (p-value)	(0.170)	(0.040)	(0.840)

Notes: The dependent variable is the percentage of adults in households with below half of median 1979 real consumption expenditure (source: Family Expenditure Survey). Standard errors in parentheses. All variables are in levels not logs, unemployment and inflation are proportions. Median real wage is taken from the Family Expenditure Survey. Inflation = annual change in CPI (average of four quarter change in year). UR = claimant unemployed (SUACCC)/workforce.

predict late 1980s poverty rates. The model in column (1) is completely unable to forecast the post-1985 experience (a formal 20-quarters forward forecast test failed dramatically with a $\chi^2(20)$ statistic of 91.1; 5 per cent criti-

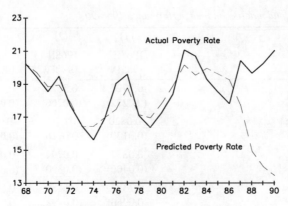

Figure 3.4 Actual and predicted poverty rates, 1968–90

cal value = 19.3; 10 per cent critical value = 37.6). Indeed, it was not possible to estimate the model for the 1968–90 sample period and then pass a standard parameter stability test.

For the full sample from 1986 to 1990 column (2) of the table incorporates a time trend starting in 1986 which renders the coefficients of the model to be stable over time but induces serial correlation in the residuals. Column (3) demonstrates that the basic structure of the results is unchanged after the inclusion of a lagged dependent variable which allows for different short and long-run effects.

Given the historical precedent that poverty follows a countercyclical time path, the late 1980s boom period, characterised by low inflation, rapidly rising real wages and falling unemployment, should have seen absolute poverty at an all-time low instead of reaching an all-time high (see figure 3.4). Rather, the results in columns (2) and (3) suggest that there has been a significant unexplained rise in the poverty rate in the mid- to late-1980s. The magnitude of the effect is large and of the order of 8 percentage points; this is an extremely large rise when compared to the 1979 base which had 17 per cent of families below half of the median of 1979 real consumers' expenditure.

These results are very much in line with the US work of Cutler and Katz (1991) who report that, whilst real living standards and unemployment could account for aggregate rise in US poverty between 1947 and 1982, this relationship broke down from 1983 onwards when poverty rose at an unexpectedly rapid rate. Hence, trends in the aggregate UK poverty rate have similarities to trends in the United States poverty rate, though timing of the breakdown of the macroeconomic relationship differs, with the US breakdown occurring somewhat earlier.

Table 3.3 *Income inequality and macroeconomic performance 1958-90*

	(1) 1957-84	(2) 1957-90	(3) 1958-90
Constant	31.625 (1.409)	31.861 (1.283)	25.205 (5.924)
Real GDP	0.0017 (0.0032)	0.0011 (0.0030)	0.0005 (0.0032)
Inflation rate	4.107 (4.926)	4.715 (4.568)	3.751 (4.833)
Unemployment rate	37.665 (9.524)	38.326 (7.532)	32.676 (9.385)
Post-1984 trend	-	0.967 (0.146)	0.7705 (0.2356)
Income inequality (t - 1)	-	-	0.2146 (0.1802)
R^2	0.735	0.940	0.941
Mean of dependent variable	34.211	35.394	35.394
Diagnostics			
Functional form: $\chi^2(1)$ test (p-value)	0.112 (0.738)	0.016 (0.898)	0.028 (0.868)
Heteroskedasticity: $\chi^2(1)$ test (p-value)	2.068 (0.150)	2.299 (0.129)	2.583 (0.108)
Normality: $\chi^2(2)$ test (p-value)	2.447 (0.294)	3.959 (0.138)	2.135 (0.344)
Serial correlation: $\chi^2(4)$ test (p-value)	1.285 (0.257)	1.543 (0.214)	1.138 (0.286)

Notes: The dependent variable is the Gini coefficient for gross weekly income as re-ported in Stark (1992). Standard errors in parentheses. All variables are in levels not logs, unemployment and inflation are proportions. The median real wage is taken from the Family Expenditure Survey. Real GDP = level of GDP at factor cost in 1985 prices. Inflation = annual change in CPI (average of four quarter change in year). UR = claimant unemployed/workforce, where we use seasonally adjusted unemployment data that are consistent with current coverage.

As remarked above, it is important to question whether the observed rise in poverty rates can be attributed to data inconsistencies (especially the 1986–7 jump in the data). One should immediately notice that the trends appear to be very strong and do not depend on any big changes for any single observation. It is clear that the models estimated up to the end of 1985 forecast poverty rates which increasingly diverge from the observed pattern of the data right through to 1990 (see figure 3.4 which is based on the regression in column (2) of table 3.2): hence there is a not a single step change explanation for this change of direction.

Comparing the FES data with other data sources also engenders confidence in the results. Firstly, Stark (1992) details the share of gross weekly normal income received by the poorest 10 or 20 per cent of the population and reports that the share of income held by the poorest quintile fell by 25 per cent between 1980 and 1990 with all the fall occurring after 1983 (the lowest decile experienced a 27 per cent fall).[3] Secondly, the Government Statistical Service (GSS) analysis of incomes reported that, between 1979 and 1989, real incomes of the poorest decile fell by around 6 per cent after adjusting for housing costs (the next poorest decile only experienced a 2 per cent rise over the same period). Both of these pieces of information point to rising poverty and tend to support the FES evidence — both in terms of direction and timing — on poverty trends in the 1980s.

Table 3.3 reports regressions relating income inequality to various macroeconomic variables between 1957 and 1990. Column (1) regresses the Gini coefficient on real GDP, the inflation rate and the unemployment rate for the period 1957–84. Again, like the US work of Cutler and Katz (1991), the principal macroeconomic influence on income inequality is unemployment (periods of higher unemployment are associated with increased income inequality). In line with the absolute income level regressions in table 3.2 this equation (explaining relative income trends) is unable to forecast the mid- to late-1980s (formal forecast test = 38.1; χ^2 (6) 5 per cent critical value = 12.6). This is largely because, in the period from 1985 onwards, unemployment was flat and then falling, yet inequality rose sharply.

In column (2) this is captured through a time trend starting in 1985. The coefficient attached to the post-1984 trend is positive and significant and suggests an unexplained rise in the Gini coefficient of 0.97 percentage points per year: this is extremely large given that the pre-1984 mean of the dependent variable was 34.2. This suggests that over the period 1985–90 the Gini coefficient measure of inequality rose by one sixth. (The additional of a lagged dependent variable in column (3) does not change the results as it is not significant.)

The simple regressions in tables 3.2 and 3.3 suggest that, whilst one can identify some important macroeconomic indicators that are linked to absolute and relative measures of inequality, the main reason for the rise in inequality in the 1980s was not changing macroeconomic performance.

Some recent studies of income inequality have used micro-data and suggested (at least) four groups of candidate arguments to explain these changes: first, changes in the tax and benefit system; second, changes in family composition; third, changes in the distribution of work; and fourth changes in the distribution of earned and unearned income.

Among income distribution specialists the consensus appears to be that the microeconomic structure of earnings definitely matters and some authors (notably Atkinson, 1993, and Jenkins, 1991b) argue that it is the single most important factor (Jenkins also stresses the importance of earnings from self-employment). Johnson and Webb (1993) use cross-sectional evidence from the Family Expenditure Survey and also claim an important role for the tax system (but not for benefits). Consideration of other potential explanations seems to suggest they are probably less important.[4] Absolute poverty is not, however, greatly affected by taxation changes and the UK Gini coefficients reported in figure 3.1 and used in the regressions in table 3.3 are defined pre-tax. Therefore, whilst it is certainly true that taxation changes may have influenced the post-tax income distribution, the large change in pre-tax income inequality identifies changes in the inequality of wages as the principal cause of increased inequality. In the next section we therefore go on to consider changes in the structure of earnings in the UK.

The rise in inequality: the distribution of earnings

In this section we focus specifically on the distribution of earnings and both draw on existing work and report on original material to consider changes in the structure of earnings in the UK. We first document the observed changes in the wage structure, then present some evidence on the mechanisms behind such changes. It appears that many of the arguments that have been applied to explain the US rise in wage inequality also apply in the UK.

Trends in UK wage inequality

The increase in wage inequality in the UK in the last decade or so has been dramatic. Table 3.4 draws out the magnitude of the increase by reporting data on the ratios of the 90th and 10th percentiles to the median of the male manual earnings distribution for selected years from 1886-1990. Earnings inequality was remarkably flat in the UK from the end of the last century up until about 1970, followed by a slight compression in the 1970s, but post-1979 a massive widening occurred. According to the measures in table 3.4 (the only ones available as far back as the 1880s) wage inequality is now greater than it was 100 years ago. This of course is all the more striking given the considerable technical changes and improvements in average living standards that

Table 3.4 *Wage inequality in the UK, 1886-1990*

Year	10th percentile/median	90th percentile/median
1886	0.686	1.431
1906	0.665	1.568
1938	0.677	1.399
1970	0.673	1.475
1976	0.702	1.449
1979	0.683	1.485
1982	0.683	1.526
1988	0.643	1.565
1990	0.637	1.591

Sources: New Earnings Survey, British Labour Statistics.
Note: These are based on male manual full-time weekly earnings.

have occurred through the century. The increase in dispersion is apparent at both the bottom and the top of the distribution. It is evident that the 1980s saw a huge turnaround of sufficient magnitude to dwarf any moves towards equality that were seen in the 1970s. Figures 3.2a and 3.2b demonstrate that this pattern emerges for both male and female earnings over the 1980s (if anything, the rise for women is somewhat smaller and therefore consistent with a fall in the gender pay gap in the 1980s).

In table 3.5 we report the standard deviation of the log of real hourly earnings for each year between 1982 and 1990 for all full-time workers and then for various sub-groups. For all groups considered the wage distribution widened out considerably over this time period. The dispersion has widened out dramatically for men, women, young men, old men, manual and non-manual workers, who work within both manufacturing and non-manufacturing industries.

Returns to education

The supply and demand explanations of the US rise in wage inequality suggest that the changing wage structure has been driven (at least partially) by an increased supply of highly educated workers but that this has gone hand-in-hand with rising returns to schooling (Katz and Murphy, 1992; Murphy and Welch, 1992). In order to rationalise this in terms of supply and demand it is argued that there must also have been a more than offsetting rise in the

Table 3.5 *Changes in the UK wage structure 1982–90: based on New Earnings Survey micro-data*

	Standard deviation of ln (real hourly full-time earnings) (Sample size in parentheses)			
	Men and women	Men	Younger men (below 25)	Older men (25 or more)
1982	0.442 (116549)	0.430 (79902)	0.366 (14014)	0.406 (65888)
1983	0.448 (114191)	0.439 (77768)	0.386 (13394)	0.411 (64374)
1984	0.455 (111720)	0.448 (75902)	0.394 (13072)	0.417 (62830)
1985	0.456 (107772)	0.449 (72400)	0.387 (12268)	0.420 (60132)
1986	0.463 (111120)	0.457 (74741)	0.399 (12594)	0.429 (62147)
1987	0.473 (111158)	0.472 (74132)	0.394 (12425)	0.446 (61707)
1988	0.481 (116905)	0.482 (77469)	0.398 (13090)	0.457 (64379)
1989	0.488 (116333)	0.490 (76446)	0.407 (12617)	0.468 (63829)
1990	0.488 (116779)	0.492 (76220)	0.409 (12558)	0.470 (63962)
	Men, manufacturing	Men, non-manufacturing	Men, manufacturing manuals	Men, manufacturing non-manuals
1982	0.374 (29614)	0.460 (50288)	0.305 (20670)	0.407 (8944)
1983	0.382 (28067)	0.467 (49701)	0.308 (19419)	0.414 (8648)
1984	0.395 (27568)	0.476 (48334)	0.317 (19063)	0.419 (8501)
1985	0.398 (26003)	0.475 (46397)	0.319 (17818)	0.423 (8185)
1986	0.410 (27190)	0.482 (47551)	0.322 (18640)	0.439 (8550)
1987	0.415 (26778)	0.501 (47354)	0.326 (18214)	0.441 (8564)
1988	0.419 (27700)	0.513 (49769)	0.327 (18915)	0.443 (8785)
1989	0.427 (27419)	0.521 (49027)	0.327 (18745)	0.455 (8674)
1990	0.428 (26998)	0.524 (49222)	0.328 (18409)	0.450 (8589)

Notes: We would like to thank Richard Dickens for obtaining these New Earnings Survey micro-data from the Department of Employment's NES files. We are extremely grateful to the Department of Employment for letting us have access to these data.

demand for skilled workers. In this section we evaluate whether the supply-side features have occurred in the UK. Later, we consider relative changes in demand.

With respect to changes in the relative supply of skills and returns to education table 3.6 draws on two UK micro-data sources. Schmitt (1993) analyses this issue using data on males from the General Household Survey be-

Table 3.6 *Changes in the distribution of education and in the wage returns to education for UK males in work*

	1978-80	1986-88
Evidence from General Household Survey data (Schmitt, 1993)		
Proportion of men with university qualification	0.079	0.109
Proportion of men with no educational qualification	0.464	0.323
Ln (weekly wage) returns to university degree relative to no qualifications	0.576	0.643
Evidence from Family Expenditure Survey data (based on data used in Machin, Meghir and Whitehouse, 1993)		
Proportion of men with at least 5 years of post-compulsory education	0.083	0.129
Proportion of men with no years of post-compulsory education	0.580	0.510
Ln (hourly wage) returns to at least 5 years of post-compulsory education compared to none (standard error)	0.420 (0.012)	0.501 (0.013)
Ln (hourly wage) returns to an extra year's schooling (standard error)	0.059 (0.001)	0.069 (0.002)

Notes: The estimated returns are based on standard human capital based earnings functions for the two pooled cross-sections. Sample sizes for FES results are: FES 1976–8 12 064; FES 1986–8 10 606. Sample sizes for GHS are not reported in Schmitt (1993).

tween 1974 and 1988; Machin, Meghir and Whitehouse (1993) use Family Expenditure survey data between 1968 and 1990.

The upper panel of table 3.6 reports on data from Schmitt (1993) describing changes between the late 1970s and the late 1980s in the proportion of workers with a university qualification and those with no educational qualification. As in the US situation the 1980s in the UK did see an increase in the relative supply of highly educated workers (with the percentage of workers having a degree rising from 8 to 11 per cent and the proportion with no qualification dramatically falling from 46 to 32 per cent). As in the US the returns to a university education (as compared to no education) rose.

The lower panel of the table conducts a similar exercise using Family Expenditure Survey (FES) information. Rather than having data on exact qualifications, the FES data contain information on years of post-compulsory education completed. These data also suggest an important rise in relative supply, with the proportion of men with at least five years of post-compulsory education (broadly degree level) rising from 0.08 to 0.13, and the corresponding fall in the proportion with no post-compulsory years dropping from 0.58 to 0.51. Based on FES data, wage returns to education also rose. The wage returns from an extra year's schooling rose significantly.

Hence, when comparing the late 1970s to the late 1980s one observes a sharp rise in the relative supply of highly educated workers, but also a rise in the returns to schooling. This is clearly the same as the US situation: it also confirms the kind of patterns observed in some other countries where wage inequality has risen (for example, Sweden: see Edin and Holmlund, 1993). On the other hand, in Canada, for example, where wage inequality has risen by less, such a pattern has not been observed (Freeman and Needels, 1991, report much less of a rise in returns to schooling, of the order of one fifth of that observed in the US). Furthermore, in Italy, where wage inequality has reduced through the 1980s, returns to schooling appear to have fallen (see Erickson and Ichino, 1992).

Table 3.7 *The sensitivity of real wages to education group based unemployment. General Household Survey 1974–88*

	Male unemployment rates by education group, 1974-88 (Figures in brackets are rates relative to row 1)			Coefficient (standard error) on ln (unemployment rates by education group) in separate ln (male weekly wage) equations for each education group	
	1974-80	1981-85	1986-88	1974-88	1980-88
University degree or equivalent	1.93	4.24	3.56	-0.004 (0.013)	-0.035 (0.023)
Intermediate (vocational, A-levels, O-levels, nursing or clerical)	3.35 (1.74)	8.74 (2.06)	7.72 (2.17)	-0.027 (0.007)	-0.70 (0.012)
No qualifications	6.46 (3.35)	17.65 (4.16)	16.40 (4.61)	-0.034 (0.009)	-0.093 (0.014)

Notes: Columns 4 and 5 are based on semi-ln(wage) regressions over the period 1974–88 and 1980–88 including controls for experience and its square, marital status, regional dummies and a time trend. Sample sizes are (for the 1974–88 samples): 6786 for university degree; 40505 for intermediate group; 33443 for no qualification group.

The sensitivity of real wages to education specific unemployment

One might reasonably question whether the observed relative decline in the real wages of less educated workers is related to the high unemployment of the 1980s. It is important to know whether the apparent contradiction of rising relative supply of skills coupled with an increase in the relative returns to such skills can be explained by a changing demand for such highly educated workers vis-à-vis their less educated counterparts.

The first three columns of table 3.7 suggest that this is indeed the case by reporting male unemployment rates by education group using the General Household Survey data of Schmitt (1993). Whilst unemployment amongst workers with a degree did rise from 2 per cent in the 1970s to around 4 per cent in most of the 1980s, it is evident that much of the incidence of higher unemployment observed in the 1980s fell on the less educated. Indeed, unemployment amongst male workers with no education reached as high as 18 per cent by the early 1980s (and stayed almost as high later in the decade).

The last two columns of the table also make it clear that this reduced demand for less educated workers did manifest itself in significantly lower real wages. The last two columns report the coefficient (and associated standard error) on the education specific unemployment rate in separate wage equations for highly educated, intermediate education and no education groups over two time periods, 1974–88 and 1980–88. In the highly educated case an increase in graduate unemployment has no effect on the real wages of workers with a university qualification. There is a negative impact for both the intermediate and no education groups, with the largest coefficient (in absolute terms) in the no education group. This is similar to the US and UK 'wage curve' results of Blanchflower and Oswald (1993), who also report a more marked downward impact of unemployment on the wages of less skilled groups. The wage-unemployment elasticities appear to have become larger (in absolute terms) in the 1980s, with a very large effect for the uneducated group between 1980 and 1988.

Changes in the manufacturing relative wage structure

One can obtain good quality employment data on manual and non-manual workers at 3-digit manufacturing industry level from the annual Census of

Notes to table: The New Earnings Survey wage data are for full-time male manufacturing workers; the Census of Production wage data is for all workers. Wages are deflated by a consumer price index by year. Heteroskedastic consistent standard errors in parentheses. The sample is restricted to those 3-digit industries which have at least fifty workers in the New Earnings Survey.

Table 3.8 *Changes in the structure of wages in UK manufacturing in the 1980s (sample = 85 3-digit manufacturing industries, 1982-90)*

Dependent variable	Coefficient (standard error) on time trend	R^2
Average real wages, NES and CoP		
ln (average hourly wage) NES	0.023 (0.002)	0.13
ln (average annual wage), CoP	0.027 (0.003)	0.12
ln (average manual hourly wage), NES	0.019 (0.002)	0.14
ln (average non-manual hourly wage), NES	0.030 (0.002)	0.23
ln (average manual annual wage), CoP	0.023 (0.003)	0.14
ln (average non-manual annual wage), CoP	0.034 (0.002)	0.30
ln (average non-manual hourly wage) - ln (average manual hourly wage), NES	0.010 (0.002)	0.05
ln (average non-manual annual wage) - ln (average manual annual wage), CoP	0.011 (0.002)	0.04
Percentiles of the real hourly wage distrihbution, NES		
ln (10th percentile)	0.015 (0.002)	0.06
ln (25th percentile)	0.017 (0.002)	0.09
ln (50th percentile)	0.022 (0.002)	0.13
ln (75th percentile)	0.026 (0.002)	0.14
ln (90th percentile)	0.030 (0.003)	0.13
Percentiles of the real manual hourly wage distribution, NES		
ln (10th percentile)	0.013 (0.002)	0.05
ln (25th percentile)	0.016 (0.002)	0.08
ln (50th percentile)	0.019 (0.002)	0.14
ln (75th percentile)	0.023 (0.002)	0.18
ln (90th percentile)	0.024 (0.002)	0.17
Percentiles of real non-manual wage distribution, NES		
ln (10th percentile)	0.020 (0.003)	0.07
ln (25th percentile)	0.023 (0.002)	0.14
ln (50th percentile)	0.029 (0.002)	0.23
ln (75th percentile)	0.034 (0.002)	0.23
ln (90th percentile)	0.040 (0.003)	0.21
Inequality measures, NES		
Standard deviation (ln hourly wages)	0.006 (0.0008)	0.07
Standard deviation (ln manual hourly wages)	0.003 (0.0006)	0.03
Standard deviation (ln non-manual hourly wages)	0.008 (0.0010)	0.07
ln (90th percentile of hourly wage distribution) minus ln (10th percentile of hourly wage distribution)	0.015 (0.002)	0.05
ln (90th percentile of manual hourly wage distribution) minus ln (10th percentile of manual hourly wage distribution)	0.011 (0.002)	0.04
ln (90th percentile of non-manual hourly wage distribution) minus ln (10th percentile of non-manual hourly wage distribution)	0.019 (0.003)	0.05

Production. We therefore decided to examine changing pay and employment structures for these broad occupational definitions using a data source that we recently assembled using the Census as its starting point.

The Census of Production data is available on a consistent (1980 Standard Industrial Classification, SIC) basis from 1979 to 1990. To the basic Census data we matched in information on percentiles (10th, 25th, 50th, 75th and 90th) of the hourly wage distribution, and measures of dispersion by 3-digit industry from the New Earnings Survey data described in table 3.5. The matching could only take place from 1982 onwards given the fact that the New Earnings Survey only switched to the 1980 SIC Classification in 1982. The advantage of this data source is then that we have good quality employment data in a panel of 3-digit industries, together with information on the distribution of pay within industries. We also matched other information on the proportion of workers by education group from the Labour Force Surveys of 1981 and 1983 onwards and other information described below.

After deleting industries for whom we had fewer than fifty NES observations we have usable pay data for eighty-five 3-digit industries between 1982–90 (we lose fifteen industries for this reason). Table 3.8 documents the wage structure for male full-timers across these eighty-five manufacturing industries. We adopt an extremely simple method of data description and simply run a log(wage) regression on a constant and a time trend between 1982 and 1990 for various pay variables. The coefficient on the time trend gives the average real wage growth of the group in question over the estimation period. Comparison with its standard error allows one to ascertain the statistical significance of this real wage growth.

The first panel of table 3.8 reports various average real wage equations. We use information on hourly wages from the New Earnings Survey (NES) but to ensure that a similar pattern emerges we also report average annual wage equations using the Census of Production data (CoP). The first row of the table suggests that average hourly wages grew by about 2.3 percentage points a year between 1982–90; the analogous number for the annual CoP data is reassuringly similar but slightly higher (as might be expected for an annual measure as compared to an hourly one) at about 2.7 percentage points.

Turning to the main comparison of interest, that between manual and non-manual wages, the results in the table isolate higher average real wage growth for non-manuals as compared to manual employees. This is the case for both NES and CoP measures of average wages. Using the NES data, non-manuals appear to have achieved higher average wage growth of about 1 percentage point a year over the sample period. This differential is highly significant in conventional statistical terms.

The next three sections of the table consider the evolution of different percentiles of the wage distribution, for all men and then for manuals and non-manuals separately. The smallest real wage growth (1.3 percentage points a year) is for the 10th percentile of the manual distribution: growth then rises in a monotonic manner to approximately 2.4 percentage points for the 90th percentile. For non-manuals growth is higher for all percentiles as compared to the same percentile in the manual distribution, but there is also a much wider spread, going from about 2 percentage points a year for the 10th percentile to a huge 4 percentage points a year for the 90th percentile of the non-manual real wage distribution. This suggests not only a widening out of the non-manual/manual relative wage but also a wider dispersion of real wages amongst manuals and non-manuals.

The final section of the table makes it clear that inequality has increased within these two broad groups. The standard deviation of the log manual real hourly wage increased by 0.3 of a percentage point per year: compared to the 1982 initial value this amounts to a very large 10.7 per cent increase between 1982 and 1990. The rise in the non-manual distribution is even greater at almost 0.8 percentage points per annum (or 17.2 per cent compared to the 1982 level). Similar results emerge for the other inequality measure reported, the 90–10 log wage differential.

These changes in the manufacturing industry wage structure are striking. Big increases in the non-manual/manual relative wage advantage were seen between 1982 and 1990. Furthermore, large increases in within-group inequality were observed. These increases become even more dramatic when one considers the descriptive data reported in table 3.5 which suggested that the smallest (though still big) rise in inequality for the groups considered there was for male manual manufacturing workers which is the group on which we focus in table 3.8.

Changes in the relative demand for labour in manufacturing

We next consider changes in the structure of employment in manufacturing. The upper panel of table 3.9 documents changes in the relative shares of non-manual workers in terms of total employment and the wage bill and changing shares by education group. The first row uses data from the Census of Production on manual and non-manual employment in 100 manufacturing industries between 1979 and 1990. This time period saw a shift away from the use of manual labour as the share of non-manual employment in total employment rose by an average of almost 0.2 percentage points a year. Compared with the 1979 mean of 0.274, this amounts to a cumulative rise of 8.3 per cent over the sample period. This occupation-based shift in the demand for labour, coupled with the accompanying relative rise in the pay of

Table 3.9 *Changes in the structure of employment in UK manufacturing in the 1980s*

Dependent variable	Coefficient (standard error on time trend	Number of industries (sample period)	Mean of depend-ent variable	R^2
(a) All industries				
Share of non-manual employment in total employment	0.0019 (0.0009)	100 (1979-90)	0.296	0.01
Share of non-manual wage bill in total wage bill	0.0040 (0.0010)	100 (1979-90)	0.359	0.01
Share of workers with degree in total employment	0.0025 (0.0007)	81 (1981-90)	0.089	0.02
Share of workers with intermediate qualification in total employment	0.0252 (0.0011)	81 (1981-90)	0.441	0.43
Share of workers with no educational qualification in total employment	-0.0278 (0.0013)	81 (1981-90)	0.470	0.34

Dependent variable	Number of industries with positive significant impact	Number of industries with no impact	Number of industries with significant negative impact
(b) Individual industries	*Estimated effect of time trend*		
Share of non-manual employment in total employment	44	41	15
Share of non-manual wage bill in total wage bill	62	32	6
Share of workers with degree in total employment	25	51	5
Share of workers with intermediate qualification in total employment	76	5	0
Share of workers with no educational qualification in total employment	0	6	75

Note: 10% significance level used to denote statistical significance.

non-manuals and a big rise in inequality amongst non-manuals documented in the previous section, is entirely analogous to the results presented earlier in terms of education-based shifts in the pay and employment structure of the UK labour market. Of course it implies that the demand curve for such labour must have shifted out. It is also entirely in line with the US work on this issue (see Berman *et al.*, 1993, for similar evidence on relative shifts in the demand for skilled — that is, non-manual —labour in US manufacturing).

The second row of table 3.9 shows that the share of the non-manual wage bill in the total wage bill rose by about 0.4 percentage points per annum between 1979 and 1990. The greater magnitude of the coefficient on the time trend as compared to that in the first row of the table clearly illustrates the coincident rise in non-manual/manual relative wages and employment.

The remainder of the upper panel of the table is devoted to the changing shares of educated and non-educated labour in total employment (based on Labour Force Survey (LFS) data: we use a smaller sample of industries, 81 rather than 100, due to not having cell sizes of at least 50 workers from the LFS in nineteen industries). The results are very strong. A small but statistically significant (0.3 percentage points a year) rise in the relative share of graduates occurred between 1979 and 1990. Such effects are small, however, compared with the shift away from uneducated workers: a massive 2.8 percentage points a year drop in the share of workers with no educational qualification in total employment occurred between 1979 and 1990.

These patterns very much mirror the changing US employment structure in manufacturing (see Berman *et al.*, 1993). In the US literature several possible explanations have been proposed to explain shifts in the relative demand for skilled labour. Two schools of thought currently dominate the current US work. One asserts that it is essentially due to product demand shifts that have a greater effect on industries with a greater share of manuals (the strongest case being the rise of import competition which has hit the traditionally manual industries — like the car industry — more). The second is that skill upgrading has occurred due to skill biased technical changes (the most common example used here is the increased use of computer technologies). The key distinction between these two arguments is that the first concerns across-industry changes whilst the second really refers to a within-industry effect. Hence, examining whether the variation in changing employment shares can be attributed to the reallocation of labour between industries or whether it is due to shifts within industries can shed some light on the relevance of these two views. To examine this we followed two approaches. First, we ran separate regressions for each industry to explore within-industry trends in the nature of employment. The results are summarised in the lower panel of table 3.9. There seems to be a positive significant

Table 3.10 *Changes in the structure of employment in UK manufacturing in the 1980s: between and within industry decompositions*

Variable	Total change (annualised) for whole of manufact- uring in percentage points	Between industry component	Within industry component	% contri- bution of within industry component to total change
Share of non-manual employ- ment in total employment	0.367	0.066	0.301	82
Share of non-manual wage bill in total wage bill	0.668	0.114	0.554	83
Share of workers with degree in total employment	0.320	0.000	0.320	100
Share of workers with inter- mediate qualification in total employment	2.476	0.043	2.433	98
Share of workers with no educational qualification in total employment	-2.797	-0.042	-2.755	98

Note: The decomposition is described in the text.

(at the 10 per cent level) shift towards non-manual labour in around half of the industries considered; just over half saw a rise in the share of the non-manual wage bill. The education-based regressions are even more clearcut. For example, in 75 out of 81 industries there was a significant shift away from the use of uneducated labour. The majority was upgrading to using in- termediate education workers. In about one third of industries the share of graduates in total employment rose significantly.

The second approach is to decompose changes in the structure of em- ployment into within-industry and between-industry components of the total change (as in Berman *et al.*, 1993). For N manufacturing industries one can decompose the aggregate change in employment shares, ΔE, as follows:

$$\Delta E = \sum_{i=1}^{N} \Delta S_i \bar{E}_i + \sum_{i=1}^{N} \Delta E_i \bar{S}_i$$

where $E_i = NM_i / N_i$ is the share of non-production employment (NM) in to- tal employment (N) for industry i. $S_i = N_i / N$ is industry i's share of employ- ment in total manufacturing industry employment. Hence, the first expression gives changes in E that are due to changes in the share of employment between industries; the second is the within-industry component due to changes in share of non-production labour in industries.

This decomposition is reported in table 3.10. For all five share variables the within-industry component is far and away the most important. The percentage contribution of the within-group component to the total change ranges from 82 per cent for the non-manual employment share to the entire 100 per cent for the graduate share in total employment. It seems that much of the shift away from relatively unskilled labour occurred within given industries. Again, this is especially true of moves away from the use of workers with no educational qualifications.

Hence it appears that the majority of the change in employment and the average skill upgrading of workers is a within-industry phenomenon. Again this is entirely in line with the US work on this issue. Berman *et al.* (1993) report that 70 per cent (0.387 of the overall 0.552 percentage points a year) of the shift in the relative share of non-manual labour between 1979 and 1987 can be attributed to within-industry factors. The UK experience suggests a comparable figure of 82 per cent (or 0.301 of the 0.367 percentage points a year rise). The dominance of the within component implies that any explanation of rising inequality which relies on industry-level shocks (e.g import penetration) is probably of little relevance. The implication is that much of the change in the structure of employment is driven by factors within industries such as technical change (Bound and Johnson, 1992), changing firm size distributions (Davis and Haltiwanger, 1992) or trade union activity. It is the latter we turn to next.

The decline in union presence

The results to date certainly suggest that one can go some way in explaining the big changes in the UK wage structure in terms of the increased supply of more skilled workers, taken together with a rise in the demand for such skilled workers. A further route that has been noted in the literature on wage inequality is the decline in the importance of labour market institutions. The two which are usually focused on, as here, are trade unions and minimum wages. In this section we look at the role of unions, and in the next we consider the system of minimum wage legislation that existed in the UK in the 1980s, the Wages Councils.

It is well established that, at a given point in time, unions are likely to be associated with more compressed wage structures (see Freeman, 1980, 1982, for the US; Metcalf, 1982, or Gosling and Machin, 1993, for the UK). The 1980s in the UK saw a big fall in union presence. Aggregate union member-

Table 3.11 *Trade unions and the dispersion of semi-skilled earnings in UK establishments, 1980-90*

	1980	1990
Raw data		
s.d of ln (real semi-skilled earnings); establishments with recognised unions	0.245	0.290
s.d of ln (real semi-skilled earnings): establishments with no recognised unions	0.274	0.356
Difference (standard error)	-0.028 (0.16)	-0.066 (0.021)
Regression corrected (based on s.d. of residuals from Maximum Likelihood Earnings equation		
s.d. of ln (real semi-skilled earnings): establishments with recognised unions	0.188	0.211
s.d. of ln (real semi-skilled earnings): establishments with no recognised unions	0.201	0.269
Difference (standard error)	-0.013 (0.012)	-0.058 (0.021)
Union structure		
Percentage of plants with recognised unions (weighted/unweighted)	74/51	64/41

Notes: Results from Gosling and Machin (1993). Semi-skilled earnings regressions are estimated separately for union and non-union private sector establishments and include: five establishment size dummies, whether in manufacturing, a single-site, UK owned, member of an employer's association, whether any shift work, manual, female, part-time, semi-skilled workforce proportions, whether the majority sex worker is male, payment-by-results, and (in the union sector) dummies indicating the presence of pre-entry or post-entry closed shop arrangements. Weights are based on the Censuses of Employments of 1977 and 1987 to correct for the deliberate oversampling of large establishments (see Millward *et al.*, 1992).

ship fell from 13.2 million employees in 1980 to 9.9 million in 1990; aggregate union density fell from 54 to 38 per cent over the same time period.

Hence a natural question to ask is to what extent the fall in unionism goes hand-in-hand with the rise in wage inequality. Some recent US work has addressed this question. Card (1991) and Freeman (1991) both reach extremely similar conclusions. Freeman reports that 21 per cent of the 1978–88 rise in the standard deviation of log earnings can be attributed to falling union density; Card gets exactly the same number, that between 1973 and 1987, 21 per cent of the rise in the variance of earnings can be explained by the fall in union density. A third extremely interesting comparison is that of the US and Canada by Lemieux (1992). He reports that about 40 per cent of the faster rising inequality in the US can be put down to the fact that density there is declining while in Canada it remains relatively stable.

In this section we report on some work by Gosling and Machin (1993) which has explored this issue for the UK. They report semi-skilled pay dispersion measures based on establishment-level data from the 1980 and 1990 Workplace Industrial Relations Surveys. These are reproduced in table 3.11. In 1980 the standard deviation of log(real semi-skilled earnings) was 0.028 (or 10.2 per cent of the non-union mean) lower in unionised plants. By 1990 this gap had widened to 0.066. When one controls for various establishment-level characteristics (see the notes to the table) the same pattern emerges.

It is important to note that these results come about from a rise in inequality in both the union and non-union sectors, but that the rise is much larger in the non-union sector. For the regression-based models, the magnitude of the effects are rises of 0.018 (or 9 per cent of the 1980 standard deviation) in the union sector, but a huge rise of 0.067 (or 34 per cent) in the non-union sector. As the table shows the incidence of union recognition fell by about 10 percentage points between 1980 and 1990.

One can evaluate the impact of union decline by considering the following question: what would inequality be predicted to be in 1990 if the 1980 union structure was still present? Consider the following variance decomposition:

$$V(w) = UV(w^u) + (1-U)V(w^n) + U(1-U)(\overline{w}^u - \overline{w}^n)$$

where $V(w)$ is the variance of log(real wages), U is the unionised proportion, u and n superscripts denote union and non-union status and a bar denotes a mean. Using the conditional regression-based standard deviations and measuring the average union wage effect by Stewart's (1992) estimate of 0.062 produces a $V(w)$ of 0.0544 in 1990. In 1980 the analogous figure is 0.0384 (using Stewart's (1991) estimate of the wage mark-up of 0.075). Replacing the 1990 U and the wage mark-up with their 1980 values but using the 1990 standard deviations produced a $V(w) = 0.0515$. One can thus compute the impact of declining union structure as $(0.0544 - 0.0515) = 0.0029$, which amounts to 18 per cent of the 1980–90 rise in the conditional variance of semi-skilled earnings.

Hence, the decline in unionisation is associated with about one fifth of the coincident rise in semi-skilled wage inequality. This is clearly very much in line with the US estimates outlined above.

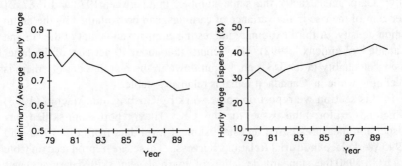

Figure 3.5 The ratio of minimum to average wages and wage dispersion for workers covered by Wages Councils, 1979-90

Table 3.12 *Wages Council minimum pay rates and the dispersion of earnings of workers covered by Wages Councils, 1979–90*

Determinants of the ln (standard deviation of hourly earnings) in 14 Wages Council sectors, 1979-90		
	(1)	(2)
Constant	3.320 (0.106)	3.710 (0.133)
ln (minimum wage/average wage)	-0.912 (0.137)	-0.395 (0.187)
Trend	0.012 (0.005)	0.014 (0.004)
GDP growth	0.077 (0.667)	0.136 (0.552)
Female council	-0.180 (0.041)	-0.312 (0.060)
Manual council	-0.057 (0.033)	
Wage Council dummies included	No	Yes
R^2	0.746	0.838
Number of observations	122	122

Notes: Standard errors are in brackets below the estimated coefficients. See Machin and Manning (1992) for more details.

The declining importance of minimum wages

The other labour market institution which has been highlighted in other work (for example, Katz *et al.*'s, 1993, discussion of the relative stability of the French wage structure) is the role of minimum wages. In the UK in the 1980s the Wages Councils provided a system of minimum wages, an industry-based system of minimum pay setting for around 2.5 million workers in low paid sectors (catering, retail and hairdressing being the largest covered sectors). Machin and Manning (1992) have investigated the evolution of the Wages Council minimum rates through the 1980s and related them to the rise in inequality and to the evolution of employment in the Wages Council industries.

Figure 3.5 reports the ratio of the minimum to the average wage in the Wages Councils sectors using data from the New Earnings Survey and information on minimum wages from various Incomes Data Services reports. This ratio clearly declines during the 1980s, reflecting a failure to uprate minimum wages in line with average pay in these sectors.

Machin and Manning (1992) investigate the relationship between wage dispersion in the Wages Councils sectors and the ratio of the minimum to the average wage. The measure of wage dispersion they use is the standard deviation of log(hourly earnings) from the New Earnings Survey. This measure is plotted in figure 3.5; it clearly rises through the decade and as such is yet another example of inequality rising within well-defined groups in the economy.

Table 3.12 reproduces two regressions from Machin and Manning (1992). In the first the log of wage dispersion is regressed on the log of the minimum/average wage ratio, a time trend, aggregate GDP growth and dummy variables indicating whether or not the Council is for females or manuals (vis-à-vis males or non-manuals). The second includes dummies for each Council to control for time-invariant fixed effects.

In both specifications, the coefficient on the minimum/average ratio is estimated to be significantly negative. The ratio of the minimum to the average declined by about 0.23 log points between 1979 and 1990 thus suggesting that this variable can account for somewhere between 9 per cent (column (2)) and 20 per cent (column (1)) of the rise in dispersion amongst these low pay sectors over the sample period. The fact that the 1993 Employment Rights and Trade Union Reform Bill will abolish the remaining twenty-six Wages Councils suggests further rises in inequality for these low paid workers.

The decline in minimum wages seems important for low paid workers in the United States. Bound and Freeman (1992) suggest that 1980s declines in the real value of US minimum wages were an important factor in explaining the fall in the relative wages of black workers. This was observed to be especially important for less skilled black workers (who, since they are located in the lower tail of the earnings distribution, are more likely to be affected by minimum wage legislation): the declining importance of minimum wages was found to be an extremely important determinant of the changing wage structure for high school dropouts.

Comparisons with experiences of other countries

The most striking feature of the results described in the two previous sections is how they appear to suggest very close similarities with the US experience. We stated earlier that the level of inequality and the date at which it began to rise are very different across the two countries, but many of the determinants of the rise in inequality seem to apply to both countries. Firstly, whilst macroeconomic indicators can predict the time-series evolution of aggregate poverty and income inequality indicators up to the early to mid-1980s it appears to be the case that this relationship broke down during the economic upswings of the 1980s in both countries. Secondly, recent changes in the labour market seem to be similar. There has been a considerable rise in the relative supply of more highly skilled/educated workers in both countries and this has gone hand-in-hand with rising returns to education and a simultaneous increase in the demand for skilled workers. It seems that the application to the UK of the simple supply and demand framework which has been used widely in the US work is a reasonable one. Thirdly, there have been considerable increases in wage inequality within different groups of workers (for example, even though the relative wages of non-manuals have grown faster than manuals, pay dispersion has widened most amongst non-manual workers). Fourthly, the decline of labour market institutions has contributed to bigger gaps between the high-paid and low-paid workers in the UK and the US economies.

One should, however, note that this discussion refers to broad trends. There are, of course, notable differences. For instance, in the US the real wages received by workers in the lowest deciles of the distribution have been falling for some time: in the UK workers at all points in the wage distribution still received positive real wage increases through the 1980s. Nevertheless, some of the patterns observed, especially in terms of economic developments of the nature of the labour market, do have similarities. If anything, it seems that the changes in the UK in the 1980s have progressed at a faster rate than the continuing shifts in the US (see the rises in 90–10 log wage differentials in table 3.1). The move towards flexibility in the UK labour market seems to have produced the marked rises in inequality that have been observed for some time in the more flexible US labour market.

Other countries have also experienced shifts in the relative demand and supply of skilled workers, in conjunction with a decline in labour market institutions. There is far less research on other countries but it suggests that Sweden and Australia appear to have been experiencing the same trends. They have also seen large increases in inequality in the 1980s. Edin and Holmlund (1993) document the Swedish situation and argue that there have

been large supply and demand shifts and that the breakdown of
solidaristic union wage policies that have traditionally compressed the wage
structure have led to rising wage inequality in the late 1980s.

Similarly, Australia has seen large rises in inequality in the 1980s. There
has also been an upsurge in the relative supply and demand for highly
skilled workers (Aungles *et al.*, 1991). Furthermore, unions and labour market institutions in Australia have interacted in a unique way to contribute to
this rise in inequality. The Accord-based incomes policy only applies to
the 80 per cent of employees whose wages are regulated by 'awards' made
by industrial tribunals. High income earners, who are generally 'award-free',
were not affected by the real wage cuts agreed to by the union movement under the Accord in the second half of the 1980s. Earnings of the well-off were
therefore unrestrained during the period of strong growth that occurred in
Australia at this time.

Hence it seems that these countries have had rapidly rising inequality and
seem to have simultaneously experienced shifts in relative supply and demand,
but also a decline in the importance of labour market institutions (or, in
the case of Australia, a change in the way these institutions interacted with
unions to regulate wages in a period of strong growth).

This seems all the more relevant when one considers the experiences of
other countries which have not suffered such big inequality increases or have
even observed moves towards greater equality. In Canada, for example,
much smaller rises in inequality have occurred. At the same time Canadian
skill differentials have not risen by anywhere near as much as in the US (Freeman and Needels, 1991, estimate increases of about one fifth of the magnitude
of those in the US) and another of the potential explanatory factors, union
density, has stayed relatively constant (Lemieux, 1992). In France a
(strongly binding) national minimum wage operates and pay dispersion has
not widened out to anywhere such an extent as that experienced by the US
and the UK (see Katz *et al.*, 1993).

Some other countries have experienced moves in the other direction. In
Italy, for example, wage inequality has fallen through the 1980s
(Erickson and Ichino, 1992, report that the standard deviation of the log wage
was 0.46 in 1977, 0.42 in 1982 and 0.37 in 1987). Erickson and Ichino report a closing of the white collar/blue collar wage gap and, though some increases in the relative supply of highly educated workers are observed, they
find no coincident rise in the returns to education. Rather, returns to education appear to have been falling through the 1980s. Hence changes in the
distribution of education appear to reconcile the different Italian experience
from that of the rising inequality group described above. Finally, they
state that 'labour market institutions .... have not been deregulated or

otherwise dismantled to the extent they have been in the US' (Erickson and Ichino, 1992, p. 34). Hence, many of the trends that have been apparent in the UK and other countries where inequality has risen sharply have actually not altered or even moved in the opposite direction in Italy. This clearly adds more credence to the notion that shifts in supply and demand and the role of labour market institutions in wage setting can explain a large part of changes in inequality across countries. Of course, in a deep sense, there is still a large residual portion of the rise in inequality left unexplained. Hopefully, future work will attempt to unravel this and consider additional avenues and potential culprits in accounting for the observed changes.

Finally, returning to the UK, it seems that if (as the UK government seems to want) one wishes to go further down 'flexibility' road then union decline and removal of minimum wage legislation are likely to induce further inequities in the distribution of earnings and income. It also seems likely to push more people into poverty and, if this route is followed, there seems no reason why the UK should not move further towards the US situation (though, given the new US government's pledges to raise taxes and to help the poor, the UK may catch up faster in terms of inequality than one might previously have thought). Of course, as noted by other commentators on this issue (Blanchflower and Freeman, 1993) at least in the US there is some element of 'sharing the inequality around' since inflows and outflows from unemployment are much faster than in the UK (or indeed than in any European country). It seems that the UK is experiencing big rises in inequality much like the US but without the equalising impact of rapid transitions between employment states. Hence it still suffers from the European-wide problem of high unemployment persistence among individuals but now has massive and widening wage inequality as well. This does not appear to be very encouraging for the future health of the UK labour market.

Notes

1   We would like to thank Richard Freeman, Alan Manning, Jane Waldfogel and especially Stephen Jenkins and Andrew Oswald for many useful comments. We would also like to thank Patricia Apps, John Buchanan, Martin Conyon, Lorraine Dearden, Richard Dickens, Amanda Gosling, John Van Reenen, John Schmitt and Jonathan Wadsworth for providing us with some of the data used and for pointing us to some of the references used in this paper, and Karen Gardiner for helping us out with some of the numbers reported in table 3.1. Richard Dickens and Steve Woodland provided extremely good research assistance. We are very grateful to the Department of Employment for giving us access to the New Earnings Survey data used in this chapter.

2 But see Pissarides (1990) who discusses many of the issues and provides some descriptive data.
3 Again the nature of the data (and various definitions) means that one should be careful only to draw broad conclusions about trends: see Jenkins (1991) for more details.
4 Historically 30–40 per cent of the poorest households were pensioners. As such one may think that the ageing of the population may imply that household composition has raised the number of households in poverty. This does not appear to be the case: the increased availability of occupational and other pension incomes have moved this group increasingly out of poverty. For example, between 1979 and 1989 the proportion of the poorest 10 per cent of households where the head of household was a pensioner fell from 32 per cent to 16 per cent (see also Jenkins, 1991a). The distribution of work is a more plausible contender. Yet Jenkins (1991b) and Atkinson (1993) both suggest that the late 1970s fall in unemployment is hard to reconcile with the continual 1980s rise in inequality.

References

Atkinson, A. (1993), 'What is happening to the distribution of income in the UK?', STICERD Discussion Paper no. 87.
Aungles, P., Dearden, L., Karmel, T. and Ryan, C. (1991), 'Through a real vision mirror darkly: occupational employment in Australia 1971–86', Australian Department of Employment, Education and Training, Economic and Policy Analysis Division.
Berman, E., Bound, J. and Griliches, Z. (1993), 'Changes in the demand for skilled labour within US manufacturing industries: evidence from the Annual Survey of Manufacturing', NBER Discussion Paper no. 4255.
Blanchflower, D. and Freeman, R. (1993), 'Did the Thatcher reforms change British labour market performance?', chapter 2 of this volume.
Blanchflower, D. and Oswald, A. (1993), *The Wage Curve*, MIT Press.
Blank, R. (1989), 'Disaggregating the effect of the business cycle on the distribution of income', *Economica*, 56, 141–64.
Blank, R. and Blinder, A. (1986), 'Macroeconomics, income distribution and poverty', in Danziger, S. and Weinberg, D. (eds), *Fighting Poverty: What Works and What Doesn't*, Cambridge, Mass., Harvard University Press.
Blank, R. and Hanratty, M. (1992), 'Down and out in North America: recent trends in poverty rates in the United States and Canada', *Quarterly Journal of Economics*, 107, 233–54.
Bound, J. and Freeman, R. (1992), 'What went wrong? The erosion of relative earnings and employment among young black men in the 1980s', *Quarterly Journal of Economics*, 107, 201–32.
Bound, J. and Johnson, G. (1992), 'Changes in the structure of wages in the 1980s: An evaluation of alternative explanations', *American Economic Review*, 82, 371–92.
Card, D. (1991), 'The effect of unions on the distribution of wages: Redistribution or relabelling', Princeton University Industrial Relations Section Discussion Paper no. 287.

Cutler, D. and Katz, L. (1991), 'Macroeconomic performance and the disadvantaged', *Brookings Papers on Economic Activity*, 1–74.

Davis, S. (1992), 'Cross-country patterns of change in relative wages', *NBER Macroeconomics Annual*, 239–300.

Davis, S. and Haltiwanger, J. (1992), 'Wage dispersion between and within US manufacturing plants, 1963–86', *Brookings Papers on Economic Activity: Microeconomics 1991*, 201–40.

Edin, P.-A. and Holmlund, B. (1993), 'The Swedish wage structure: the rise and fall of solidaristic wage policy?', NBER Discussion Paper no. 4257.

Ellwood, D. and Summers, L. (1986), 'Poverty in America: is welfare the answer?' in Danziger, S. and Weinberg, D. (eds), *Fighting Poverty: What Works and What Doesn't*, Cambridge, Mass., Harvard University Press.

Erickson, C. and Ichino, A. (1992), 'Wage differentials in Italy: market forces, institutions and inflation', NBER Working Paper, forthcoming in Freeman, R. and Katz, L., *Changes and Differences in Wage Structures*, University of Chicago Press.

Freeman, R. (1980), 'Unionism and the dispersion of wages', *Industrial and Labor Relations Review*, 34, 3–24.

Freeman, R. (1982), 'Union wage practices and wage dispersion within establishments', *Industrial and Labor Relations Review*, 36, 3–21.

Freeman, R. (1991), 'How much has deunionisation contributed to the rise in male earnings inequality', NBEResearch Discussion Paper no. 3826.

Freeman, R. and Needels, K. (1991), 'Skill differentials in Canada in an era of rising wage inequality', NBER Discussion Paper no. 3827.

Gosling, A. and Machin, S. (1993), 'Trade unions and the dispersion of earnings in UK establishments, 1980–90', Centre for Economic Performance, LSE, Discussion Paper no.140.

Jenkins, S. (1991a), 'Income inequality and living standards: changes in the 1970s and 1980s', *Fiscal Studies*, 12, 1–28.

Jenkins, S. (1991b), 'Accounting for inequality trends: decomposition analyses for the UK, 1971–86', University College Swansea mimeo.

Johnson, P. and Webb, S. (1993), 'Explaining the growth in UK income inequality: 1979–88', *Economic Journal Conference Volume*, 103, 429–35.

Katz, L. and Krueger, A. (1992), 'The effect of the minimum wage on the fast-food industry', *Industrial and Labor Relations Review*, 46, 6–21.

Katz, L., Loveman, G. and Blanchflower, D. (1991), 'A comparison of changes in the structure of wages in four OECD countries', forthcoming in Freeman, R. and Katz, L., *Changes and Differences in Wage Structures*, University of Chicago Press.

Katz, L. and Murphy, K. (1992), 'Changes in the structure of wages, 1963–87: supply and demand factors', *Quarterly Journal of Economics*, 107, 35–78.

Lemieux, T. (1992), 'Unions and wage inequality in Canada and the United States', Princeton University, mimeo.

Levy, F. and Murnane, R. (1992), 'US earnings levels and earnings inequality: a review of recent trends and proposed explanations', *Journal of Economic Literature*, 30, 1333–81.

Machin, S. and Manning, A. (1992), 'Minimum wages, wage dispersion and employment:

evidence from the UK wages councils', Centre for Economic Performance, LSE, Discussion Paper 80.

Machin, S., Meghir, C. and Whitehouse, E. (1993), 'Changes in the UK wage structure 1968–90: identifying macroeconomic effects across and within groups', Institute for Fiscal Studies draft.

Metcalf, D. (1982), 'Unions and the distribution of earnings', *British Journal of Industrial Relations*, 20, 163–9.

Millward, N., Stevens, M., Smart, D. and Hawes, W. (1992), *Workplace Industrial Relations in Transition*, Dartmouth.

Murphy, K. and Welch, F. (1992), 'The structure of wages', *Quarterly Journal of Economics*, 107, 285–326.

Nolan, B. (1986), 'Unemployment and the size distribution of income', *Economica*, 53, 421–46.

Pissarides, C. (1990), 'Macroeconomic adjustment and poverty in selected developed countries', Centre for Economic Performance, LSE, Discussion Paper No. 13.

Raskall, P. (1992), 'Inequality in Australia—what we know and what we don't' in Raskall, P. and Saunders, P. (eds.), *Economic Inequality in Australia, Volume I: Government and Redistribution*, SSEI Monograph No. 1, Centre for Applied Economic Research and the Social Policy Research Centre, University of New South Wales.

Saunders, P., Stott, H. and Hobbes, G. (1991), 'Income inequality in Australia and New Zealand: International comparison and recent trends', *Review of Income and Wealth*, 37, 63–79.

Schmitt, J. (1993), 'The changing structure of male earnings in Britain, 1974-88', forthcoming in Freeman, R. and Katz, L., *Changes and Differences in Wage Structures*, University of Chicago Press.

Slesnick, D. (1993), 'Gaining ground: poverty in the post-war United States', *Journal of Political Economy*, 101, 1–38.

Stark, T. (1977), 'The distribution of income in eight countries', Royal Commission on the Distribution of Income and Wealth, Background Paper no. 4.

Stark, T. (1992), 'Income and wealth in the 1980s', Fabian Society.

Stewart, M. (1991), 'Union wage differentials in the face of changes in the economic and legal environment', *Economica*, 58, 155–72.

Stewart, M. (1992), 'Do changes in collective bargaining arrangements imply declining union wage differentials', University of Warwick, mimeo.

4   Transformation of British industrial relations? Institutions, conduct and outcomes 1980–1990

DAVID METCALF[1]

'There can be no doubt about the transformation which has taken place in British industrial relations in the past decade.' Michael Howard, Secretary of State for Employment, *Hansard* 166(39), 29 January 1990, col. 38.

'What Thatcherism appears to have produced is neither new realism nor flexibility but a system of workplace industrial relations with much the same features as were previously seen as responsible for Britain's economic decline ... there is surprisingly little evidence of a dramatic shift of bargaining power away from the unions.' John MacInnes, *Thatcherism at Work*, Open University Press 1987, pp. 133, 136.

No consensus exists concerning the extent and consequences of change in British industrial relations in the last decade or so. There is no doubt that there has been a transition away from the traditional system, although towards what is unclear. Millward *et al.* (1992, summary p.6) write that 'the distinctive "system" of British industrial relations based on collective bargaining is no longer characteristic of the economy as a whole.' But transition towards an unknown destination is not necessarily the same as transformation.

In the next section we examine the alterations in industrial relations structure (institutions) and conduct (processes). This covers unions, management, bargaining and the environment. In the second section we analyse the links between the modifications to the institutions/processes and the performance outcomes of the system. The two major outcomes concern the pay/jobs trade-off and the performance of workplaces and companies. These are dealt with in turn. Much of the evidence is taken from successive Workplace Industrial Relations Surveys (WIRS) covering approximately 2 000 workplaces in 1980 (WIRS1), 1984 (WIRS2) and 1990 (WIRS3, see Millward *et al.*, 1992).

Institutions and conduct

Union presence

In 1991 37 per cent of employees were union members (Beatson and Butcher 1993). Union membership rose by some three million during the 1960s and 1970s, reaching its zenith in 1979. Since then it has fallen back such that in 1990 membership and density was similar to its 1960 figure (see table 4.1).

Table 4.1 *Trade union membership (thousands) and density (per cent)*

	UK	GB corrected	TUC affiliated	GB density
	(1)	(2)	(3)	(4)
1960	9835	8852	8299	41.3
1965	10 181	9163	8868	40.5
1970	11 178	10 060	10 002	48.2
1975	12 184	10 966	11 063	49.4
1979	13 289	11 960	12 173	52.9
1985	10 821	9739	9581	46.6
1990	9947	8952	8230	40.0
Membership loss 1979-90	3342	3008	3943 (3608)	12.9

Notes and Sources:
(1) Membership of UK trade unions. Annual article in *Employment Gazette* (for example, April 1992, p. 187). Information supplied by unions themselves to the Certification Officer.
(2) Union membership among employees in employment in Great Britain. This is derived from column (1), suitably corrected. It is necessary to deduct (a) self-employed and unemployed, and (b) members in Northern Ireland and overseas. 10 per cent of union members as defined in column (1) fall into categories (a) and (b), so column (1) is multiplied by 0.9. It should be noted that unions may either over-report their membership (for example, to boost their importance in the TUC and Labour party) or under-report (to reduce affiliation fees). No full information exists on the direction of bias and no correction is made.
(3) Membership of unions affiliated to the TUC as supplied by the unions themselves. Figure in brackets is for information. It 'adds back' EETPU membership to control for the expulsion of the EETPU in 1988.
(4) Column 2 as a percentage of GB employees in employment, *Employment Gazette*, table 1.2.

Table 4.2 *Union presence 1984 and 1990*

Indicator	1984 %	1990 %
Recognition		
Establishments with recognised trade unions for any workers as % of all establishments	66	53
Density (% of all employees who were union members)		
All employees	58	48
Manual	66	53
Non-manual	61	43
Private manufacturing	56	48
Private services	30	27
Public sector	80	72
Multiple unions (number of recognised unions, excluding workplaces with no recognised unions)		
Manual 1	65	66
2	21	19
3+	14	15
Non-manual 1	39	45
2	28	31
3+	33	23
Closed shop		
Number of employees (millions)	3.6	0.4
% of establishments where all or some groups have to be union members:		
Manual	20	4
Non-manual	9	1

Source: Millward *et al.* (1992) tables 3.7, 3.2, 3.8, 3.9, 3.17.
Note: Information based on representative sample of some 2000 workplaces with 25+ employees in 1984 and 1990.

Profound changes in union presence occurred between 1984 and 1990. The WIRS evidence focuses on workplaces with twenty-five or more employees. Table 4.2 documents the decline. The number of establishments recognising unions for collective bargaining fell from two thirds to one half. Putting it another way, by 1990 collective industrial relations were the norm for only half of workplaces (with over twenty-five employees). There is some evidence of partial or complete derecognition in smaller workplaces, engineering, printing and establishments which were independent of any larger organisation (Gregg and Yates, 1991, Millward *et al.*, 1992). More important is the lack of new recognition. In the private sector, workplaces that were less than ten years old recognised unions in only 23 per cent of cases compared with 52 per cent of those that were more than twenty years old.

Density fell virtually hand-in-hand with this decline in the fraction of workplaces recognising unions: it waned for both manual and non-manual workers, and for private and public services and manufacturing. Taking a longer perspective, the period since 1979 represents the longest ever continuous period of declining union membership. Future analysis of industrial relations will have to pay far greater attention to the non-union sector.

Among workplaces which recognised unions the extent of multiple unionism was unchanged for manual workers. But among non-manuals multi-unionism diminished, particularly in the public sector. In 1990, focusing just on workplaces with recognised unions, we find:

Number of recognised unions	1	2	3	4+	Mean
% of establishments	36	31	12	20	2.5

Thus only one third of establishments had single unionism and a fifth had four or more unions. It is clear that 'single union deals' are not as pervasive as might be thought from the publicity and controversy they generate. However, an increasing proportion of workplaces with multiple unions engage in single table bargaining (Marginson and Sisson, 1990) which can be thought of as a halfway house towards single unionism.

Closed shops represent the pinnacle of union strength. In 1979 over five million workers were covered by these arrangements. The majority were in post-entry shops, where union membership was required once in the job. Around one in six were in pre-entry shops where membership was required to get a job. Table 4.2 shows that this totem of union power has virtually withered away and legislative changes since 1990 have outlawed all closed shops.

Union organisation has also altered since 1979. First, membership has become more concentrated (Bird, Kirosingh and Stevens, 1992). In 1990 there were only 287 unions, down from 453 in 1979 (and only a fifth of the peak number of 1384 in 1920). Four in five union members now belong to a union with over 100 000 members and three in five to one with over 250 000 members. Second, the central union hierarchy has reasserted control over constituent workplaces (Elgar and Simpson, 1993), largely to ensure that union funds are not put at risk from unlawful industrial relations acts. Third, union finances are a cause for concern. Willman (1990) terms unions' net worth (assets minus liabilities) as a multiple of spending the 'acid test' measure because it indicates how long a union could operate if it had no revenue coming in. This indicator has consistently declined in the postwar period.

Explanations for shrinking union influence have exercised industrial relations academics and other scholars. A full treatment would require a separate chapter. Instead, the focus here is more narrow, on density. The intersection of Thatcherite policies with long-run trends is the cause of lower trade union membership. More specifically, density has contracted because of the complex interaction of five factors: macroeconomic variables; labour force composition; and policies of the state, employers and unions themselves.

Carruth and Disney (1988) examined movements in density from 1896 to 1984. They found that, when unemployment and real wage growth were high relative to trend, this exerted a depressing influence on density. They went as far as to state that: 'the downturn in membership [in the 1980s] is entirely a cyclical phenomenon'. This seems a bit strong. Further, the slow-down in real wage growth and rapid fall in unemployment 1988–90 should — according to business cycle theory — have caused membership to increase, but it did not.

Composition arguments are deceptively seductive. The probability of belonging to a union is higher for full-timers than for part-timers, for men than for women, for manuals than for non-manuals, in manufacturing than in services, in large workplaces than in small ones, in northern Britain than in southern. Therefore, so the argument runs, because the mix of jobs and workers moved unfavourably with respect to union membership on all counts, membership was bound to decline. Booth (1989) ascribes nearly half the decline in density 1980–86 to such composition effects. This begs two questions. First, most of the trends noted above were in operation in the 1970s when membership rose rapidly. Second, why have unions not been able to get recognised, organise and recruit in expanding areas of employment?

The study of the effects of legislative onslaught against unions was advanced by Freeman and Pelletier (1990). They analysed fluctuations in density between 1948 and 1986. The control variables included macroeconomic variables, industry composition, and the political complexion of the government. The authors calculated a 'legislation index' according to how favourable or unfavourable various strands of labour law were to unions in each year. Changes in the law were held to be 'responsible for the entire decline' in density levels — clearly inconsistent with the identical claim of Carruth and Disney concerning macroeconomic factors.

Employer policies towards unions are crucial. Recognition is the fulcrum on which membership moves. In the WIRS panel, de-recognitions were twice as likely as new recognitions over the period 1984–90. Encouragement of human resource management among employees in unionised workplaces (see next section) has further undermined the traditional collective approach to industrial relations.

Finally, unions' own policies surely count. In recent years, many unions have adopted a 'market share' approach. They have attempted via mergers, amalgamations and transfers of engagements to boost their share of a declining pool. This may well be a sensible defensive tactic, but it does not boost aggregate membership. It is noteworthy that the most successful union in the 1980s — The Royal College of Nursing — trebled its membership to 300 000 by emphasising its professional ethos and exclusive craft status.

Management

'The main feature of industrial relations in the 1980s was that managers were firmly in charge.' So conclude Kessler and Bayliss (1992) in their exhaustive study of industrial relations in the last quarter of a century. The ascent of management cannot be quantified in the way that the decline of union organisation is measurable, but certain features of management practice during the 1980s and 1990s stand out. Dunn (1993) shows how management has frequently de-incorporated itself from previous pluralist practices involving joint regulation with unions. This de-incorporation is associated with greater decentralisation, a spread of human resource management practices and changes to the substantive clauses in collective bargaining.

Consequent upon the findings of the Donovan (1968) Report into our industrial relations, 'management "sponsorship" of shop stewards in the 1970s became the vogue ... previously feeble stewards found themselves with the procedural wherewithal to do something to satisfy their members' demands' (Dunn, 1993). Studying over fifty companies in 1979, Dunn traces how a 'live and let live' principle evolved such that managerial ambition was stunted and its imagination unionised. In surveys in the 1970s managers generally stated they were content, but this was because 'stewards defined the terms of the truce and management rationalised their compliance.' When he revisited these companies in 1990–91 he noted the re-assertion of managerial prerogative. This was not simply a consequence of greater product market competition and higher unemployment. Rather it had involved great effort — not just getting rid of restrictive working practices, but 'breaking the routine of conforming with bargaining rituals and of deferring to steward power'.

One such ritual that was ruptured was multi-employer bargaining. Purcell (1991) shows that the 1980s witnessed the culmination of the process of collapse of multi-employer bargaining and simultaneous decentralisation to local units. Further, 'it is extremely rare for the trade unions to have initiated the restructuring of collective bargaining. In most cases they have opposed it, unsuccessfully.' This decentralisation of management is evidenced by the fact that membership of employers' organisations halved between 1980 and 1990.

Although some decentralisation was going on before 1980 its pace accelerated around then. Management experts such as Purcell indicate that the dominant force for this change in industrial relations is the 'development of business policies and corporate strategies concerned with the structure, shape, and control systems of the firm which have forced personnel and industrial relations managers, often reluctantly, to restructure collective bargaining'. This is especially the case with large enterprises which dominate the British economy to a greater extent than in other OECD countries.

While the change to decentralised management is self-evident, there is more debate concerning the extent to which it has been accompanied by human resource management (HRM). Evidence from WIRS3 (Millward *et al.*, 1992) shows that HRM practices are on the increase, but that — paradoxically — they are more prevalent in union than in non-union workplaces (see Sisson, 1993, for further details).

The decline in union density and recognition was outlined in the first section. Workplace-level joint consultation committees (JCCs) provide an alternative mechanism to conduct collective industrial relations. The fraction of workplaces with such arrangements rose in the 1970s, but these committees have also been in decline subsequently

| | % of workplaces with JCC | |
	1984	1990
Union workplaces	41	37
Non-union workplaces	21	19
All workplaces	34	29

Thus there is no evidence that JCCs have filled the institutional vacuum left by the decay in collective bargaining.

By contrast 'individual' practices — usually thought of as components of HRM — are spreading. Examples include team briefings, now regularly used by nearly half of all workplaces, and line managers spending more time on personnel matters.

Possibly more important are the changes in payment systems (see table 4.3). There was no overall increase in payments-by-results (PBR) between 1984 and 1990 but it is notable that one third of establishments had some form of merit pay — dependent on the subjective judgement of a supervisor

Table 4.3 *Changes in payment systems*

	Per cent of establishments	
	1984	1990
Payments by results		
Any worker paid by results on individual, group or organisational basis		
Manual	31	32
Clerical, administrative, secretarial	16	19
Individual payments: any worker with:		
Individual PBR	n.a.	27
Merit pay	n.a.	34
Either	n.a.	45
Profit sharing		
Cash-based or share-based profit sharing, establishments in industrial and commercial sectors	18	43
Employee share ownership schemes		
Share ownership or share option schemes	23	32
Eligibility: % of workforce eligible where schemes exist	68	62
Participation: % of workforce participating	22	34

Source: Millward *et al.* (1992) tables 7.19, 7.20, pages 264, 265.
Note: See note to table 4.2.

or manager — by 1990. Profit sharing schemes and employee share ownership plans (ESOPs) both expanded.

However, these 'individual' elements in pay probably account for only a
tiny fraction of the total wage bill. In 1990 a third of establishments had an
ESOP and in these workplaces a third of employees participated (see table
4.3). If the ESOP accounted for, say, 10 per cent of total pay, this implies
that ESOPs total only around 1 per cent of the aggregate British private
sector wage bill. If merit pay and profit sharing represent similar fractions
it can be readily seen that these HRM elements have a shallow hold.

Contents of collective agreements provide one indication of the tilt in the
balance of power towards management in the 1980s and 1990s. Such analysis confirms that it is vital not to associate procedural stability with a lack of
dynamism in industrial relations. Wright (1993) has studied over 100 such
agreements for the same fifty companies operating in 1979 and 1990. He
found that procedural clauses were rather robust: clauses relating to state-

ments of intent and the parties recognised had changed little. There were some procedural extensions concerning dispute resolution, check-off and shop steward constituencies and time off. Closed shop clauses were the most likely to be deleted, although in the majority of cases they remained extant. It is noteworthy that there was virtually no extension of 'new style deal' procedures incorporating clauses covering, for example, cooperative statements of intent, single status, and final offer arbitration to resolve disputes.

By contrast, there was a noticeable shift in the substantive clauses towards greater flexibility of work organisation. Sometimes such flexibility was achieved via formalisation of more flexible job descriptions but more often the 1990 clauses emphasised managerial prerogative in determining job tasks.

Collective bargaining

The diminution of unionisation and developments in managerial practices outlined above leads naturally to a consideration of changes in the coverage, structure and quality of collective bargaining.

Official attitudes towards collective bargaining have altered dramatically over the past quarter of a century. Brown (1993) — from where the following quotes are taken — charts these views. The Royal Commission on Trade Unions and Employers Associations 1965–8 stated:

'Properly conducted, collective bargaining is the most effective means of giving workers the right to representation in decisions affecting their working lives. While therefore the first task in the reform of British industrial relations is to bring greater order into collective bargaining in the company and plant, the second is to extend the coverage of collective bargaining and the organisation of workers on which it depends.' (Donovan, 1968, para. 212).

Yet twenty-four years later we find the Secretary of State for Employment reporting to Parliament that:

'Traditional patterns of industrial relations, based on collective bargaining and collective agreements, seem increasingly inappropriate and are in decline.' (Department of Employment (1992), Cm. 1810, para. 1.15).

Donovan certainly got its wish to extend collective bargaining during the 1970s but subsequently the coverage of collective agreements decayed rapidly, particularly in the second half of the 1980s. Brown (1993) assembled

Table 4.4 *Percentage having most recent pay rise determined by collective bargaining*

Sector	Manual		Non-manual		All employees	
	1980 Estabs.	1990 Estabs.	1980	1990 Estabs.	1984	1990
Private manufacturing	65	45	27	24	64	51
Private services	34	31	28	26	41	33
Public sector	91(a)	78	98(a)	84	95	78
All	55	48	47	43	71	54

Source: Millward *et al.* (1992) tables 3.15, 3.16, 7.2, 7.5, 7.8.
Note: (a) 1984 (not 1980) Information based on representative sample of some 2000 workplaces with 25+ employees in 1984 and 1990.

these figures from a variety of sources:

	% of all employees covered by collective agreements
1968	65
1973	72
1984	64
1990	47

Collective bargaining is also now the norm in only a minority of workplaces and it has ebbed in importance in both private manufacturing and services and in the public sector in the last decade (table 4.4). Where pay in the private sector is still determined by collective bargaining, two features stand out. First, multi-employer bargaining has decayed but, second, there is also less fragmentation of internal company bargaining.

Many multi-employer ('national') agreements have collapsed or been greatly reduced in influence or coverage since 1986 (Brown and Walsh, 1991). Examples include engineering, buses, banking, cotton textiles, independent television, food retailing and manufacturing, docks, cement, newspapers, merchant shipping and wholesale meat. Around half of all employees in the private sector have their pay determined by collective bargaining and, of these, four in five are now covered by single employer bargaining.

This decentralisation has not, however, extended to workplace level. Rather the reverse. Most multi-plant employers bargain at division rather than workplace level, so moderating the fragmentation of bargaining inside the firm. And where there is decentralisation to the workplace — perhaps to be congruent with profit-related product centres — 'companies have tended to introduce higher level coordination of ostensibly decentralised pay control points' (Brown and Walsh, 1991). Thus the switch away from multi-employer negotiations has gone hand-in-hand with the extension of negotiating structures at enterprise or company level.

This corporate control of decentralised bargaining is potentially important. It has been asserted that greater coordination of pay bargaining is required to improve the macroeconomic trade-off between pay and jobs (Layard, 1990, Soskice, 1990). Leaving aside the merits of the case for coordination, some critics have suggested it is an impossible dream consequent on the decentralisation of pay bargaining (see, for example, the debate in IRS *Employment Trends* 485, 5 April 1991). This criticism is probably wrong. Although the number of 'pay control points' — a more useful concept here than bargaining groups — rose when multi-employer bargaining collapsed, this increase was partially offset by the lower degree of fragmentation of bargaining inside the company. If it were held to be desirable, coordination could probably be achieved by focusing on the largest 100 or so private sector companies.

The quality of collective bargaining encompasses (Brown, 1993) the degree of union security provided by employers, the depth of union involvement in the administration of bargaining, the scope of bargaining, and the degree of control exercised by collective agreements. The evidence is mixed.

We have already seen that union security has waned. Where collective bargaining remains unions are still deeply involved through shop stewards, office facilities and check-off. However, as Brown (1993) points out, this could represent either union strength or weakness — workplace organisation being dependent on management for legitimacy and other resources. The scope of bargaining contracted between 1980 and 1990 such that fewer issues were subject to joint regulation. Finally, single employer bargaining — accompanied by greater procedural formality — has greatly increased the degree of control of agreements on both pay and non-pay matters.

Considerable disagreement exists concerning the factors underpinning pay determination (Blanchflower and Oswald, 1988). Those who emphasise bargaining — one version of which is the 'insider–outsider' theory — stress the importance of the company's own economic and financial performance. In this approach, pay is set, in large part, by how well the employer is doing. By contrast, the competitive (or classical) theory stresses that the wage cannot be controlled by either the employer or the worker. As Blanchflower and Oswald put it (p. 364): 'The going rate of pay is fixed by conditions in the whole economy, and most especially by the total demand for and supply of labour. Each firm must pay the going rate. It has no need to raise wages when its productivity increases or its sales boom; if it did so it would be inundated with applicants from other sectors. In this kind of world "insiders" have no power.' In general, industrial relations specialists prefer the bargaining approach while many economists emphasise competition (though in recent years some economists have been stressing the importance of institutions, see for example, Blanchflower *et al.*, 1990, Carruth and Oswald, 1987). WIRS3 provides excellent information on this debate (Millward *et al.*, 1992, table 7.11). Pay setting is influenced by *both* competitive pressures and bargaining. Typically, labour market factors like recruitment and retention and a link to other settlements — the going rate — emphasise the importance of competition. But the economic performance of the workplace or company is mentioned just as often as labour market factors, and given equal weight in both the union and non-union sectors. Further, 'individual performance' is mentioned by a substantial fraction of managers in non-union workplaces. This WIRS3 evidence supports — for both union and non-union labour markets — Blanchflower and Oswald's statement (p. 367), using information from WIRS2, that 'these results are difficult to reconcile with the wage taking firm of classical theory'.

This evidence on the extent, structure and quality of collective bargaining confirms the views of Millward and his co-authors concerning the aims and achievements of successive governments since 1979: 'Government policy, both through its dealings with its own employees and through persuasion and advocacy to other employers, encouraged a move away from national, multi-employer pay settlements towards more locally determined ones which were more sensitive to local labour markets and the circumstances of the employer' (Millward *et al.*, 1992, p. 217). The objective has been accomplished. Whether this has improved the outcomes of the industrial relations system — particularly concerning pay and jobs — will be examined in the second part of this chapter.

Environment

The environment in which industrial relations are conducted is sharply different now from what it was in the decade following the Donovan Report in 1968. There are three main elements. First, the composition of the workforce has altered and high unemployment casts a fearful shadow. Second, unionised firms now face much greater international and domestic competition than previously. Third, the state has mounted a sustained attack on collectivism. The legislative onslaught against unions is the best known component of this assault, but there are others including privatisation, contracting-out and the withdrawal of collective bargaining for many public sector workers. It is probably the combination of these three environmental factors which has contributed to the changes in outcomes discussed below.

At the time of the Donovan Report, employees in employment accounted for 89 per cent of the total workforce; that figure now is 75 per cent. Then, women represented a little over one third of employees; now they account for nearly half. In the 1960s two employees in five were in manufacturing, twice today's proportion. There has also been a substantial increase in part-timers, self-employed and those on temporary contracts and, sadly, each successive peak of unemployment reaches a new higher total. This unemployment 'fear factor' has had a real impact on industrial relations practice.

Many trading companies — and particularly those with a strong union presence — have experienced more intense product market competition in the 1980s and 1990s. Exchange controls were removed in 1979. The exchange rate was seriously overvalued in the early 1980s and early 1990s forcing exporters and import-competing companies to improve their unit labour costs or go out of business. State subsidies to lame duck, monopolistic, highly unionised firms were simply axed. This applied particularly to firms with predominantly male workforces in coal, steel, cars, shipbuilding and aerospace, where subsidies had reached record levels in the late 1970s.

It is also possible to point to instances where cosy cartels between management and unions to boost their own profits and pay at the expense of the consumer have been breached almost overnight, leading to amazing adjustments in work practices. Proposals (now implemented) to auction, rather than to allocate by committee, the franchises to operate commercial TV networks undermined the monopoly position of the TV companies and unions. Imminent competition from the Channel Tunnel breached the cross-channel ferry duopoly leading to changed work patterns among seamen. And new technology permitted new entry into national and provincial newspaper production, causing changes in working practices and contracts among craft workers, general workers and journalists. In each of these three cases the unions — all of which previously operated closed shops — were vanquished in the bitter industrial disputes which accompanied the ending of the old regime.

Industrial relations legislation passed between 1980–93 is summarised in Dunn and Metcalf (1993). Its thrust has been to undermine collectivism by promoting individual responsibility, voice, exit from collective decision and organisation and loyalty to the organisation. At the start of the 1980s, statutory union recognition procedures were in place (albeit rather ineffective), a firm could not isolate itself from a dispute in which it was not involved, and unions as organisations were completely immune from tortious liability. Now, this position is very different. It is up to the firm to decide whether or not to recognise a trade union. That union has a legal personality, so the firm can get injunctions and damages against the union itself. The definition of a trade dispute attracting immunity has been successively reined back: it must be between workers and their own employer, subject to majority support at the workplace in a secret ballot and not designed to foster or maintain a closed shop. The firm can use the courts to insulate itself from secondary action and can selectively dismiss unofficial strikers.

State sponsored routes to spread the effects of collective bargaining have all been withdrawn. The century-old Fair Wage Resolutions which ensured workers employed by firms undertaking public contracts were paid the rate for the job were rescinded in 1982. Previously, in 1980, the comparability machinery under Schedule 11 of the 1975 Employment Protection Act was abolished. The Wage Council system was also narrowed in scope to exclude young workers and is about to be abolished.

In a nutshell, where a union is recognised, the legislation has made the firm and the union responsible for their own workplace industrial relations and where there is no union it is now harder to organise than previously. The narrowed definition of a trade dispute and outlawing of secondary action can be thought of as encouraging 'company unionism'. Employees' commitment to the company might be enhanced further by provisions in the 1982 Act which oblige the company to state in its Annual Report its policy on information, consultation and employee involvement, and by various measures in successive budgets which have encouraged profit sharing and employee share ownership schemes, discussed below.

The 'voice' of the individual member, relative to that of the activist and union official, has been given a boost through the various secret ballot provisions. Ballots are required prior to industrial action, for elections of union executive members and to decide whether a union be permitted to hold funds for political activity. Further, the individual union member can restrain the union from calling them to take industrial action which has not been supported by a majority in a secret ballot. All these strands require the official union hierarchy to exercise more control over their shop stewards at workplace level. Perhaps the most potentially far-reaching element of individual voice is the establishment of a Commissioner for the Rights of Trade Union Members. A disaffected union member can apply to the Commissioner to use public funds for court proceedings against the union, or for the Commissioner to take on the case on the member's behalf. No comparable arrangements exist for disaffected shareholders or golf club members.

Exit has been made easier for both individuals and firms. The assault against the closed shop culminated by outlawing post-entry closed shops in 1988 and pre-entry closed shops in 1990. Now, it is wholly a matter of individual choice to belong or not to belong to a union, although it is in the employer's gift to decide whether a union will be recognised. An individual union member can also exit from a dispute: he or she can continue working even in the face of an overwhelming majority in a secret ballot in favour of industrial action and the union is impotent to discipline that member. The weakening of the 'floor of individual employment rights' also means that the firm can more easily exit from the employment contract. For example, a worker does not benefit from unfair dismissal provisions until he or she has been with the company for two years, four times longer than in 1979.

It is now necessary to evaluate how reduced union presence, the harsher climate, and the other alterations to managerial strategy, tactics and bargaining structures influenced the performance outcomes of the system.

Outcomes

Pay and jobs

Modifications to unions and to the industrial relations system set out above can have, at least, three different influences on pay. First, the pay structure can be modified via changes in the pay differential achieved by unionised employees compared with their non-union counterparts. Second, the distribution of pay can be altered through union activity. Third, the industrial relations system might affect the rate of growth of nominal and/or real pay. These issues are considered in turn. In each case the related implications concerning jobs are also discussed.

There is now general agreement that, on average, unionised workplaces pay higher wages than otherwise comparable non-union ones. Fortunately, successive WIRSs, and other surveys, permit us to go well beyond this bald statement. We now know how the structure of bargaining influences the union/non-union differential; how this differential responds to changes in the bargaining environment such as increased competition or anti-union laws; and how the differential varies by demographic characteristics, permitting us to gauge the impact of unions on equality.

Semi-skilled employees in workplaces where a union is recognised for collective bargaining earned, on average in 1984, around 8 per cent more than their counterparts in non-union workplaces (see table 4.5). But this 'average' conceals as much as it reveals. In particular, we need to unravel it to examine the union effects associated with different density levels, closed shops, and with multiple or single unionism.

In workplaces without a closed shop, high density (above 95 per cent) was required in 1984 to get the wage premium associated with recognition. When unions were recognised, but density was below 95 per cent, the workplace paid no more than the corresponding non-union workplace. Where

Table 4.5 *Union/non-union wage structure, semi-skilled workers, 1984 Workplace Industrial Relations Survey*

Author	Sample	Union indicator		
Stewart (1991)	1005 private sector workplaces	Recognition	Average union cf. average non-union	8
Metcalf and Stewart (1992)	660 private sector workplaces	Recognition Density Closed shop	No closed shop: - recognition, density < 95% - recognition, density > 95% Closed shop: - post-entry - pre-entry	0 7-10 7-10 17-19
Machin, Stewart and Van Reenen (1992)	683 private sector workplaces	Single or multiple unions	Average union cf. average non-union Around which: - multiple unions bargaining separately - single bargains	10 12 8

Notes: In each case the pay measure is the typical weekly earnings of a semi-skilled manual worker. The following control variables are included: workplace size, industry, single or multiple establishment company, foreign or domestic owned, shiftwork, PBR, per cent manual, per cent part-time, per cent skilled, per cent female.

there was a closed shop, the post-entry variety yielded no extra, over and above simple recognition with 95 per cent plus density. By contrast, the pre-entry closed shop was a separate institutional form. The wage premium gained by those in the pre-entry closed shop was roughly double that for recognition alone.

The respective merits of multiple versus single unionism in a workplace, whether from the management or union standpoint, has long been a matter of debate (see for example Donovan Report paras. 672–691). Secondary analysis from WIRS2 provides evidence on this issue. Multiple unions which bargain separately achieve a significantly larger pay premium than both multiple unions which bargain jointly (often called 'single-table' bargaining) and single unions. However, multiple unions with single-table bargaining and single unions have identical wage premia over non-union workplaces.

Until recently the link between the product market and the labour market was rather neglected. Stewart (1990) helps to rectify this omission in the case of pay. In the vast majority of establishments facing competitive product market conditions, unions are unable to achieve wage levels above those paid elsewhere to comparable non-union workers. Likewise they cannot create differentials over non-union pay in establishments which operate primarily in international markets — foreign competition restrains union influence. By contrast, in establishments in firms with market power there is considerably greater scope for unions to achieve pay levels significantly above those paid to comparable non-union workers, especially where a pre-entry closed shop is present. It is monopoly power in the product market of the firm that provides a rent ('surplus') and unions are able to bargain a share of these super-normal profits.

There is less evidence concerning changes in this pay structure. The weight of what little there is points to a decline in the union mark-up. Ingram (1991) uses the CBI pay databank to show that, in every year except one, 1979–89 pay increases in unionised bargaining groups were lower than their non-union counterparts. The cumulative fall in the differential was 4 per cent. Gregg and Machin (1992) undertook their own survey of nearly 300 firms employing some two million workers and concluded that, in the 1980s, unionised firms experienced slower wage growth than non-union firms and that 'this is consistent with an erosion of the average union/non-union wage differential in these firms over the late 1980s'. Stewart (1992) analysed workplace data from WIRS2 (1984) and WIRS3 (1990). The average union differential (for semi-skilled workers) fell from 0.088 to 0.062, with a particularly noticeable collapse in the previous mark-up gained by those in pre-entry closed shops. The panel data (537 establishments) tell the same story:

	Wage growth 1984-90 Change in log median wage (mid point) Weighted means	
Overall mean		0.40
No recognition in 1984		0.42
Recognition in 1984		0.37
No recognition in 1990	0.28	
Recognition in 1990	0.38	

Thus pay rises were greater in workplaces where unions were not recognised than where they were. Further, where de-recognition occurred between 1984 and 1990 the pay rise was even lower. The differential based on industry data first estimated by Layard, Metcalf and Nickell (1978) was also lower in the second half of the 1980s than in the first half (but this series is less robust than that based on other data).

When the union wage differential is calculated from data on individuals it appears, in contrast to the above evidence, to be roughly stable. This holds for studies based on both the British Social Attitudes Survey (Blanchflower, 1991) and the Family Expenditure Survey (Symons and Walker, 1988).

The bulk of the evidence — both in terms of data sources and number of studies — therefore points to a decline in the union/non-union pay differential since 1980. What effect should this have on employment? Minford (1983) and Hayek (1984) argued that prior to 1980 pay in union workplaces was boosted by immunities and the closed shop. This, they said, lowered employment in the union sector. In turn, displaced labour put downward pressure on pay in the non-union sector making work less attractive relative to unemployment benefit, resulting in higher unemployment. They proposed, therefore, lower unemployment pay, the elimination of various immunities enjoyed by unions in connection with their activities and the outlawing of the closed shop. This, it was held, would reduce the union mark-up with beneficial effects on employment levels. Minford and Hayek seem to have got their wish — their prescriptions were enacted and the union differential is lower now than in 1980. Alas, the favourable predicted employment effects have not emerged — rather the reverse — employment is lower in the union sector than in 1980 and aggregate unemployment has at least doubled.

Blanchflower, Millward and Oswald (1991) explain the lack of success on the jobs front — given that the Hayek–Minford prescriptions have been followed — by suggesting that unions have (in addition to a positive wage differential) a negative impact on employment growth in the private sector. They state that this differential is –3 per cent a year: unionised workplaces lose 3 per cent more jobs or gain 3 per cent fewer jobs, each year, than their non-union counterparts. Their article produced an acrimonious academic exchange (see Machin and Wadhwani, 1991b). It is plausible that it is not really possible to estimate the dynamic impact of unions on jobs from the cross-section (WIRS1 and 2) data used by the protagonists. Further, the –3 per cent differential on employment growth is presumably time-specific (in their case 1980–84). Thus, Millward et al. (1992, p.322) argue that any such adverse effect was attenuated 1984–90.

Unions are a force for pay equality — they have a 'sword of justice' effect. The pay distribution is less dispersed for union than for non-union workers. Union activity narrows the wage structure as between females and males, disabled and able-bodied, blacks and whites, manuals and non-manuals (Metcalf, 1982). The ebbing of union strength has been associated with a huge increase in the inequality in pay among both individuals and workplaces between 1980 and 1990 (Gosling and Machin, 1992, Schmitt, 1993). For example, Gosling and Machin show that across-establishment inequality was much greater in 1990 than in 1980. The decline in the share of plants with recognised unions accounts for a fifth of the coincident rise in earnings inequality. Further, within-establishment wage inequality increased in both union and non-union plants, but far more in the latter. This implies that the pay-equalising effects of unions became more marked through the decade.

The growing inequality in pay occurred during the decade in which unemployment twice topped three million. The promotion of inequality has patently failed to deliver the aggregate employment goods. Further, the unemployment rate of 18- and 19-year-olds, who were removed from Wage Council coverage in 1986 because it was held that the Councils were pricing them out of jobs, is unchanged relative to the all-age rate. It seems that the causal relationship runs from higher unemployment to greater inequality rather than vice versa.

The third interaction between the industrial relations system and pay and jobs concerns the break-up of the traditional system of industrial relations. There are fewer workers covered by collective bargaining, such bargaining is more decentralised, pay is more sensitive to individual and workplace performance and to local labour market conditions than previously. This could provide one explanation of an enduring puzzle of the 1980s (Carruth and Oswald, 1989). Despite higher unemployment, the growth in competition and the legislative onslaught against unions, real wages grew faster than at any other time in the postwar period (Bayliss, 1993). The insiders changed their work practices (Ingram, 1991), and the efficiency, productivity and profits of their establishments were given a boost, at least in manufacturing. The insiders got their reward in the form of higher real earnings. But simultaneously the number of outsiders — the unemployed — was growing. Millward *et al.* (1992, table 7.11) demonstrate that the labour market is not wholly competitive — ability to pay, profitability, and productivity growth all matter too. In these circumstances the outsiders exercise less influence on the process of pay determination than previously. So successively higher levels of unemployment are required to control wage inflation.

Company and workplace performance

Connections between the industrial relations system and three dimensions of company and workplace performance — productivity, profitability and investment — are examined here. In each case we examine how the links have varied over time.

(a) Productivity

Alterations in the institutions and conduct of industrial relations outlined

above contributed to two noteworthy, interrelated, features of British productivity performance in the 1980s. First, growth in manufacturing output per head improved such that Britain was top of the OECD-major seven
nations growth league table in the 1980s, after being bottom in both the
1960s and 1970s. Labour productivity in manufacturing has continued to
grow rapidly in the 1990s (some 4 per cent per annum) reflecting the sharper
fall in employment than output. Second, averaged over the 1980s, unionised
workplaces, companies and industries had a superior productivity growth
record than their non-union counterparts.

The improved productivity performance of the manufacturing sector in the
1980s was attributable to the *interaction* of greater product market competition, high unemployment and anti-union legislation (Metcalf, 1990).
Crafts (1993) recently echoed these findings. In the most comprehensive
review yet of manufacturing industry in recent times he writes: 'Better performance came from an intensification of competitive pressures on management, a weakening of trade union bargaining power and a retreat from the unsuccessful interventionist policies of the 1960s and 1970s. There was a substantial shake-out of inefficiencies which had previously been allowed to
persist' (pp.76–7). As a consequence of this turnaround in UK performance
the gap between the level of labour productivity in Britain and in other
countries was narrowed (Crafts, 1993, table 6):

Manufacturing output per person employed (UK = 100)

	USA/UK	Germany/UK	France/UK
1977	230	149	138
1989	177	105	112

Unionised workplaces, companies and industries contributed dis-
proportionately to the reversal in the aggregate productivity growth performance of manufacturing. In the second half of the 1970s productivity
growth was lower in unionised companies than in non-union companies
(Nickell *et al.*, 1992). This resulted in such unionised firms having, on average, a lower level of labour productivity than their non-union counterparts
around 1980, particularly in large workplaces with a closed shop (Machin,
1991b). Then during the 1980s unionised companies narrowed, and quite possibly eliminated or even reversed, the favourable productivity edge previously
enjoyed by non-union companies (Gregg *et al.*, 1993).

It is likely that the differential growth in unionised workplaces and companies in the first part of the 1980s was mainly a consequence of changes in
work organisation. For example, Machin and Wadhwani (1991a) referring to
1981–4 state that 'unionised plants were more likely to have experienced a
change in work practices because they are more likely to have restrictions
on managerial discretion vis-à-vis restrictive practices in the first place'.

However, the re-assertion of managerial prerogative did not stop at the conduct of industrial relations. It has also influenced the institutions themselves. Dunn and Wright (1993), after extensive detailed case studies, describe the closed shop as 'moribund'. Gregg and Yates (1991) note the extensive, albeit usually partial, de-recognition of unions for collective bargaining in the second half of the 1980s. Purcell (1991) captures these changes when he writes — on the basis of his case studies — that 'the constraints on management action, traditionally reflected and reinforced through the institutions and procedures of industrial relations, especially collective bargaining, have been significantly weakened'. Gregg *et al.* (1993) show why these modifications to the structure of industrial relations matter. Productivity growth 1985–9 was higher in companies which recognised unions in 1985 than it was in non-union companies. But it was still higher where there had been a change in the union institutions — rescinding a previous union membership agreement (closed shop) and/or full or partial de-recognition. They conclude that 'the visible evidence of changes in union status probably acts as a signal to the workforce of a greater assertiveness on the part of management'.

It must be emphasised that much of the productivity growth in the 1980s — particularly in unionised workplaces and companies — flowed from unrepeatable sources. The conduct of industrial relations was changed by, for example, alterations to working practices. The institutions were modified in places by rescinding union membership agreements or by de-recognition of the union for collective bargaining purposes. The higher growth rates of the last decade can only be sustained in the future by either greater investment in physical and human capital or a change in the rules of the game away from adversarial towards cooperative industrial relations. Paradoxically, this offers hope. Past failures — underinvestment and a reliance by management on compliance rather than cooperation — imply considerable scope for future productivity growth.

(b) Profitability

Unanimity exists in the eight UK studies which use workplaces, firms or industries to analyse the link between profitability and industrial relations: all show a significant negative association between unionisation and financial performance or profitability. WIRS data are used in three studies, summarised in table 4.6. In two further studies the firm is the unit of observation (Cable and Machin, 1991, Machin, 1991a) while industry data are used in Conyon and Machin (1991) and Dowrick (1990). One study (Geroski *et al.*, 1991) mixes industry-level industrial relations indicators with firm-level financial data.

Table 4.6 *Studies of financial performance based on Workplace Industrial Relations Surveys*

Author	Sample	Industrial relations indicator	Controls	Results
Blanchflower and Oswald (1988)	1209 private sector establishments WIRS2 1984	Recognition Closed shop	LC/TC Plant size	Recognition and closed shopp sig -ve
	1984	Performance related pay scheme	Demand shocks International competition Industry controls Region contrrols	Pay schemes have no effect on performance
Machin and Stewart (1990)	1134 private mfg establishments	Recognition Pre-entry closed shop	Market share Demand	Recognition and closed shop sig-ve
	623 WIRS1 1980		K:L ratio	Greater effect
	511 WIRS2 1984		K:L ratio	Greater effect
			Capacity utilisation	- 1984 than 1980
			5-firm concentration ratio	- when market share high
			Industry performance	- with closed shop
			Industry TU coverage	
Machin, Stewart and Van Reenen (1992)	566 private mfg unionised establishments WIRS2 1984	Multiple unionism Multiple bargaining	As Machin and Stewart (1990)	Multple bargaining significantly worsens performance

Note: Financial performance defined by managers' assessments of their own establishments' financial performance. They were asked the following question (Q14a Management Questionnaire, p.8): How would you assess the financial performance of this establishment compared to other establishments in the same industry? They could answer: (i) better than average; (ii) about average; (iii) below average; (iv) no comparison possible.

It will be seen from table 4.6 that both union recognition and the closed shop are linked with a greater likelihood of below average performance. Possibly more interesting are the findings of Machin *et al.* (1992) concerning multi-unionism. Among unionised manufacturing workplaces, multiple unionism with single table bargaining generates a similar financial performance to a single union environment. However, when multiple unionism is accompanied by separate bargaining arrangements, financial performance is significantly worse.

The crucial question concerning this apparent link between industrial relations institutions and financial performance is: does it matter in the long run? If all we are observing is a shift in the distribution of income from capital to labour — from profits to pay — many would say 'so much the better'. But if the lower profitability results in less investment in research and development and in physical and human capital this will damage the dynamic prospects of the workplace and company. It would also tend to lead to a worse performance on job creation than would otherwise be the case.

There is tentative evidence that what we are observing is largely a matter of equity between labour and capital and that it has few implications concerning long-run economic senescence. The first batch of evidence concerns the profitability studies themselves. The second relates to the link between industrial relations systems and investment rates.

Cable and Machin (1991) conclude that the profitability results are simply the mirror image of the well-known results on the union wage differential. High density or the closed shop or multi-unionism generates a wage differential compared with otherwise similar non-union workers, but it does not lower profitability over and above this labour cost effect. There is increasing evidence that the union wage differential is associated with some degree of monopoly power in the product market (see for example, Stewart, 1990, Gregg and Machin, 1992). This, in turn, implies that unions are simply creaming off some of the firms' super-normal profits in the form of higher pay. Such a line of reasoning is reinforced by the studies of Machin and Stewart (1990), Machin (1991a) and Conyon and Machin (1991) which each finds that unions only lower financial performance, *ceteris paribus*, where the firm has some product market power.

It appears, provisionally, that this link between unionisation and financial performance became weaker as the 1980s progressed. Millward *et al.* present a cross-tabulation (from table 3.4) which shows:

Table 4.7 *Studies of investment based on Workplace Industrial Relations Surveys*

Author	Sample	Measure of investment	Union indicator	Control variables	Union effect
Machin and Wadhwani (1991a)	630 private mfg. and service workplaces WIRS2	Whether introduced 1981-4 (i) Convent-ional technical change (ii) Advanced technical change	Recognition	Capacity utilisation Product demand Organisation-al change Financial performance Size of plant Industry	Both (i) and (ii) +ve but not significant
Latreille (1992)	418 private mfg. workplaces WIRS2	Use of micro-electronic technology	Recognition Pre-entry closed shop Multi-unionism JCC Decentralised bargaining	Size of plant Subsidiary Ownership % skilled Product market	Recognition sig +ve c.12% All other indicators non-significant
Denny and Nickell (1992)	73 3-digit mfg. industries 1980-84, incorporating WIRS1 and 2 data	Investment rate	Recognition Density	Industry demand Prices Technical progress Pay Expected growth	Recognition -ve Density +ve 100% density not sufficient to offset recognition effect

Financial performance compared with other workplaces in the same industry	Average union density (%)	
	1984	1990
Lots better	29	33
A little better	44	37
About average	45	35
A little below average	52	40
Lots below average	74	63

Although average union density in workplaces reporting below average performance remains higher than it is in those reporting above average performance, the association is less pronounced in 1990 than it was in 1984.

(c) Investment

Capital accumulation is the key to long-run growth. Therefore, the impact of our industrial relations system on investment — in new technology, process and product innovation, research and development and in human capital — is of vital importance. The Department of Employment (1981, para. 1) has asserted that 'For at least a generation now our industrial relations have failed us because they have ... acted as a disincentive to investment and discouraged innovation.' That pronouncement is scrutinised here.

Unfortunately the only evidence relates to the impact of various characteristics of unions on investment. This is a pity. The evidence is ambiguous and, anyway, it is plausible that the propensities of management dominate the investment decision.

Any link between unionisation and investment is an empirical matter because the theoretical arguments cut both ways. On the one hand, union pressure on pay will cause firms to invest more heavily so as to reduce their need for expensive labour. On the other hand, union presence might lower investment directly or indirectly. The direct effect occurs if a union delays the installation of new machinery or operates inflexible work rules inhibiting the full use of the investment. Any indirect effect is less easy to spot. When a company invests in a new project, unionised workers may capture ('tax') some of the returns in the form of higher pay because, once the capital is installed or the R and D done, the process cannot easily be reversed thereby weakening the company's bargaining position.

The evidence is conflicting. In very broad terms cross-section evidence from workplaces, firms and industries suggests that unionised organisations have a superior investment performance to their non-union counterparts. By contrast, time series evidence tentatively suggests that unions have a depressing effect on investment.

WIRS2 has been used in three studies and these are summarised in table 4.7. Machin and Wadhwani (1991a) examined the incidence of different forms of investment between 1981 and 1984. Advanced technical change incorporates micro-electronics whereas the conventional variety does not. Previously Daniel (1987) noted from cross-tabulations that unionised workplaces undertook more of both types of investment than non-union workplaces in the early 1980s.

This raw positive correlation is explained by Machin and Wadhwani (1991a) by three factors operating in the early 1980s. First, unionised workplaces had higher pay than non-union workplaces, which directly encouraged greater investment. Second, unionised workplaces were experiencing more organisational change — particularly the elimination of restrictive practices — than non-union workplaces. Such organisational change frequently went hand-in-hand with more investment. Third, union voice has a background role in the higher investment via more formalised consultative procedures.

Latreille (1992) considers whether or not the workplace has ever invested in microelectronic technology (rather than such investment just in 1981–4) by studying its use. Workplaces where unions were recognised were 12 per cent more likely to use such equipment than non-union workplaces. A similar conclusion emerges from the more detailed case studies of Litner *et al.* (1987).

Denny and Nickell (1991, 1992) get the most clear-cut union effects. Their sample is drawn from manufacturing industries and incorporates information on industrial relations variables from WIRS1 and 2. They find, for 1980-84, that union recognition depresses investment, but that this adverse effect is offset as density rises. However, even 100 per cent density does not completely counter the negative recognition effect. By implication, they point out that the worst possible situation is union recognition but with only a small fraction of the workforce being union members. Fortunately, this is rather rare. Voice effects are also apparent — where many workers are covered by joint consultative councils (whether in union or non-union workplaces) investment rates are higher.

Thus three studies use information from WIRS to analyse the link between unionisation and investment. Two show, essentially, a positive association, while one reports both positive and negative links with the latter dominating. Unfortunately, time series evidence is rather inconsistent with these results. Manning (1987) and Wadhwani and Wall (1989) both report no significant associations. Denny and Nickell (1992) and Tsamourgelis (1990) disclose that union recognition and mark-ups (respectively) are negatively associated with investment. It is interesting to note, however, that such effects are attenuated in the 1980s compared with the 1960s and 1970s. By the mid-1980s the adverse association between recognition and investment was halved compared with a decade earlier.

It is clear, even from this brief survey, that the link between unionisation and investment is complex. The evidence is mixed but there is, at worst, no strong evidence of British unions adversely affecting investment in the 1980s or 1990s and, if anything, unionised workplaces use more, and invest more in, advanced capital equipment and human capital than do their non-union equivalents. Thus the quote at the beginning of this section from the

Department of Employment Green Paper on Trade Union Immunities probably no longer holds (if it ever did) concerning the link between unions and investment. This is not really surprising: investment is the *change* in capital stock and the evidence above suggests that unions are more likely to impact on levels (of pay, productivity, and so on) than on changes in these variables.

Summary and conclusions

There can be no doubt that the institutions and processes of British industrial relations has changed fundamentally in the last decade or so. In the first section the following four points emerged.

First, union membership haemorrhaged. The fourteen-year three million free-fall in membership since 1979 is the longest ever period of decline. The closed shop is almost extinct and new recognitions are rare. It should be noted, however, that two employees in five still belong to a union, an impressive figure by international standards.

Second, management prerogatives were restored. Management often extricated itself from previous pluralist arrangements involving joint regulation with unions. There was some spread of human resource management practices, mainly in unionised workplaces, but they have a shallow hold. More importantly collective agreements were altered to emphasise greater flexibility of work organisation.

Third, under half of employees are now covered by collective agreements compared with nearly three quarters in the mid-1970s. Where collective bargaining remains four in five employees are now covered by single employer agreements, reflecting the virtual collapse of multi-employer national agreements. Simultaneously the fragmentation of bargaining inside the company has been moderated: most multi-plant employers now bargain at company rather than workplace level.

Finally, the industrial relations environment has become harsher. Each successive peak of unemployment reaches a new higher level. Product market competition has intensified. State subsidies to lame duck, monopolistic, highly unionised firms have been axed. Legislative changes have undermined collectivism by promoting individual responsibility, voice, exit from collective agreements, and loyalty to the company.

Thus the institutional structure and the conduct of industrial relations have probably been 'transformed' as the Secretary of State for Employment claimed in 1990. But what of the performance outcomes? Here the story is very different.

In the 1960s and 1970s industrial relations were seen to be central to our economic performance. Our system of labour relations was subject to varieties of social engineering in the 1970s — for example, pluralism in the workplace, corporatism at national level, a stress on institutions and procedures — but the emphasis remained on collective relations. By contrast, the 1980s witnessed the rise of individualism and the rule of the market. This certainly altered company performance. In particular, any adverse links between union presence and productivity, financial performance and investment were weakened in the 1980s: it may well be that unionised workplaces now have higher levels of labour productivity and investment than their non-union counterparts. The industrial relations system — particularly concerning union presence — can no longer be held to stymie companies' achievements. Changes in the environment — the legislative onslaught, greater competition and higher unemployment — reduced any monopoly effects of unions on company and workplace performance. But this is surely not a 'transformation'. The changed outcomes seem to be mainly the result of compliance by labour in the conduct of workplace relations. What is still needed for a transformation is a change of gear by management — greater emphasis on co-operation and more investment in physical and human capital.

The impact of changes in industrial relations institutions and processes on the pay/jobs trade-off are even more acutely depressing. The pay-setting institutions have certainly been transformed: fewer workers are in collective agreements, bargaining is decentralised, the century-old tradition of 'the rate for the job' has been ruptured, Fair Wage Resolutions and comparability machinery have been withdrawn, there is greater sensitivity to the fortunes of the company and the performance of the individual. The government and its acolytes have achieved virtually all they set out to do yet unemployment rises inexorably to a postwar record high.

Here there can only be two conclusions. Either the government got it wrong concerning the link between pay-setting institutions and procedures and the employment outcomes, in which case the emphasis on individual and company performance and the undermining of collective organisation should be reversed. Instead, there should be greater stress on a national economic assessment and coordination and synchronisation of bargaining. Alternatively, the government got it right about pay setting. In this case its macroeconomic policy must be a shambles. Either way it is a tragedy that more than three million unemployed are needed to implement government policy.

Note

1 I am grateful to the Nuffield Foundation Small Grant Scheme for financial assistance; to Sue Fernie and Simon Milner for research assistance and to the following colleagues for helpful comments on an earlier draft: Rachel Bailey, Stephen Dunn, Paul Gregg, John Kelly, Stephen Machin, Neil Millward, Andrew Oswald, Marcus Rubin.

References

Bayliss, F. (1993), *Does Britain Still Have a Pay Problem?*, Employment Policy Institute, January.

Beatson, M. and Butcher, S. (1993), 'Union density across the employed workforce', *Employment Gazette*, January, 673–89.

Bird, D., Kirosingh, M. and Stevens, M. (1992), 'Membership of trade unions in 1990', *Employment Gazette,* April, 185–90.

Blanchflower, D.G. (1991), 'Fear, unemployment and pay flexibility', *Economic Journal*, 101, May, 483–96.

Blanchflower, D.G., Millward, N. and Oswald, A. (1991), 'Unionism and employment behaviour', *Economic Journal*, 101, July, 815–34.

Blanchflower, D. and Oswald, A. (1988), 'Internal and external influences upon pay settlements', *British Journal of Industrial Relations*, 26 (3), 363–70.

Blanchflower, D., Oswald, A. and Garrett, M. (1990), 'Insider power in wage determination', *Economica*, 57, 143–70.

Booth, A. (1989), 'What do unions do now?', Brunel University, March, mimeo.

Brown, W. (1993), 'The contraction of collective bargaining in Britain', *British Journal of Industrial Relations*, 31 (2), June.

Brown, W. and Walsh, J. (1991), 'Pay determination in Britain in the 1980s: the anatomy of decentralisation', *Oxford Review of Economic Policy*, 7 (1), Spring, 44–59.

Cable, S. and Machin, S. (1991), 'The relationship between union wage and profitability effects', *Economic Letters*, 37, 315–21.

Carruth, A. and Disney, R. (1988), 'Where have two million trade union members gone?', *Economica*, 55, 1–19.

Carruth, A. and Oswald, A. (1987), 'On union preferences and labour market models: insiders and outsiders', *Economic Journal*, 97, 431–45.

Carruth, A. and Oswald, A. (1989), *Pay Determination and Industrial Prosperity*, Oxford, Clarendon Press.

Conyon, M. and Machin, S. (1991), 'The determination of profit margins in UK manufacturing', *Journal of Industrial Economics*, 39 (4), 369–82.

Crafts, N. (1993), *Can De-Industrialisation Seriously Damage your Wealth?*, IEA, Hobart Paper 120.

Daniel, W.W. (1987), *Workplace Industrial Relations and Technical Change*, Frances Pinter and Policy Studies Institute, London.

Denny, K. and Nickell, S. (1991), 'Unions and investment in British manufacturing industry', *British Journal of Industrial Relations*, 29 (1), 113–22.

Denny, K. and Nickell, S. (1992), 'Unions and investment in British industry', *Economic Journal,* 102, 874–87.

Department of Employment (1981), *Trade Union Immunities,* Green Paper Cmnd 8128, London, HMSO.

Department of Employment (1992), *People, Jobs and Opportunity,* Cm. 1810, London, HMSO.

Donovan Commission (1968), *Royal Commission on Trade Unions and Employers Associations, Report,* Cm 3623, London, HMSO.

Dowrick, S. (1990), 'Wage pressure, bargaining and price-cost margins in UK manufacturing', *Journal of Industrial Economics,* 38 (3), 239–67.

Dunn, S. (1993), 'From Donovan to ... wherever', *British Journal of Industrial Relations,* 31 (2), June.

Dunn, S. and Metcalf, D. (1993), 'Labour legislation 1980-1993: intent, ideology and impact', Centre for Economic Performance, LSE, Working Paper 12 (revised).

Dunn, S. and Wright, M. (1993), 'Managing without the closed shop' in Metcalf, D. and Milner, S. (eds), *New Perspectives on Industrial Disputes,* London, Routledge.

Elgar, J. and Simpson, R. (1993), 'The impact of the law on industrial disputes in the 1980s' in Metcalf, D. and Milner, S. (1993).

Freeman, R. and Pelletier, J. (1990), 'The impact of industrial relations legislation on British union density', *British Journal of Industrial Relations,* 28 (2), July.

Geroski, P., Machin, S. and Van Reenen, J. (1991), 'The profitability of innovating firms', Forthcoming *RAND Journal of Economics.*

Gosling, A. and Machin, S. (1992), 'Trade unions and wage dispersion in UK establishments, 1980-90', Centre for Economic Performance, LSE, Working Paper, December.

Gregg, P. and Machin, S. (1991), 'Changes in union status, increased competition and wage growth in the 1980s', *British Journal of Industrial Relations,* 29 (4), December, 603–12.

Gregg, P. and Machin, S. (1992), 'Unions, the demise of the closed shop and wage growth in the 1980s', *Oxford Bulletin of Economics and Statistics,* 54 (1), February, 53–72.

Gregg, P., Machin, S. and Metcalf, D. (1993), 'Signals and cycles? Productivity growth and changes in union status in British companies, 1984–89', *Economic Journal,* 103.

Gregg, P. and Yates, B. (1991), 'Changes in wage setting arrangements and trade union presence in the 1980s', *British Journal of Industrial Relations,* 29 (3), September, 361–76.

Hayek, F. (1984), *1980s Unemployment and the Unions,* Hobart Paper 87, second edition, LEA.

Ingram, P. (1991), 'Ten years of manufacturing wage settlements 1979-89', *Oxford Review of Economic Policy,* 7 (1), Spring, 93–106.

Kessler, S. and Bayliss, F. (1992), *Contemporary British Industrial Relations,* London, Macmillan.

Latreille, P. (1992), 'Unions and the inter-establishment adoption of new microelectronic technologies in the British private manufacturing sector', *Oxford Bulletin of Economics and Statistics,* 54 (1), 31–51.

Layard, R. (1990), 'How to end pay leapfrogging', *Employment Institute Economic Report,* 5 (5), July.

Layard, R., Metcalf, D. and Nickell, S. (1978), 'The effect of collective bargaining on relative and absolute wages', *British Journal of Industrial Relations*, 16 (3), November, 287–302.

Litner, V., Pokorny, M., Woods, M. and Blinkhorn, M. (1987), 'Trade Unions and technological change in the UK mechanical engineering industry', *British Journal of Industrial Relations*, 25 (1), 19–30.

Machin, S. (1991a), 'Unions and the capture of economic rents: an investigation using British firm level data', *International Journal of Industrial Organisation*, 9, 261–74.

Machin, S. (1991b), 'The productivity effects of unionisation and firm size in British engineering firms', *Economica*, 58, 479–90.

Machin, S. and Stewart, M. (1990), 'Unions and the financial performance of British private sector establishments', *Journal of Applied Econometrics*, 5, 327–50.

Machin, S., Stewart, M. and Van Reenen, J. (1992), 'The economic effects of multiple unionism: evidence from the 1984 Workplace Industrial Relations Survey', Centre for Economic Performance, LSE, Discussion Paper, no. 66.

Machin, S. and Wadhwani, S. (1991a), 'The effects of unions on investment and innovation: evidence from WIRS', *Economic Journal*, 101, 324–30.

Machin, S. and Wadhwani, S. (1991b), 'The effects of unions on organisational change and employment', *Economic Journal*, 101, July, 835–54.

Manning, A. (1987). 'A bargaining model of wages, employment and investment for UK manufacturing', Department of Economics, Birkbeck College, mimeo.

Marginson, P. and Sisson, K. (1990), 'Single table talk', *Personnel Management*, May, 46–9.

Metcalf, D. (1982), 'Unions and the distribution of earnings', *British Journal of Industrial Relations*, 20 (2), July, 163–69.

Metcalf, D. (1990), 'Industrial relations and the 'productivity miracle' in British manufacturing industry in the 1980s', *Australian Bulletin of Labour* 16 (2), June, 65–76.

Metcalf, D. (1993), 'Industrial relations and economic performance', *British Journal of Industrial Relations*, 31 (2), June.

Metcalf, D. and Milner, S. (1993), *New Perspectives on Industrial Disputes*, Routledge.

Metcalf, D. and Stewart, M. (1992), 'Closed shops and relative pay: institutional arrangements or high density?', *Oxford Bulletin of Economics and Statistics*, 54 (4), November, 503–16.

Millward, N., Stevens, M., Smart, D. and Hawes, W. (1992), *Workplace Industrial Relations in Transition*, Aldershot, Dartmouth.

Minford, P. (1983), *Unemployment: Cause and Cure*, Martin Robertson.

Nickell, S., Wadhwani, S. and Wall, M. (1992), 'Productivity growth in UK companies 1975–86', *European Economic Review,* 36, 1055–85.

Purcell, J. (1991), 'The rediscovery of management prerogative: the management of labour relations in the 1980s', *Oxford Review of Economic Policy*, 7 (1), Spring, 33–43.

Schmitt, J. (1993), 'The changing structure of male earnings in Britain 1974–88' in R. Freeman and L. Katz (eds), *Changes and Differences in Wage Structures*, University of Chicago Press.

Sisson, K. (1993), 'In search of HRM', *British Journal of Industrial Relations*, 31 (2), June.

Soskice, D. (1990), 'Wage determination: the changing role of institutions in advanced industrial companies', *Oxford Review of Economic Policy*, 6 (4), Winter, 36–61.

Stewart, M. (1990), 'Union wage differentials, product market influences and the division of rents', *Economic Journal*, 100 (403), December, 1122–37.

Stewart, M. (1991), 'Union wage differentials in the face of changes in the economic and legal environment', *Economica*, 58, May, 155–72.

Stewart, M. (1992), 'Do changes in collective bargaining arrangements imply declining union wage differentials into the 1990s?', University of Warwick, December, mimeo.

Symons, E. and Walker, I. (1988), 'Union/non-union wage differentials 1979-84: evidence from the FES', Keele University, mimeo.

Tsamourgelis, E. I. M. (1990), 'Unions and investment in the UK manufacturing sector', DPhil Thesis, St Catherine's College, Oxford.

Wadhwani, S. and Wall, M. (1989), 'The effects of unions on corporate investment', Centre for Labour Economics, LSE, Discussion Paper 354, August.

Willman, P. (1990), 'The financial status and performance of British trade unions 1950–1988', *British Journal of Industrial Relations*, 28 (3), November.

Wright, M. (1993), 'Maintaining the "status quo"? An analysis of British collective agreements 1979–1990', CEP Working Paper XX, January.

5   Low pay and minimum wage protection in Britain and the EC

MARY GREGORY and VÉRONIQUE SANDOVAL[1]

Differing approaches to the functioning of the labour market and the role of regulation affecting terms and conditions of employment are highlighted in the divergent attitudes of the governments of the UK and the other members of the EC towards the Social Chapter of the Maastricht Treaty. The Social Chapter, incorporating the Community Charter of Basic Social Rights for Workers (the Social Charter) has the support of eleven of the twelve member states, while the UK government, which has negotiated the opt-out agreement on it within the Treaty, remains firmly opposed.

The Social Charter is designed to establish the framework of legal rights for workers throughout the EC. Its provisions cover a wide range of social and economic issues, including the right to choice of occupation, fair remuneration, and the restriction of maximum working hours; to belong to a trade union and to engage in collective action; to equal treatment, for men and women; to social protection, to health and safety protection at work, and to information, consultation and participation. These general principles are elaborated into more specific proposals in the accompanying Action Programme on the Social Charter, and in Commission Opinions. Commission Opinions are not binding on member states, but may at a later date be the basis of a legally enforceable Directive. They therefore provide important pointers to the direction of Commission thinking. While the general motivation leading to the drawing up of the Social Charter was a concern with social justice, the immediate impetus was the fear that pressure of competition following the completion of the Single Market would progressively erode established rights of workers — the process of 'social dumping'.

On remuneration the Social Charter specifies the right of workers to 'an equitable wage', interpreted narrowly but explicitly as a minimum wage:

'workers should be assured of an equitable wage, that is to say remuneration sufficient to ensure them and their families a decent standard of living'. (Article 4.1).

The Action Programme and, more recently, the Commission's Opinion on the Equitable Wage delivered in December 1991, make it clear that the Commisssion sees the role of the Community as to secure common acceptance of the principle of workers' legal rights to an equitable wage, and not direct intervention in the process of wage regulation or the harmonisation of wage outcomes. It is affirmed explicitly that the determination of the appropriate level of a minimum or reference wage and the mode of implementation remain national concerns:

'It is not the task of the Community to fix a decent reference wage. This concept corresponds to different criteria from one country of the Community to another and should be defined at the level of the member state.'

The Commission confirms as its basic stance that pay determination is a matter for the social partners, management and employee representatives, through collective bargaining. It specifically warns that any attempt to enforce convergence in wage levels which is not consistent with relative productivity levels will have adverse effects on employment in lower-productivity countries. However, it also acknowledges that collective bargaining may provide insufficient protection for vulnerable groups, noting that in a number of member states this has already led to additional measures of wage regulation. As competitive pressures accentuate with the completion of the Single Market vulnerable groups may be increasingly at risk. The Commission's view is therefore that there 'may be a case' for requiring member states to have in place some form of minimum wage regulation in order to ensure wage protection for vulnerable groups.

It should be noted that all the member countries of the EC, including the UK, are signatories to the ILO Convention, article 131 of which requires them to ensure that mechanisms exist to fix minimum rates of pay for the lowest paid workers. In this respect the Social Charter merely reiterates a commitment of some decades' standing. As with the Social Charter, the ILO Convention enunciates the general prescription, but leaves the manner, and indeed the extent, of conformity as a national matter. But unlike the EC, at least potentially, the ILO has no powers of enforcement.

Therefore, while the Community is moving towards recognition of minimum remuneration as a legal right, in its present stage of development Community policy goes no further than current practice among member countries. However, all member states, with the exception of the UK and Ireland, already have in place provisions for systematic minimum wage protection. In the UK, by contrast, not only is minimum wage regulation at its most partial, but the thrust of government policy in recent years has been clearly and deliberately to further restrict its scope. The objective of the UK government continues to be to reduce intervention in pay-setting in general, including, very specifically, for the low-paid.

The purpose of this chapter is to review the incidence of low pay in the individual countries of the EC, particularly in comparison with the UK, and to identify the groups involved. We then outline the various modes of wage determination, collective bargaining and minimum wage provisions, which regulate low wages in member countries, and assess the relationship between the modes of pay determination and the incidence of low pay.

The incidence of low pay within the EC

There are many possible definitions of low pay, but the EC approach clearly focuses on earnings which are low in the context of the relevant national distribution rather than in absolute terms or in an EC-wide context. Our definition of the incidence of low pay will therefore be the proportion of employees whose earnings fall below specified percentile points in the overall distribution of earnings in the country concerned.

To compare the incidence of low pay across member states on this basis ideally requires data on the distribution of earnings for each country, standardised at the EC level. Unfortunately, only two EC-based surveys are available in this area, neither of them suitable for this purpose. The Structure of Earnings Survey (SES) (Eurostat, 1986) contains data on individual earnings and their distribution for each country, derived from a large survey of establishments. However this enquiry was last carried out for 1978-9 and omits the newer members (Spain, Portugal and Greece); moreover its coverage is limited to establishments with ten or more employees and to manufacturing, with partial coverage of the service sector through a parallel survey of financial services. The Labour Force Survey is a survey of households, held at four-yearly intervals. This gives information on average earnings which is comparable across countries, and improved coverage of employees in small firms and atypical workers by comparison with the SES. However, its household basis makes it poorly adapted to the analysis of the distribution of individual earnings. The Commission's Opinion on the Equitable Wage has given a commitment to improve the quality and comparability of Community statistics on the distribution of earnings.

Due to the lack of appropriate data from an EC source the data used here have been collated from national sources, adapted as far as possible to a comparable basis. The sources for the individual countries are heterogeneous and, in spite of some access to unpublished records, on occasion less than perfectly suited to the enquiry in hand. In three countries they are derived from offical social insurance records (Germany, France, Belgium), in three from surveys of employers (Britain, Netherlands, Portugal), and in four from household surveys (Ireland, Italy, Greece, Spain). Luxembourg is omitted. Details of the sources for individual countries are given in the appendix at the end of this chapter.

Social insurance records are comprehensive and accurate for the categories of employee involved, but major groups may be excluded. In France these comprise civil servants and public sector employees (18 per cent of full-time employees), along with agricultural workers and domestic servants (12–15 per cent); in Germany, a more restricted group of civil servants (8 per cent), as well as holders of 'small jobs', including domestic servants; and in Belgium, railway employees and seamen. The net effect of these exclusions on the estimated incidence of low pay is unclear, but the balance of high- and low-paying occupations suggests that any bias is unlikely to be large. In the case of surveys of enterprises, the earnings data are of good quality, but small businesses and family firms may be deliberately under-sampled, or even excluded, on grounds of cost, or incompletely covered due to their high 'birth' and 'death' rates. Atypical workers, those in part-time, temporary and casual jobs, tend to be less fully reported. Even in larger enterprises recent job-changers are liable to go unrecorded. Since many of the low-paid are employed in small firms, have high rates of turnover and work on a part-time or casual basis, enterprise-based surveys are liable to under-record the incidence of low pay (for Britain, see Gregory et al., 1990). In the case of the Netherlands, however, any tendency in this direction will be heavily offset by the exclusion of managers and heads of firms (21 per cent of full-time employees). Household surveys are better adapted to capturing earnings from all types of employment, including part-time and casual work, although reporting may not be fully reliable, particularly for small incomes derived from several sources. The focus on household incomes may also lead to the inadequate recording of individual earnings.

Social insurance records and employer surveys typically record gross earnings. These may be based on the day (Belgium), week (Britain), month (Portugal) or year (Germany, France, Netherlands). Earnings reported on a full-year basis typically include any annual supplements (Germany, France, Netherlands), but where the reference period is shorter these may be included (Portugal), excluded (Belgium) or liable to partial coverage (Britain). The effect of these differences in measured earnings is unclear, but where the low-paid are high-turnover groups they are less likely to qualify for annual supplements. In France earnings are recorded net of social security contributions, although gross of taxes, but since these are proportional to gross earnings the distribution is unaffected. Household surveys tend to record

Table 5.1 *The incidence of low pay among full-time employees within the EC*

	Year	Percentage with earnings		
		Below 50% of median	Below 66% of median	Below 80% of median
Britain (a)	1989	7	20	35
Ireland (b)	1987	10	18	30
Germany (c)	1986	6	13	25
France (d)	1987	0	14	28
Italy (e)	1987	9	14	25
Belgium (f)	1988	0	5	19
Netherlands (g)	1988	5	11	24
Luxembourg		n.a.	n.a.	n.a.
Denmark		n.a.	n.a.	n.a.
Greece (h)	1988	10	16	26
Spain (i)	1985	9	19	32
Portugal (j)	1985	4	12	31

Sources: CERC (1991) and national sources, see appendix at end of chapter.

(a) Based on gross weekly earnings; may exclude certain non-regular bonuses.

(b) 'Normal' weekly gross earnings; may exclude certain non-regular bonuses.

(c) Annual gross earnings including supplements. Private sector employees only, excluding apprentices and those with their current employer for less than one year.

(d) Annual earnings, inclusive of annual supplements, net of social security contributions but gross of personal income tax. Excludes trainees and public employees.

(e) Annual gross pay.

(f) Daily earnings; excludes holiday and year-end bonuses. Excludes apprentices, railway employees and seamen.

(g) Estimated gross annual earnings, including annual supplements; based on a reference pay week. Excludes trainees, managers and heads of firms.

(h) Earnings net of social security and personal income tax. Also includes part-time workers.

(i) Earnings net of social security contributions and personal income tax. Includes domestic servants.

(j) Gross monthly pay, inclusive of annual supplements.

earnings on a net basis (Greece, Spain) and progressivity in the fiscal system will reduce the incidence of low pay measured through the distribution of net earnings. In Ireland the earnings reported are 'standard' earnings for a 'normal' week, not the actual earnings in any period.

Given the differences of coverage and definitions in the data for individual countries emphasis should not be placed on minor differences in the incidence of low pay across member states or on the strict ranking of individual countries.

The incidence of low pay among full-time employees in the member states of the EC is shown in table 5.1. The figures are for varying dates in the later 1980s, as available; for Britain the reference date is 1989. More or less stringent definitions of low pay can be adopted. To give a reasonably broad perspective, three reference points have been chosen: one half, two thirds and four fifths of the median earnings of all employees, males and females combined. Because of the lower quality of data for them, and the differing labour markets in which they are employed, part-time workers will be treated separately.

Even with allowance for differences in coverage, the spread across member countries in the incidence of low pay, on each measure, is striking, from negligible to 10 per cent for very low pay (earnings below one half of the median), from 5–20 per cent for low pay (two thirds of the median) and from 19-35 per cent at 80 per cent of the median.

For extremely low pay, below 50 per cent of median earnings, the incidence is generally low. In France and Belgium it is negligible. Britain falls into the intermediate group, along with pre-unification Germany, the Netherlands and Portugal, while the highest incidence, 9–10 per cent, is recorded by Ireland, Greece, Italy and Spain.

However, on the central definition of low pay, earnings below two thirds of the median, Britain's position changes sharply, its 20 per cent incidence being the highest within the EC. Britain, along with Ireland and Spain, emerge as the high-incidence group on this basis (although it should be noted that the figures for Spain include domestic servants, a very low-paid group with income received partly in kind, giving an upward bias to the measured incidence of low pay there relative to most other national definitions, including the British and Irish, where they are excluded). On this central definition of low pay Belgium stands alone, with the conspicuously low incidence of 5 per cent, while the remaining six countries form an intermediate group, with the incidence of low pay ranging between 11 and 16 per cent.

Broadly similar groupings apply for pay below 80 per cent of median earnings, with Britain again showing clearly the highest incidence, and followed in the high-incidence group by Spain, Portugal and Ireland. Belgium again records a conspicuously low incidence.

Table 5.2 *Major groups comprising the low-paid (percentages of all low-paid full-time employees)*

		Percentage of those with earnings		
High incidence countries		Below 50% of median	Below 66% of median	Below 80% of median
Britain	Women	n.a.	63	55
	Young people under 25	n.a.	49	39
	Clerical workers	n.a.	35 (a)	34
	Personal service workers	n.a.	18 (a)	12
	Salespersons	n.a.	12 (a)	7
Ireland	Women	54	51	47
	Young people under 25	70	62	54
	Personal service jobs	23	15	11
	Retail trade	26	24	19
Spain	Women	70 (b)	n.a.	49
	Young people under 25	47 (b)	n.a.	38
	Primary education not completed	61 (b)	n.a.	60
	Domestic servants	40 (b)	n.a.	17
	Less than 1 year with employer	47 (b)	n.a.	34
Low incidence countries				
Belgium	Women	-	62	38
	Young people under 25	-	37	20
	Labourers	-	37	19

Source: CERC (1991).

Notes: Figures in the table show the percentage of all low-paid employees in each country who are in the various categories. Countries are grouped by the incidence of low pay at two thirds of median earnings.

(a) Less than 62 per cent of median earnings.

(b) Less than 40 per cent of median earnings.

(c) Net earnings.

(d) Full-time plus part-time workers.

(Table 5.2 continued)

		Percentage of those with earnings		
Medium incidence countries		Below 50% of median	Below 66% of median	Below 80% of median
Germany	Women	95	82	72
	Young people under 30	42	49	49
	With primary schooling only	25	28	21
France	Women	-	51	n.a.
	Young people under 25	-	43	37
	Workers without qualifications	-	26	27
	Enterprises with 1-5 workers	-	25	20
Italy	Women	64	62	58
	Primary schooling only	74	73	73
	Manual workers	74	72	70
	Resident in the South	32	29	26
Netherlands	Women	56	53	47 (c)
	Young people aged 16-24	97	89	62 (c)
	Retail trade	25	20	14 (c)
	With enterprise < 2 years	n.a.	55	43 (c)
Greece (d)	Women	52	55	58
	Young people under 25	32	37	36
	Unemployed	23	14	9
	Agricultural workers	30	19	13
	In Anatolia, Macedonia, Thrace	40	26	19
Portugal	Women	44	49	52
	Young people under 25	82	65	44
	Primary schooling only	97	91	90

Table 5.3   *Low pay: high-incidence groups by country (full-time employees)*

		Percentage of those with earnings		
High incidence countries		Below 50% of median	Below 66% of median	Below 80% of median
Britain	All employees	7	20	35
	Women	13	40	57
	Young people under 25	n.a.	41	67
	Personal service jobs	n.a.	45 (a)	72
	Salespersons	n.a.	31 (a)	50
Ireland	All employees	10	18	30
	Women	17	29	45
	Young people under 25	28	45	65
	Agriculture	30	47	65
	Personal service jobs	44	52	66
	Retail trade	27	44	60
Spain	All employees	9	19	32
	Women (b)	29 (c)	n.a.	60
	Young people under 20 (b)	52 (c)	n.a.	89
	Illiterates (b)	21 (c)	n.a.	57
	Domestic servants (b)	70 (c)	n.a.	90
	6-12 months in post (b)	29 (c)	n.a.	63
Medium incidence countries				
Germany	All employees	6	13	25
	Women	18	33	53
	Agriculture	34	47	64
	Food industries	15	29	42
	Textile industries	14	36	58
France	All employees	0	14	28
	Women	-	20	n.a.
	Clothing trades	-	31	59
	Hotels, cafes	-	30	53
	Food retailing	-	27	53
	Personal service jobs	-	35	62
	Enterprise with < 5 workers	-	20	51

(Table 5.3 continued)

Italy	All employees	9	14	25
	Women	15	23	38
	Young people under 20	56	73	87
	Agriculture	36	45	57
	Manual workers	14	23	39
	Resident in the South	14	20	32
Netherlands	All employees	5	11	24
	Women	n.a.	28	51
	Young people under 25 (d)	17	40	74
	Agriculture	8	19	42
	Retail trade	20	39	59
	With enterprise < 1 year	n.a.	32	50
Greece (b)	All employees	10	16	26
	Women	15	26	45
	Young people under 20	61	74	95
	Agriculture	81	81	93
	Anatolia, Macedonia, Thrace	77	81	93
Portugal	All employees	4	12	31
	Women	6	19	50
	Young people under 20	33	67	87
	Agriculture	5	50	71
	Primary schooling only	9	19	36
	Enterprise with 1-4 workers	15	39	66
	With enterprise < 1 year	16	32	55
Low incidence countries				
Belgium	All employees	0	5	19
	Women	-	10	31
	Young people under 20	-	30	61
	Unskilled	-	22	59

Source: CERC (1991).
Notes: Countries are grouped by the incidence of low pay at two thirds of median earnings.
(a) Less than 62 per cent of median earnings. (b) Full-time plus part-time workers. (c) Less than 40 per cent of median earnings. (d) Earnings measured as net pay.

Who are the low-paid?

While the overall incidence of low pay varies quite widely across the members of the EC, a relatively small number of groups make up a substantial proportion of the low-paid in each country, as shown in table 5.2. The preponderance of women is striking. At least 45 per cent of the low-paid among full-time employees in every country of the EC are women. In Germany women comprise virtually all of the low-paid, 95 per cent of those whose earnings fall below half of the median and 82 per cent of those below two thirds. In the UK, Italy and Belgium the proportion of women is around 62 per cent. Young people also feature prominently, comprising at least one in three of the low-paid in each member country. In the Netherlands they constitute virtually the whole group, 97 per cent of the very low-paid and 89 per cent of the low-paid. Differences in national definitions and coverage restrict the range of direct comparisons, but it is clear that other major groups among the low-paid are those working in parts of the service sector, notably personal services and retail trade, those working for individual proprietors and in small firms, those with short job-tenure and those with limited education and skills. A very high proportion of the low-paid in Italy, Spain and Portugal have at most primary schooling. The role of agriculture tends to be under-represented by the exclusion of self-employed small proprietors in most countries. In general the role of individual groups among the low-paid diminishes as the earnings threshold rises, the groups affected becoming more diversified, although the presence of women among the low-paid in Greece and Portugal is an exception to this.

In order to identify the most vulnerable groups table 5.3 indicates those groups in each country among whom the incidence of low pay is particularly high. Again women and young people feature prominently in most countries, although the incidence of low pay for women ranges from a high of 40 per cent in Britain to a low of 10 per cent in Belgium. Other groups among whom low pay is extensive include agricultural workers, employees in the service sector in personal service jobs, retail trade, hotels and catering, and within manufacturing in textiles and clothing. The incidence is systematically high for those with limited education, low skills, high job turnover and working in small enterprises. In this respect the Commission's concern for 'vulnerable groups' on an EC-wide perspective has a practical basis.

Two groups clearly systematically at risk in terms of low pay are women and the young. The social issues posed are, however, rather different, with the low earnings status of young people often transitory, even when they do not formally have trainee or apprenticeship status. In the case of women the issue is a more fundamental one, and emerges in spite of the strong role which the

Table 5.4 *Women and low pay in the EC (full-time employees)*

	Activity rate in full-time employ-ment(%)	Unemp-loyment rate relative to men	Women as % of all low-paid (a)	Incidence of low pay among women (a)(%)	Risk indices for earnings		
					Below 50% of median	Below 66% of median	Below 80% of median
Britain	27	0.5	63	41	190	200	160
Ireland	27	0.6	51	29	170	160	150
Spain	26	2.0	70(c)	29(c)	220(c)	n.a.	150
Germany	28	1.4	82	33	290	250	220
France	34	1.8	51	20	-	145	140
Italy	30	2.3	62	23	165	160	150
N'lands	16	1.8	53	28	275	260	230
L'bourg	28	1.4	n.a.	n.a.	n.a.	n.a.	n.a.
Denmark	34	1.1	n.a.	n.a.	n.a.	n.a.	n.a.
Greece	31	2.6	55(b)	26(b)	n.a.	n.a.	n.a.
Portugal	40	2.2	49	19	140	155	165
Belgium	26	2.2	62	10	-	200	170

Source: CERC (1991).
(a) Low pay as two thirds of median earnings.
(b) Full-time plus part-time employees.
(c) Earnings less than 40 per cent of the median.

Commission continues to play in promoting the commitment to equal pay in member states.

The position of women is further illustrated in table 5.4. To give greater precision to the degree of risk to which women are exposed this includes an 'index of risk'. This expresses the incidence of low pay within the group as a ratio to its incidence in the workforce as a whole. Thus in Britain 40 per cent of women are low-paid against 20 per cent of all full-time employees, giving a risk index for women of 200. (The risk index is, of course, a purely statistical measure, ignoring what can be regarded as relevant causal factors, such as the differential skills, work experience, location and non-wage aspects of work.) In every country the incidence of low pay among women is greater by at least 40 per cent than in the workforce as a whole. The relative risk of low pay for

women is greatest in the Netherlands and Germany, at more than 2.5 times
the risk for the workforce as a whole; this is substantially greater than in
France, Italy and Portugal, and in spite of the fact that relative unemployment
for women is approximately equal between the Netherlands and France, and
lower in Germany than in Italy and Portugal. In Britain and Belgium women
are twice as much at risk as the workforce as a whole, in spite of these countries'
contrasting overall incidence of low pay, but in Britain the low relative
unemployment rate for women may appear an offset to their high incidence of
low pay. The level of risk for women is rather higher at 50 per cent of median
earnings, but falls slightly in most member countries at 80 per cent. Thus the
lower the earnings threshold, the more women are at risk (although Greece
and Portugal are marked exceptions to this). As a particularly discouraging
prospect, there appears to be an inverse relationship between women's
participation in full-time paid employment and their risk of being low-paid.

Atypical workers

A category left out of account so far is that of part-time, temporary and casual
workers, the atypical workers found mostly in secondary labour markets.
Part-time employment is substantial in Britain, the Netherlands and Denmark,
where it involves one worker in four, predominantly women, but is relatively
rare in the southern EC countries; in Italy, for example, part-time work
involves only 5 per cent of workers, mostly young people (table 5.5).

Data on earnings for atypical workers are scantier and of lower reliability.
For Britain, although the coverage of full-time workers in the New Earnings
Survey is around 93 per cent, for part-timers it is estimated to be only around
60 per cent. Moreover, the appropriate measure for the analysis of the
earnings of part-time workers is hourly pay, but distributional data on this is
rarely available. In the case of France, for example, social security records
provide comprehensive coverage of employees and their earnings, but do not
record the actual hours worked by part-timers.

In those countries for which hourly earnings data are available for both full-
time and part-time workers, low pay emerges as almost twice as frequent
among part-timers. This characterises low as well as high incidence
countries. In Ireland, for example, one part-time worker in three is low-paid,
and one in five receives very low pay, against one in ten full-time workers. A
similar disproportion applies in the Netherlands, although the overall
incidence of low pay there is low. However, the most marked increase in
incidence of low pay for part-time as against full-time employees occurs in
Britain, where no less than 60 per cent of part-timers are low-paid. This is well

Table 5.5 *Atypical workers and low pay*

	Part-time employment as % of total	Part-time employment as % of total: women	Temporary employment as % of total	Temporary employment as % of total: women	% of part-timers with less than 66% of full-time median hourly earnings(a)
Britain	23	43	5	7	60(17)
Ireland	8	15	9	12	33(19)
Spain	5	11	26	31	n.a.
Germany	13	30	11	12	n.a.
France	12	23	8	9	n.a.
Italy	5	10	6	9	n.a.
Netherlands	29	58	8	11	23(11)
Luxembourg	6	17	3	5	n.a.
Denmark	25	41	10	10	n.a.
Greece	4	7	17	16	n.a.
Portugal	4	8	19	21	n.a.
Belgium	11	28	5	8	9(5)

Souurce: CERC (1991).
(a) Figures in parentheses are percentages of full-time workers with earnings below two thirds of median.

over three times higher than the incidence for full-time workers in what is already a high-incidence country.

Part-time work is a predominantly female activity and, as has been frequently documented, the earnings of men tend also to be low in female-dominated employment. This also characterises part-time work. As a result, the difference between men and women in the incidence of low pay is much lower among part-time than full-time workers in most countries, conspicuously including Britain. The incidence of low pay among part-time men in Britain (a small group) is 58 per cent, against 61 per cent among women, while for full-time work the incidence among women is 2.5 times greater than among men.

Since earnings from part-time employment are low overall and with a much less dispersed distribution than for full-time work, the incidence of low pay measured within the distribution of part-time earnings only is greatly reduced. However, this basis conceals the serious disadvantage which characterises part-time work as a whole.

Other groups of atypical workers are those employed on a seasonal or temporary basis. Relatively rare in northern countries, casual work involves around one worker in five in the southern European countries. It is particularly common in Spain, but also frequent in Greece and Portugal, involving women only slightly more than men (table 5.5). The incidence of low pay in these groups is high; in Spain 86 per cent of casual workers and 51 per cent of temporary workers receive less than 80 per cent of median earnings, against 32 per cent of full-time employees. Beyond them are the groups of black-economy workers, illegal immigrants and other hidden groups.

Minimum wage regulation within the EC

This review of the incidence of low pay indicates that while many of the same groups are at risk in each country the incidence of low pay varies substantially across the member states of the EC. The purpose in the remainder of the chapter is to relate the pattern of low pay to the nature of wage-setting in the member countries and in particular to measures of wage protection for vulnerable groups. Modes of wage-setting vary widely, in terms of both the structure of collective bargaining and the role of the state. We will confine our outline to the key aspects which affect the position of the low-paid, and particularly the establishment of minimum rates.

The two principal methods of regulating low pay among the member states of the EC are through a national minimum rate, or through a series of industry or sectoral minima, possibly also different:..ied by region. It would be possible to regard the lowest of the sectoral minima as the national minimum, but since sectoral wage-setting does not incorporate rates from other sectors this is not a useful definition. Both national and sectoral approaches are widely used. The national minimum is typically legally enforceable, with its level most commonly set by government but sometimes by the social partners. Sectoral minima are set by collective bargaining, but may be made comprehensive in scope by statutory enforceability on all employers in the sector.

Seven countries have instituted a national minimum wage. In five of these (France, the Netherlands, Luxembourg, Spain and Portugal) this is set by the government and has the force of law. In Belgium and Greece it is set by a centralised collective accord at the national level. Where the approach is by way of sectoral minima, these can be either negotiated, as in Germany, Italy and Denmark, or statutorily regulated, as in the UK and Ireland. Negotiated minima can have virtually universal coverage, as in Germany and Italy, while statutory regulation at the sectoral level, as in the UK, can leave many gaps. The regulation of low pay among the member countries of the EC thus involves the interaction of collective bargaining with state intervention, with the balance between the two varying widely. A simple division based on the presence or absence of a national, legally enforceable minimum wage is therefore a rather poor guide to the nature and extent of minimum wage protection in the member countries.

The essential elements of pay-setting arrangements as they affect the low-paid in the EC will be summarised through a four-way classification incorporating both the mode of minimum wage protection and the collective bargaining context (CERC, 1991). The basic distinction is between those countries with a national minimum and those with sectoral minima, and within each category distinguishing restricted as against wide roles for the minima. Further details for each country individually are given in table 5.6.

The first category is characterised by the existence of a national minimum wage, but one which serves in a safety-net role only, with substantive wage protection for the low-paid being through collective bargaining in individual sectors. The countries in this category are Belgium, the Netherlands and Luxembourg, each of which has a strong tradition of collective social action. The national minimum is taken as the baseline, with the rates set in the sectoral collective agreements typically exceeding it. The role of the national minimum is to safeguard the position of those not covered by sectoral agreements. The level of the minimum is typically over 60 per cent of median earnings. The numbers whose pay is actually determined by the national minimum are small, well under 5 per cent of employees, and for the most part atypical workers.

In the second category, collective bargaining is less highly developed and comprehensive, and the national minimum plays a more prominent role. In this group, which comprises France, Spain, Portugal and Greece, the national minimum becomes the mode of pay determination for a significant number of workers. This arises partly because union weakness in certain areas leads to sectoral minima below the national rate, which are then superseded by the national minimum. Bazen and Benhayoun (1991) have estimated that in France the national minimum exceeded the lowest rates set in 134 out of 164 main sectoral agreements in 1990. In these situations workers are paid the national minimum, but remain on that rate until they reach the grade where the collectively bargained rate exceeds this. In addition the absence of collective bargaining coverage for certain groups of workers leads to their pay being set

Table 5.6 *Low wage regulation in the EC*

UK	26 sectoral Wages Councils set minimum hourly rates for workers over 21. No regulation of rates for those under 21. Rates vary, on average around 60% of median earnings for full-time men and 75% for full-time women.
Ireland	14 Joint Labour Committees set legally enforceable sectoral rates for workers over 20 periodic reviews. Rates variable, eg 40% of average weekly pay in hotels and hairdressing, 60% in flour-milling.
Germany	Industry-level agreements negotiated at regional level set legally binding minimum rates for all employees under the agreement. Wide differences between sectors.
France	A statutory national minimum 'salaire minimum interprofessionel de croissance' (SMIC) set after consultation. Defined as an hourly rate, but applied to a standard working month (169 hrs). Covers all workers over 18, including part-timers but excluding trainees and temporary workers. 16 and 17-year-olds entitled to 70-90% of the minimum. Annual adjustment is by at least half the growth of average earnings, plus automatic adjustment whenever prices rise by more than 2%, plus intermittent discretionary reviews. The SMIC has increased relative to average earnings (see Bazen and Martin, 1991). Statutory national minimum is 61% of median earnings. 11% receive the minimum.
Italy	Industry-level collective agreements set legally binding minimum rates. Full and part-time workers, including young workers who have completed training. Indexed to inflation.
Belgium	National accord sets legally binding minimum 'salaire minimum interprofessionel garanti' (SMIG) or 'revenu minimum mensuel moyen' (RMMM) for workers over 21 in full-time employment with 6 months' service. Excludes some trainees. Younger worker rates reduced by 7.5% for each year under 21. 8% receive the minimum, B.frs.36,856 per month in 1990 minimum is 66% of median earnings. Indexed to prices, with intermittent review.
N'lands	Statutory national minimum, 'wet minimum loon'. Daily, weekly or monthly rate in spite of variable length of the standard work-week. Applies to workers over 23. Young people aged 15-22 receive 30-85% of adult rate. Excludes part-timers working less than 13 hours per week. The level of the minimum was cut in 1984 and has since been frozen with the suspension of formal indexation to average earnings; the real value has fallen by 15% since 1980. Statutory national minimum is 60% of median earnings. 4% receive the minimum.
L'bourg	Statutory national minimum, 'salaire social minimum' (SSM) set by govt after consultation. Hourly rate. Applies to full and part-time workers over 18. 16-18-year-olds receive 60-80% of adult rate. Supplemented for marital status and dependants. Automatic indexation to prices.

(Table 5.6 continued)

Denmark	Collective bargaining sets minimum rates for workers over 18. Over 600 agreements, renegotiated every 2 years. In practice very few receive only the minimum.
Greece	National collective agreement sets minima for manuals and non-manuals separately, which are legally enforceable. Covers manuals over 18, non-manuals over 19. Varies by age, occupation, marital status. Entitlement depends on completed training and service. Reduced rates for 15-19-year-olds. Minimum is 67% of median. Indexed to inflation. 15-20% receive the minimum.
Spain	Statutory national minimum, 'salario minimo interprofessionanel' (SMI). Defined for a standard working day. Applies to workers aged over 18. A lower wage set as an absolute amount applies for younger and temporary workers. Annual adjustment on the basis of forecast inflation, national productivity growth and the general economic situation, often disputed. The level has tended to fall in real terms. Statutory national minimum is 54% of median. 15% receive the minimum.
Portugal	Statutory national minimum, 'salario minimo nacional' (SMN). Hourly rates, at different levels for industry and services, agriculture and domestic service, with harmonisation in progress. Enterprises with fewer than 5 employees can implement the agricultural rate. Applies to workers aged over 18, reduced by 25% for those under 18. Excludes trainees. Annual adjustment on the basis of forecast inflation, national productivity growth and the general economic situation. The level has tended to fall in real terms. Statutory national minimum is 73% of median (1985). 10% receive the minimum.

Source: Individual country studies prepared for CERC (1991).

at the national minimum. This national minimum again tends to lie around two thirds of median earnings, rather higher in Portugal and rather lower in Spain. In the countries in this group the national minimum wage in this sweeping-up role sets pay for between 10 and 20 per cent of the workforce.

The countries in the third category, Germany, Italy and Denmark, have no national minimum wage but are characterised by highly developed systems of collective bargaining through which sectoral minima are set. The coverage of these negotiated sectoral agreements is extremely high: essentially the whole workforce in Germany and Italy, and over 80 per cent in Denmark. In Italy the coverage of the sectoral agreement is extended automatically to all employers. In Germany implementation of the minimum set in the relevant collective agreement is mandatory on all employers belonging to the employers' federation, and conventionally applied also by non-members. In Denmark, where not all workers are covered by sectoral collective agreements, a safety net is provided by the negotiation of sectoral minima for the unskilled. Unlike other rates, which are typically open to renegotiation upwards at the level of the enterprise, these minima remain fixed.

In the final category, comprising the UK and Ireland, not only is there no national minimum wage but collective bargaining is diverse and the regulatory framework limited. By contrast with the third group above, industry-level collective agreements have only partial coverage, in that they do not feature in all industries and, even where they exist, they are not binding on the individual employer. Wage protection for the low-paid outside collective agreements is provided through the twenty-six Wages Councils in the UK and the fourteen Joint Labour Committees in Ireland. These comprise equal numbers of representatives of employers and employees, with at least one independent member who acts as chairman. The system is very partial in coverage, being confined to a list of specified industries selected originally on the basis of their weakly developed collective bargaining. There is thus a fundamental difference in the approach to minimum wage protection between the UK and Ireland on the one hand and the rest of the EC on the other, specific selection for protection via a 'positive list' approach contrasting with the concept of universality. The degree of intervention and the role of the Wages Councils in the UK are being progressively curtailed. The Employment Protection Act of 1975 which had required employers to pay wages in line with those specified in the relevant national, industry or local agreement, was repealed in the 1980 Employment Act. The number of Wages Councils has been reduced, and in the 1986 Wages Act their powers were further limited, to setting a single minimum hourly rate for adult workers, where previously they had been able to set rates for different jobs and for juveniles. In spite of these curtailments, an estimated 2.5 million workers, 12 per cent of the workforce, are in principle covered by Wages Councils in Britain. In Ireland the Joint Labour Committees apply to 6 per cent of the workforce. Implementation of the minimum rates, by a wages inspectorate, is acknowledged to be weak, in spite of their statutory status, and the number of inspectors has been reduced by more than half since 1979. The current intention of the UK government is to abolish the remaining Wages Councils.

Low pay and wage-setting procedures

The impact of minimum wage regulation on the incidence of low pay depends on the level set, its coverage and the degree of compliance. In several cases comparison of the incidence of low pay with the level of the minimum wage apparently indicates workers receiving less than the minimum (Belgium, the Netherlands, Portugal; possibly also France, Greece and Spain). In a number of cases the discrepancy can be attributed to specific exclusions in the coverage of minimum wage provisions. In the Netherlands, for example, minimum wage provisions are age-related for workers under 23, and in France and Portugal apprentices and certain categories of trainee are excluded from the minimum wage provisions, but included in the earnings distribution. Beyond this, one must suspect, in unknown proportions, non-compliance with minimum wage requirements and the under-reporting of earnings. Non-compliance is particularly suspected in the countries of Southern Europe where the informal sector is large.

Certain correlations can be noted between the incidence of low pay and the use of one particular mode of pay determination rather than another. Two of the three countries in the high-incidence group, Britain and Ireland, have neither a national minimum wage nor comprehensive coverage of collective agreements; rather they are characterised by extensive firm-level wage-setting, with or without collective bargaining, and no requirement on employers to adhere to sectoral collective agreements, whether they are party to these or not. However, Spain, the third country in the group, has a statutory national minimum wage policy and a high incidence of low pay. The level of the statutory minimum, around 54 per cent of median earnings, and the limited protection of younger workers, explain part of the incidence of low pay; in addition, however, a degree of non-compliance must be inferred.

The incidence of low pay within the EC is clearly least frequent in Belgium, on the figures given. However, the incidence for both Belgium and the Netherlands is reduced almost to zero when young people (37 per cent of the low-paid in Belgium, 89 per cent in the Netherlands) are separated out. Both countries have similar wage-setting procedures, a national minimum wage serving in a safety-net role beneath comprehensive sectoral collective bargaining, indicating this combination is highly effective in reducing the incidence of low pay.

The largest, middle, group of countries in terms of the incidence of low pay includes France, Portugal and the Netherlands, where a statutory national minimum is in place, along with Italy and Germany where there is no national minimum, but industry-level collective agreements have comprehensive coverage. This suggests that either a national minimum wage or full-coverage collective agreements can achieve a substantial degree of protection against low pay, relative to the loose structures which characterise the UK and Ireland, but that neither system has a clear advantage.

However this picture has to be modified in considering the incidence of very low pay. On this criterion those countries with a statutory minimum wage (Benelux, France, Portugal) each have an incidence below 5 per cent (again leaving aside Spain), while those with less interventionist systems (Germany and Italy as well as Ireland and Britain) all have a higher incidence. This suggests that a statutory minimum is a more powerful instrument than collective bargaining for restricting the incidence of very low pay.

On a cautionary note it should be borne in mind that the figures cited give a snapshot picture for the late 1980s from a distribution which itself is evolving. Lack of data for several countries precludes a systematic comparison, but since the end of the 1970s the incidence of low pay has fallen in France and Ireland while remaining fairly constant in Germany and the Netherlands, and rising in Belgium and Britain, where the earnings distribution has become more dispersed. These developments do not align at all closely with the systems of pay determination or the degree of intervention. In particular, those countries without a statutory minimum wage (Germany, Italy, Ireland, Britain) have not universally seen an increase in the dispersion of earnings in the 1980s under the impact of high unemployment and skill shortages, while the case of Belgium shows that the institution of a minimum wage is perfectly consistent with an increasing incidence of low pay.

Our conclusions will remain provisional until more closely standardised data are available, but nonetheless the present evidence is that a national minimum wage is neither necessary nor sufficient for a low incidence of low pay, although it is an effective regulator in eliminating very low pay. Full-coverage collective bargaining provides a comprehensive framework in which pay rates at all levels are integrated. The most comprehensive defence against low pay is the combination of a national minimum wage in a safety-net role with comprehensive collective bargaining.

Appendix: Data sources on earnings in individual EC countries

Great Britain

Earnings data are taken from the New Earnings Survey, a survey of employers conducted by the Department of Employment in April of each year. Northern Ireland is surveyed separately and the results are not collated with those for Great Britain. The NES comprises a 1 per cent sample of national insurance numbers, an NI number being issued to each employee on taking a first job. Categories excluded from the Survey are members of the armed forces, domestic servants and those whose hours of work and pay fall below the PAYE threshold. Employers are required by law to complete the Survey return. While 93 per cent of questionnaires are returned, usable returns relate to only 85 per cent of full-time employees and a considerably smaller proportion, probably around 60 per cent, of part-time employees. The final sample is around 180 000 employees. The most common reason for uncompleted returns is that the employee is no longer with the contacted employer, implying lower coverage of job-changers.

The measure of pay is gross weekly earnings, including overtime, incentive and premium pay, and periodic bonuses where they can be attributed to the Survey pay week. Normal and overtime hours are recorded, allowing the calculation of hourly pay, including and excluding overtime.

Ireland

Data are taken from a survey of 3300 households carried out by the Economic and Social Research Institute, Dublin. The sampling frame is the electoral register. The total sample comprised 2800 employees who had worked at least one hour during the reference week, of whom 89 per cent had worked full-time. Domestic servants are excluded.

The earnings recorded are 'normal' or 'standard' gross weekly pay.

Germany

Data have been collated by the Federal Statistical Office from official records of annual salaries as reported to pension funds. These cover all salaries, full and part-time, on which contributions are payable, involving 87 per cent of employees. Categories excluded are certain state employees (the BEAMTE), domestic servants and apprentices, and those working less than two months or fifty days in the year or less than fifteen hours per week. For full-time employees a 1 per cent sample is taken, but only of those who have been employed by the same employer throughout the year. The proportions of full-time employees in the various categories not covered by the earnings statistics are estimated to be:

(a) small jobs, including domestic service — 10 per cent
(b) the BEAMTE
   in the public sector — 8 per cent
   trainees and employees with less than one year's service — 9 per cent.

Earnings are measured as gross annual earnings, inclusive of bonuses.

France

Data are taken from the official records of the Annual Return on Social Contributions completed by employers and collated by the Social Security office. The sample is 1 in 24. Coverage excludes civil servants, local community employees, agricultural workers, domestic servants, trainees and

the unemployed on job programmes. Newly engaged workers tend to be
omitted. The proportions of full-time employees in the various categories
not covered by the earnings statistics are:
(a) local community employees, agricultural workers, trainees, domestic
servants — 12–15 per cent
(b) civil servants and state employees — 18 per cent.
Earnings are reported as annual pay, inclusive of all bonuses, net of social
security contributions but gross of personal taxes. For workers with their
employer for less than a year earnings are converted to a 'year equivalent'
basis.

Italy

The only available data on individual earnings are drawn from a 1987
household survey by the Bank of Italy. This covered 7000 households,
comprising 6000 employees. Only personal servants are excluded:
(a) domestic servants — 2–5 per cent of full-time employees.
Earnings are gross annual pay.

Belgium

Data on individual earnings are taken from the offical records of social security
contributions held by the Institut National de Maladie et d'Invalidité
(INAMI). Excluded categories are railway employees, seamen, domestic
servants and apprentices. The unemployed on job programmes are not
classified as employees. The proportions of full-time employees in the various
categories not covered by the earnings statistics are estimated to be:
(a) domestic servants, apprentices, the unemployed on work programmes —
4–5 per cent
(b) railway employees, seamen — 2 per cent.
Earnings are recorded as gross daily pay, excluding year-end and holiday
bonuses.

The Netherlands

Data are taken from the annual survey of enterprises conducted by the Central
Statistical Bureau. All enterprises are covered. Excluded categories are
domestic servants, the unemployed on special programmes, trainees, handi-
capped workers, and those who have joined or left the firm during the survey
month (October). Managers and heads of firms are also excluded. The
proportions of full-time employees in the various categories not covered by
the earnings statistics are estimated to be:
(a) domestic servants, trainees — 2–3 per cent

(b) managers — 21 per cent.

Earnings are recorded as annual, including all supplements, based on weekly earnings for those in full-time employment during the survey month.

Luxembourg

Not included.

Denmark

Data are available only on employees in firms belonging to the employers' confederation; this covers around 50 per cent of employees in the private sector. This is supplemented by information from the government statistical service. Earnings are measured inclusive of premia. While indicative figures can be derived, data for the systematic analysis of the incidence of low pay are not available.

Greece

Data are taken from a 1988 household survey conducted by the National Centre for Social Science Research. This was based on a representative sample of 3000 households, comprising 2000 employees. All employees are covered, including domestic servants. Earnings are reported net of tax.

Spain

Data are taken from a 1985 household survey of living standards and work. 60 000 households were surveyed. The entire population is covered, including domestic servants.

Earnings are reported as monthly pay, excluding non-regular bonuses, and net of tax.

Portugal

Data are drawn from a survey of 40 800 employees through employer pay records collated by the Ministry of Labour. Excluded categories are some civil servants, domestic servants, and employees in some small agricultural operations. The proportions of full-time employees in the various categories not covered by the earnings statistics are estimated to be:

(a) employees in small agricultural operations — 1–2 per cent

(b) civil servants — less than 1 per cent

Earnings are measured as average gross monthly pay, inclusive of overtime pay and annual bonuses.

(a) denotes groups with a high incidence of low pay

(b) denotes groups with a low incidence of low pay.

Note

1 This paper draws extensively on the report *Les Bas salaires dans les pays de la Communauté Economique Européenne* (CERC 1991) commissioned by the Commission of the European Communities, Directorate-General V (Employment, Industrial Relations and Social Affairs) from the Centre d'Etudes des Revenus et des Coûts, Paris. The report was prepared by a working group under the direction of Véronique Sandoval, assisted by Nicole Lanfranchi and Guy Neyret. The national representatives on the working group were: UK — Mary Gregory, Oxford University; Ireland — Gerard MacMahon, Dublin Institute of Technology; W. Germany — Claus Shäfer, W.S.I., Dusseldorf; France — Gilbert Benhayoun, Centre d'Economie Régional, Aix-en-Provence and Steve Bazen, University of Bordeaux I; Italy — Claudio Lucifora, Catholic University of Milan; Belgium — Bernard Delvaud, IRES, Louvain Jean Verly, IST, Louvain; Netherlands — Wiemer Salverda, Faculty of Economics, Groningen; Denmark — Niels Ploug, Danish National Institute of Social Research, Copenhagen; Greece — John Ifantopoulos, University of Athens; Spain — Fernando Frenandez, Universidad autonoma de Madrid; Portugal — Alberto Castro, Facultate de Economia do Porto.

Their contributions on their individual countries and to the collective discussions within the group are gratefully acknowledged.

References

Bazen, S. and Benhayoun, G. (1991), Les Basses rémunerations en France, mimeo, Centre d'Economie Regional.

Bazen, S. and Martin, J. (1991), 'The effect of the minimum wage on employment and earnings in France, 1963–85', *OECD Economic Studies,* no. 16, Spring.

CERC (Centre d'Etudes des Revenus et des Coûts) (1991), *Les Bas salaires dans les pays de la Communauté Economique Européenne,* Report to the Commission of the European Communities, Directorate General for Employment, Industrial Relations and Social Affairs.

Eurostat (1986), *Structure of Earnings, 1978–79,* Statistical Office of the European Communities.

Gregory, M, Houston, S., Sanjines, C. and Thomson, A. (1990), 'The New Earnings Survey', in Gregory, M. and Thomson, A. (eds.), *A Portrait of Pay: An Analysis of the New Earnings Survey,* Oxford, Clarendon Press.

6　Direct and indirect effects of active labour market policies in OECD countries

DAVID GRUBB[1]

Introduction

The OECD has focused attention on the importance of active labour market policies (ALMPs) by publishing data for public spending on labour market programmes and recommending an 'active' stance (OECD, 1990). This chapter briefly reviews the data set and conventional views on how each main category of labour market programme works and how programme effectiveness can be assessed. It then evokes some of the many complicating factors which can make ALMPs more or less effective in reducing unemployment, and discusses some specific country experiences.

The OECD figures for ALMP spending

Table 6.1 shows, for 1985 and 1990, labour market spending for seven principal categories. As notes to the table suggest (and as discussed further below), there are many borderline cases of programmes which combine labour market functions with other functions. The general rule is that the data in table 6.1 cover labour market policies that are explicitly focused on unemployed persons or those at risk of becoming unemployed.

'Active' labour market programmes (ALMPs) refer conventionally to the first five categories in table 6.1, administration and public employment service work, training, youth measures, job creation (and job subsidisation) and measures to help place and directly employ the disabled. The last two categories, unemployment benefits and payment of early retirement pensions for labour market reasons, are then labelled 'passive'. Some regression coefficients (with t-statistics in brackets) given below illustrate the correlation, across the twenty-three countries shown in table 6.1, of total active spending AC (active spending, columns 1–5 in table 6.1) and

Table 6.1　*Patterns of spending on labour market policy, 1985 and 1990*

1985

(b)	Labour market spending as a % of GDP								Unemployment rate(a)
	Training		Job creation	Disabled	Unemp. benefits	Early retirement	Total		
	Admin & PES	Youth measures							
	1	2	3	4	5	6	7		%
Australia	0.11	0.01	0.07	0.19	0.04	1.30	0.00	1.73	8.2
Austria	0.11	0.06	0.06	0.03	0.02	0.83	0.13	1.23	3.6
Belgium	0.17	0.11	0.00	0.79	0.15	2.56	0.87	4.66	11.3
Canada	0.24	0.31	0.06	0.02	0.00	1.87	0.00	2.50	10.4
Denmark	0.08	0.51	0.23	0.01	0.25	2.65	1.26	5.00	9.0
Finland	0.08	0.26	0.05	0.42	0.09	0.87	0.46	2.25	5.0
France	0.13	0.25	0.17	0.06	0.05	1.20	1.21	3.07	10.2
Germany	0.21	0.20	0.05	0.17	0.19	1.41	0.01	2.23	7.2
Greece	0.08	0.03	0.03	0.06	0.00	0.43	0.00	0.63	7.8
Ireland	0.18	0.67	0.54	0.19	0.00	3.69	0.00	5.27	17.0
Italy	0.08	0.05	0.32	0.00	0.00	0.75	0.28	1.48	9.6
Japan	0.03	0.03	0.00	0.10	0.01	0.40	0.00	0.57	2.6
Luxembourg	0.05	0.00	0.11	0.13	0.29	0.31	0.74	1.63	1.6
Netherlands	0.08	0.19	0.04	0.06	0.72	3.24	0.00	4.32	10.6
New Zealand	0.10	0.09	0.01	0.62	0.01	0.65	0.00	1.48	4.1
Norway	0.12	0.11	0.05	0.21	0.18	0.50	0.00	1.17	2.6
Portugal	0.08	0.20	0.05	0.04	0.04	0.41	0.00	0.81	8.5
Spain	0.09	0.02	0.00	0.22	0.01	2.87	0.02	3.23	21.4
Sweden	0.25	0.50	0.21	0.43	0.72	0.75	0.12	2.97	2.8
Switzerland	0.08	0.01	0.00	0.00	0.11	0.28	0.00	0.48	0.8
Turkey	0.01	0.02	0.04	0.07	0.01	0.00	0.00	0.15	11.3
UK	0.14	0.09	0.26	0.22	0.03	2.05	0.05	2.84	11.2
US	0.07	0.12	0.03	0.02	0.04	0.57	0.00	0.84	7.1

(Table 6.1 continued)

1990

(b)	Labour market spending as a % of GDP								Unemployment rate(a)
	Training			Job creation	Disabled	Unemp. benefits	Early retirement	Total	
	Admin & PES		Youth measures						
	1	2	3	4	5	6	7		%
Australia	0.09	0.06	0.04	0.05	0.04	1.12	0.00	1.39	6.9
Austria	0.11	0.09	0.02	0.05	0.05	0.87	0.11	1.29	3.2
Belgium	0.18	0.14	0.00	0.59	0.16	1.96	0.75	3.78	7.2
Canada	0.23	0.25	0.04	0.02	0.00	1.91	0.00	2.44	8.1
Denmark	0.09	0.51	0.26	0.07	0.34	3.18	1.22	5.67	9.5
Finland	0.11	0.25	0.05	0.45	0.13	0.63	0.50	2.12	3.4
France	0.13	0.33	0.22	0.07	0.06	1.32	0.56	2.68	9.0
Germany	0.22	0.37	0.04	0.15	0.23	1.14	0.02	2.17	4.9
Greece	0.08	0.25	0.03	0.14	0.01	0.43	0.00	0.94	7.0
Ireland	0.13	0.48	0.45	0.28	0.14	2.79	0.05	4.33	13.4
Italy	0.08	0.03	0.69	0.00	0.00	0.40	0.32	1.51	10.3
Japan	0.02	0.03	0.00	0.07	0.01	0.32	0.00	0.45	2.1
Luxembourg	0.03	0.02	0.12	0.06	0.13	0.17	0.57	1.10	1.1
Netherlands	0.10	0.21	0.06	0.05	0.64	2.20	0.00	3.27	7.5
New Zealand	0.16	0.39	0.09	0.19	0.06	1.90	0.00	2.79	7.9
Norway	0.14	0.36	0.12	0.18	0.20	1.17	0.00	2.17	5.2
Portugal	0.11	0.14	0.13	0.08	0.06	0.31	0.00	0.83	4.6
Spain	0.13	0.10	0.07	0.45	0.00	2.43	0.00	3.18	15.9
Sweden	0.21	0.54	0.07	0.13	0.76	0.81	0.08	2.60	1.5
Switzerland	0.06	0.01	0.00	0.00	0.14	0.14	0.00	0.35	0.6
Turkey	0.01	0.05	0.05	0.04	0.00	0.00	0.00	0.16	10.0
UK	0.15	0.23	0.18	0.02	0.03	0.95	0.00	1.57	6.8
US	0.08	0.09	0.03	0.01	0.04	0.50	0.00	0.74	5.4

Source: OECD *Employment Outlook*, 1992, table 2.B.1, with some minor statistical revisions.
Notes: see next page.

unemployment benefit spending UB (column 6 in table 6.1) with the unemployment rate (many countries have no spending in the last category, early retirement). Variables are in logarithms (log) and changes in logarithms (dlog) which refer to 1990 values less 1985 values, t-statistics in brackets.

$\log(AC85) = c + 0.25(1.3)\log(U85)$
$\log(AC90) = c + 0.38(2.3)\log(U90)$
$\mathrm{dlog}(AC) = c + 0.32(1.4)\mathrm{dlog}(U)$
$\log(UB85) = c + 1.48(3.5)\log(U85)$
$\log(UB90) = c + 1.24(2.8)\log(U90)$
$\mathrm{dlog}(UB) = c + 0.95(3.9)\mathrm{dlog}(U)$

A 1 per cent increase in unemployment is associated in these international comparisons of levels and changes through time with much less than a 1 per cent increase in ALMP spending. By contrast a 1 per cent increase in unemployment is associated with a more than 1 per cent increase in spending on unemployment benefit in level terms.

Since higher unemployment probably leads to an increase in spending while higher 'active' spending reduces unemployment and higher 'passive' spending increases unemployment, the possible causalities run in both directions. It is not possible to infer from such regressions, without further identifying information, the impact of labour market policies on unemployment.[2]

Notes to table 6.1 on previous page

(a) Standardised unemployment rate where available: otherwise (Austria, Denmark, Ireland, Luxembourg, New Zealand 1985, Switzerland, Turkey) a rate on a national basis.

(b) A more detailed description of intended coverage of the programme categories is as follows: (1) employment services (placement, counselling, vocational guidance and mobility support) and administration of the other labour market programmes (including unemployment compensation). (2) Labour market training of unemployed workers and employed workers at risk for reasons of labour market policy. This excludes provisions open to all adults or which provide general support for enterprise training. (3) Youth measures: this covers only measures for youth who have already encountered employment problems, but more or less generally available support of apprentice training has been included in some cases. (4) Direct job-creation and employment subsidies. Only subsidies targeted on the unemployed or other groups defined according to labour market priorities are included. Grants to enterprises for capital costs are not included. (5) Measures for the disabled: this covers only measures restricted to the disabled. In countries where spending on this heading is low or zero, the disabled are typically helped by measures appearing in the other categories here. (6) Unemployment compensation. (7) Early retirement for labour market reasons.

A conventional view of how labour market programmes work

Introduction

This section attempts to describe a 'conventional' view of how labour market programmes work for the main categories of programmes, in particular the public employment service (PES), labour market training, direct job creation and incremental and/or targeted subsidies to employment in the private sector, and early retirement (although this last is not 'active'). This is not a complete list of labour market programmes, since in some countries, specific measures of work-sharing (reduction of average weekly hours and expansion of part-time work) and 'contractation' (the legalisation of particular forms of employment contract) have at least as much, probably more, importance in the national debate.[3]

In a standard view, the public employment service (PES) increases employment and reduces unemployment by facilitating vacancy-filling and job-finding with a minimum of delay and cost. Among the arguments for public funding of the job-broking service may be, first, that job broking is a natural monopoly because the centralisation of all vacancy and jobseeker information in a single agency is the most efficient arrangement (where there are many agencies, employers and jobseekers have to contact them all to be sure of identifying the best match); second, that private agencies may engage in abusive practices; and third, that only a free public service can provide special help to people with otherwise poor labour market prospects. (Similar arguments have sometimes been advanced to justify not just public funding but also a legal monopoly for the PES, that is, a ban on private placement agencies and/or a legal requirement that employers should notify all vacancies to the PES).

Labour market training of unemployed adults reduces unemployment for the duration of the training (by taking the participants out of the labour market), but this in itself only interrupts unemployment spells. Overall unemployment spell lengths are reduced if participation in training programmes reduces the expected subsequent duration of unemployment. Training should not only increase the probability of exit from unemployment, but also (because workers are made more productive) reduce the probability of re-entry to unemployment. Training may work by improving participants' level of general education, or by providing the specific skills needed in growing sectors — in the latter case it reduces mismatch unemployment. Apprenticeship and youth training work similarly. All forms of training should contribute to productivity and competitiveness in the economy as a whole.

Direct job creation (usually in the public sector) should increase total employment directly. When participation is temporary (which is the normal practice), such schemes are sometimes called 'work experience', and they should then enhance future employability, although the requirements of 'additionality' (see below) may imply that work conditions do not well approximate those in regular jobs.

Subsidies to regular employment in the private sector need to be selective: otherwise they become equivalent to a change in employer contributions or payroll taxes. Purely incremental employment subsidies, for example subsidies paid to firms which increase this year's payroll relative to last year's, are rather rare. One more common method of targeting is to pay the subsidy only for hires from particular groups such as the long-term or otherwise difficult-to-place unemployed. This may make it possible to employ people whose productivity is temporarily below benefit or minimum wage levels, and thus increase the equilibrium level of total employment. Subsidised placement of the unemployed in a private firm should improve the individual's employability by providing work experience in a real business situation and, since it leads to the acquisition of firm-specific skills, it may lead to a permanent position in the firm. A second common method of targeting restricts payment to firms in temporary difficulty on condition (for example during a recession) that they retain workers who would otherwise have been made redundant until business recovers. For both forms of targeting, problems such as 'deadweight' and 'displacement' are major concerns. 'Deadweight' normally refers to the proportion of the target group which would have become (in the latter case, would have remained) employed even in the absence of the subsidy. 'Substitution' in the case of a programme for hiring the long-term unemployed may refer to a reduction in hiring of the short-term unemployed. 'Deadweight' might also refer to the difference between the number of subsidised hires and the net increase in employment in the firms using the subsidy. 'Displacement' may then refer to indirect effects on employment in firms which do not use or are not granted the subsidy.

Early retirement for labour market reasons involves grants of early pensions to the unemployed above a certain age. If unemployment is analysed as an equilibrium phenomenon, grants of pension to workers who would otherwise be or become employed must be seen as a form of 'deadweight' reducing the effectiveness of the measure. However, the average unemployment rate should still be reduced by concentrating reductions of the labour force on a group with a high expected unemployment rate, such as the long-term unemployed already close to retirement age. A simpler view may be that withdrawals from the labour force have no effect on total employment and thus result mechanically in a fall in total unemployment. In this case, any employment losses among older workers will lead to jobs being filled by unemployed younger workers — a positive form of 'displacement'.

Microeconomic evaluation procedures and findings.

Corresponding to standard views about how ALMPs work are two well-known methods of evaluation for ALMPs. One compares re-employment probabilities (and/or some other outcomes) between participants in training and job creation programmes and a control group that did not participate. Another method involves calculations of deadweight and displacement effects in order to provide an estimate of 'net' hirings from the target group or a 'net' effect on employment.

Other evaluation methods — which are less specific to ALMPs — include surveys (for example, asking employers or programme participants what impact the ALMP had) and historical/statistical analysis (for example, an increase in exit rates from long-term unemployment has been cited as evidence that the United Kingdom's Restart policy, targeted on the long-term unemployed, was successful).

WHAT CAN WE LEARN FROM STUDIES OF RE-EMPLOYMENT PROBABILITIES?

Workers who participate in an ALMP, such as vocational guidance or a training course, have different characteristics from workers who do not participate, making it difficult to know whether the ALMP itself or these characteristics are responsible for differences in later outcomes for the two groups. Some summary findings from studies which use random-assignment techniques to control for this problem, or attempt to control for it statistically, are as follows.

First, studies of interviews and intensive counselling of unemployed from the United Kingdom (in 1980), and Sweden (in 1975) (Royston, quoted by Blackwell, and Delander, quoted by Björklund, both in OECD, 1991) have shown increases in the re-employment rates of a randomly selected group of unemployed; US experiments have also tended to find a significant impact on re-employment rates from intensified counselling. Because intensive counselling is a relatively cheap form of ALMP, results tend to suggest these measures are cost-effective.

Second, studies of training programmes indicate, according to the tentative conclusions of the international survey by Björklund (1991, p.59) that in general 'employment and training programmes have had their greatest impact and largest social returns for those who have had the least previous labour market experience and are most disadvantaged. Most evaluations found that programmes work better for women than for men, for those less educated and poorer than for those better educated and with higher income. For seriously disadvantaged males, there is little evidence pointing to any particular employment and training policy as effective.' Several European countries seem to have more positive results with high rates of job-finding (around 70 or 80 per cent, except in recession) among the unemployed who have learnt specific new skills in vocational training centres. In the Netherlands, De Koning *et al.* (1990) found that people leaving courses which train the unemployed in metalwork and building had only half the subsequent duration of unemployment of people who were otherwise similar (so far as could be measured) but had recently lost a job (no such impact could be detected for courses in clerical work).

Consistent with the above, OECD (1993), after reviewing the evaluation literature, finds a tendency for programmes with no estimated impact often to be those which were broadly targeted and implemented as an 'entitlement' for all unemployed, rather than in connection with special efforts of job counselling.

WHAT CAN WE LEARN FROM ESTIMATES OF PROGRAMME DEADWEIGHT AND DISPLACEMENT?

'Deadweight', at the microeconomic level, can in principle be measured by experimental techniques, for example by offering hiring subsidies only to randomly selected individuals or firms so as to observe what proportion of subsidised hires would have been made in the absence of the subsidy. Such estimates are a useful step in assessing the overall effect of an ALMP. However, there are other less immediately apparent effects which are more diffused throughout the economy. Analysis may estimate, for example, substitution in product markets (whereby a subsidy to some firms causes a reduction in employment in firms without the subsidy) or the effect of the subsidy on wage levels. There is no clear distinction between a comprehensive estimate of 'displacement' through these and other mechanisms, and a general evaluation of the overall final impact of an ALMP on unemployment.

The wider picture

The definition and coverage of the OECD's database on public spending on labour market programmes

Economists sometimes conclude a research report by saying that a lack of suitable data is the main barrier to further progress, when the real problem is that the economic model is such a crude approximation that its variables do not in fact exist in any precise sense. The variable for which suitable data is lacking — and this can apply to variables such as 'earnings' or 'unemployment' as well as to 'corporatism' or 'the strength of employment protection legislation' — is often a many-dimensioned phenomenon where the significance and even existence of particular components vary through time and across countries, depending on the institutional environment. In this context, any set of 'data' is a summary, reflecting general definitional principles and many specific definitional decisions. The definitions and detailed coverage by country of the spending categories in the OECD's labour market policy data have been well documented in OECD (1988, pp.84–114) and OECD (1990, pp.93–130), but some interpretative remarks will help explain their significance.

First, in practice, the OECD's labour market policy spending data often correspond to elements in the budget of the Labour Ministry of each country, but there is a major exception to this principle in respect of unemployment insurance benefits, which are included regardless of whether they are financed by another ministry or a non-governmental social insurance fund.

Second, various measures which do not involve public spending may be functional equivalents of other measures which do involve spending. For example, in one country regulation may prevent firms from laying off workers or closing down loss-making plants, while in another subsidies are paid to avoid layoffs and closures. 'Tax expenditures' such as exemptions from employer social security contributions in respect of employment of certain target groups may not be budgeted as a form of labour market spending. Regular public sector employment may be managed to promote employment of unemployed people: thus, in a number of countries, conventions specify that all vacancies in the public sector must be notified to the public employment service, and such an agreement may, without any specific budget allocation, be equivalent to an increase in spending on the PES. In the related area of general training of employed workers (which is not included in the OECD labour market policy spending data set), some countries have a legal obligation for employers to spend a proportion of the wage bill on training (1.2 per cent in France), others make payment of training levies into funds controlled by employers and unions obligatory, while others have training levies controlled by another Ministry, such as Japan's Ministry of Trade and Industry.

Third, a number of categories of spending which are not specifically targeted on the unemployed or employed groups at risk of unemployment (and thus are omitted from the OECD data set) may nevertheless influence unemployment or have an employment-related motivation. Spending on the training of employed people in general, mentioned above, is a prime example. Others cases are: public investment in depressed regions; local government spending to attract business to the locality; upper secondary education for 16–18-year-olds with a vocational training component (which resembles subsidies to apprenticeship schemes or Youth Training in the United

Kingdom, which are included); subsidies to adult education courses, which may provide a significant proportion of training for the unemployed; and general help to people setting up small businesses.

Some further issues arise concerning the definition of particular categories of labour market spending in the OECD data set and the allocation of particular spending items among them.

Public services and administration usually include spending on administering unemployment benefits which usually amounts to between one and two thirds of the total in this category. However, in a few countries (Denmark, Finland, the Netherlands, New Zealand) it has not been included for practical reasons (in the first three cases, non-governmental union/employer or industry-based funds are involved). This category includes mobility allowances and some lighter forms of training such as one-week 'Restart' courses in the United Kingdom.

Subsidised employment includes in Finland 'public works to support employment', which is a transfer from the Labour Administration to other bodies covering about 2 per cent of total spending on public sector investment. In Denmark this category does not include the 'job offer' scheme, which is listed as 'labour market training' even though it involves employment 'at normal contractual pay and working conditions' (CEC, 1988) in a private sector enterprise or in the public sector. This category in general covers only payments to employers; the re-employment bonus in Japan and the payments of unemployment insurance (UI) during employment (benefits paid to persons in involuntary part-time work in Belgium and Norway) are included in the 'unemployment compensation' line, and are thus not counted as 'active' spending.

Unemployment compensation in the United Kingdom includes housing benefit paid to the unemployed as well as unemployment insurance and assistance (Income Support). However, few if any other countries include housing benefits in this line. Australia, Ireland and New Zealand include all regular assistance benefits: countries such as Austria, France, Germany and Spain include unemployment insurance and unemployment assistance but not social assistance (minimum income) payments to unemployed people: the United States includes AFDC, but not Food Stamps: and in Belgium, Canada, Denmark, Finland and Norway, the data cover only UI spending.[4] As mentioned above, figures for Belgium include payments to people in part-time employment, but Family Credit in the UK (which could have a similar effect, but is not conditional on past or current employment difficulties) is not included. Some countries such as Austria and Spain budget social security contributions paid for the unemployed as unemployment compensation, whereas in other countries, where the unemployed are exempted or social security is tax-financed, the 'unemployment compensation' line represents only money finally received by the unemployed.

Early retirement for labour market reasons generally covers only explicit early retirement schemes — such as the 'unemployment pension' to which older long-term unemployed benefit claimants are entitled in Finland. Unemployment benefits paid to older long-term unemployed benefit claimants who are exempted from requirements to register unemployed, search for work or be available for work in Belgium, Germany, New Zealand and the United Kingdom are not included in this line. (In Belgium and Germany but not the United Kingdom these unemployment benefits to older workers paid under relaxed conditions are included in the 'unemployment compensation' line.) Disability pensions (often received by those with labour market difficulties) are, of course, not included either.

The complications involved in defining, and thus in measuring, 'labour market spending' go far towards explaining why a close correlation between such spending and the unemployment rate in a cross-country analysis cannot be expected. This highlights the importance of understanding individual country situations, even when using data that have been standardised as far as possible.

Some main characteristics of active labour market programmes

It would be wrong to imagine that the search for programme efficiency has led to a situation where all programmes are equally effective, at the margin; the effectiveness of an ALMP depends strongly on various of its characteristics.

DURATION OF PARTICIPATION

Job creation places, training programmes or employment subsidies are generally temporary, with six months being perhaps a typical duration. Many participants thus re-enter unemployment after this period. However, some programmes have created permanent jobs or subsidies — Japan (for coal miners), Belgium and the Netherlands currently have people employed indefinitely on job creation programmes, and Spain has had a programme since 1980 reducing employer social security contributions indefinitely for employers who hire both younger (under 26) unemployed workers and older (over 45) long-term unemployed workers. Programmes offering temporary places aim to increase chances of finding a regular unsubsidised job (perhaps by extension of the inital job, in the case of employment subsidies). Permanent job creation programmes tend to be favoured where there is a political consensus against allowing temporary contracts for regular jobs (as a principle of social protection), and on the grounds that they increase the

total volume of employment as much as temporary programmes and are targeted on people judged to be otherwise 'unemployable'.

ADDITIONALITY

This criterion implies that jobs created should be additional to spending that
would otherwise have taken place, and that output from the work should
not substitute for (or compete with) other output. Thus 'additionality'
implies a minimisation of deadweight and displacement effects. It may be
required on public policy grounds, but also by unions and business associations who want to avoid the subsidised work displacing the demand for
work by their members.

The principle of additionality tends to conflict with the aim of producing useful output, which reduces public cost per job and makes working
conditions more like those in market jobs. In practice, 'additionality' requirements tend to lead to projects such as dredging a disused canal, a project
that is considered useful but would never have been carried out if the full cost
had to be paid!

There is no general agreement that 'additionality' increases the effectiveness of labour market programmes. A measure which reserves regular
job vacancies in the public sector for unemployed people is a form of labour
market programme that runs counter to the principle of 'additionality', yet it
is often implemented through subsidies paid by the central government to
local government for hires of unemployed people into regular jobs.

REMUNERATION OR SUBSISTENCE ALLOWANCE LEVELS

Remuneration for participants on a labour market programme may be equal
to unemployment benefit, or involve some increase above benefit, or offer a
'market' wage rate. For particular categories such as youths with a training
allowance, remuneration may be below regular unemployment benefit levels.

METHOD OF INDUCTION

An ALMP may be supply-constrained (more willing applicants than places)
or demand constrained (more places than willing applicants). Decisions
about who enters an ALMP may be made mainly by the participants
themselves (if programmes are demand-constrained or roughly in balance),
by the programme managers (for example, suppliers of training) or by the
PES. At one extreme, unemployed workers can find a training programme
or study course that interests them, and the PES will then pay the fees and
provide a subsistence allowance: this will still be counted as 'active' labour

market policy spending. At the opposite extreme, the PES may operate essentially by issuing instructions to report to training courses. Of course, discussion between PES officers and the unemployed person may lead to situations in between these two extremes. ALMPs may also be targeted using objective criteria. For example training may be obligatory for all workers under 50 who have been unemployed for a year, and be available optionally for older workers in the same circumstances.

The relationship of ALMPs to other labour market institutions

In North America and the United Kingdom, particular ALMPs tend to be implemented (or dropped) on the basis of the kinds of criteria used in evaluation studies, as discussed above. However, in other countries policymakers appear to be largely indifferent to these considerations. Evaluations of programmes in terms of the post-programme employment performance of participants may not answer some important policy concerns, often those related to the interaction of ALMPs with other labour market institutions.

UNEMPLOYMENT BENEFITS

The impact of any ALMP is strongly dependent upon its relationship to unemployment benefit, the main alternative status for most participants. Remuneration on training courses, and so on, not significantly higher than unemployment benefit (after work- or course-related expenses) is one of the factors that can lead to a shortage of people willing to participate.

Participation is often obligatory in law, that is, benefit may be stopped temporarily or permanently if the worker refuses to accept a programme place as directed by the PES, yet may be largely voluntary in practice because the PES rarely uses this power. When participation is voluntary, the availability of ALMPs adds to the range of options open to unemployed people, and thus may make unemployment more attractive (or less unattractive) than it would otherwise be.[5] By contrast, if participation is effectively obligatory, ALMPs may make entry to unemployment less attractive (or more unattractive) than it would otherwise be.

In most countries the duration of unemployment insurance benefits is limited. When these end, some people (for example, those with a spouse in full-time work) are not eligible for assistance benefit, and for those who are eligible assistance benefit may involve a sharp fall in income. In some countries, ALMPs commence when unemployment (insurance) benefits end.[6] At the level of policy thinking, ALMPs may then be seen as a means of maintaining the incomes of the unemployed, more than as a means of solving unemployment — 'public works' in many countries in the earlier twentieth century were often conceived in these terms.

LOCAL GOVERNMENT

Job creation programmes are often organised by local government and subsidies for hiring unemployed people into regular jobs may be taken up by local government more often than by private sector employers. Local government involvement may be essential for the success of ALMPs because national administrations lack the management resources needed to 'create' meaningful jobs in thousands of localities. Moreover, in small communities, local government officials may themselves be familiar with the characteristics and the problems of long-term unemployed people on an individual basis.

Often, responsibility for paying assistance benefits (for unemployed people without insurance benefits) falls on some level of local government. It has, for example, traditionally fallen on municipalities in Nordic countries, on the *Länder* in Germany, on Cantons in Switzerland, on Provinces in Canada, and on municipalities in Belgium and the Netherlands. The RWW assistance benefit in the Netherlands is 90 per cent financed by central government, but this is fairly exceptional; the Minimex benefit in Belgium is only 50 per cent financed by central government (these are universal entitlement assistance benefits, like Income Support in the United Kingdom). In some other countries the situation is complex but local/regional governments bear a large proportion of the true final cost of each benefit claim.

Local government responsibility for financing assistance benefits gives it an incentive to find work for unemployed assistance beneficiaries and even insurance beneficiaries, since insurance beneficiaries if not attended to will later become assistance beneficiaries. When they are responsible for financing benefits, municipalities will take into account the benefit saving (which may cover a substantial proportion of the wage) when considering the cost of hiring an unemployed worker. They also have an incentive to withdraw benefit entitlement from workers who refuse jobs. When insurance benefits have limited duration, local governments can set up programmes where the created jobs last just long enough to requalify the workers for (centrally financed) unemployment insurance benefits. Local government action to create temporary jobs for unemployed workers, motivated partly by this consideration, seems to be a pattern of labour market behaviour in at least five OECD countries (Denmark, Finland, Norway, Canada and Germany). In Sweden, local authorities tend to avoid ever starting social welfare payment to employable claimants. People requesting welfare would, rather, be sent to the National Labour Market Board, which itself would be expected to offer a 'relief job' in the absence of any benefit.

If a local government is paying unemployment benefit to a worker, the marginal cost to it of hiring the worker is the gross wage in work less unemployment benefit. If financing of the benefit is transferred to central government, the marginal cost to a municipality of hiring the unemployed worker will rise, unless central government pays an employment subsidy equivalent to the level of benefit paid during unemployment. In countries where financing of benefit has been shifting from local to central goverment, it may be expected that increasing large subsidies from central government will be necessary to maintain an unchanged degree of job creation by local government.

As the financing of ALMPs shifts from local to central government, the incentives as regards the administration of ALMPs also change; local authorities may lose concern with deadweight (deadweight meaning in this context that central government finances work that local governments would have done anyway; this is called 'fiscal displacement' in American discussion) and cease to argue for benefit disqualification of workers who have refused the offer of a job. This may influence the administration of insurance benefits, since the local offices of the national organisation which pays unemployment insurance benefits may identify more with concerns of the local community than with concerns of their own bureaucracy at national level.

According to Schmid *et al.* (1991) 'While other comparative institutional studies have focused on systems of unemployment insurance in isolation, none has investigated the interrelationship between the financing of wage-replacement benefits and active labour market policy, which is central to our study'. Germany (home country of those authors) is exceptional in that active labour market policy is financed from unemployment insurance funds. A more general study, covering the financing of both insurance and assistance unemployment benefits and the administration of ALMPs remains to be written.

One indication that local/regional government activity may be a significant factor in the effectiveness of overall labour market policy is given in table 6.2. It shows two criteria for unemployment performance, the increase of the unemployment rate between 1967–73 and 1980–88, and the average level of unemployment over 1980–88. In all the seven countries where unemployment rose by less than 3 percentage points (Austria, Finland, Japan, Norway, Sweden, Switzerland and the United States), local/regional government receives some revenue from income tax. Except in Austria, these receipts are based on local/regional incomes, rather than incomes nationwide (this gives local governments an incentive to reduce local unemployment).

Table 6.2 *Financial autonomy of regional and local government and unemployment rates*

	Proportion of income tax received by regional and local government 1988	Unemployment rate (a)	
		Average 1980-88	Increase, 1967-73 to 1980-88
Australia (b)	0.0	7.7	5.7
Austria	(c)	3.3	1.8
Belgium	9.6	11.1	7.5
Canada (b)	37.3	9.5	4.3
Denmark	53.2	8.4	7.4
Finland	49.7	5.0	2.4
France	0.0	9.0	6.5
Germany (b)	(c)	6.1	5.1
Ireland	0.0	14.3	8.8
Italy	0.0	9.3	3.7
Japan	32.3	2.5	1.3
Netherlands	0.0	9.9	8.3
New Zealand	0.0	4.3	3.9
Norway	60.7	2.5	0.8
Spain	(c)	17.8	15.0
Sweden	70.8	2.6	0.4
Switzerland(b)	75.2	0.6	0.6
UK	0.0	10.3	6.9
US (b)	18.1	7.4	2.9

Sources: for unemployment, OECD data drawn from the CEP-OECD database: for income taxes, OECD (1993b).

(a) OECD standardised unemployment rate where available: otherwise (Austria, Denmark, Ireland, New Zealand, Switzerland) the rate on a national basis.

(b) Federal state.

(c) In these countries a share of taxes raised on personal incomes nationwide is allocated to regional governments.

The group with an average 1980-88 unemployment rate below 8 per cent is made up of the same seven countries plus Germany, Australia and New Zealand; the first two are federal states and New Zealand is, of course, a rather small and homogeneous economy.

Among the three countries with local/regional financial autonomy but poor unemployment performance (Belgium, Denmark, and Spain), Belgium and Denmark are exceptional for having a very long duration of unemployment insurance benefits (which are nationally financed), with special provisions to allow new entrants to the labour market to qualify. This shields local/regional governments from most of the direct financial consequences of local unemployment. Thus in Belgium the 'Mimimex' (assistance) benefit, which is 50 per cent financed by local authorities, is received by well under 1 per cent of the population.

PROGRAMME PROVIDERS OTHER THAN LOCAL GOVERNMENT

Providers of programme places include regional training authorities, private sector educational and training establishments, regular private sector firms, and enterprises set up specifically to create jobs. Some tension commonly arises between the programme providers, who aim to provide the courses that unemployed people want to follow and take in people with good learning abilities, and the PES which wants to see training oriented towards occupations where there are jobs, and wants trainers to take in the more difficult-to-place unemployed people.

ALMPS AND 'CONTRACTATION'

In Spain, Italy, and to some extent other countries (such as Belgium and France), one important form of labour market policy in the 1980s has been legislation which makes legal or facilitates (in terms of social security treatment or conditions to be met, for example) non-standard forms of employment contract, sometimes with subsidies provided. This concerns permanent part-time contracts as well as fixed-term contracts. The issue of what employment contracts are used, and under what conditions, is referred to, in Spanish or Italian, as 'contractation', in much the same way as in English discussion refers to 'remuneration'. In the countries concerned the impact of the subsidies is difficult to distinguish from the impact of the deregulation and even the impact on unemployment benefit eligibility (see below).

THE CYCLICALITY OF ALMP SPENDING

Schmid *et al.* (1991) discuss the cyclicality of ALMP spending at some length. They find that only in Sweden has ALMP spending consistently been adjusted countercyclically. In Germany, the financing of ALMP from insurance revenues has sometimes provoked procyclicality in ALMP spending, that is, when unemployment rises, ALMP spending is cut because spending on benefits increases.

The countercyclicality of ALMP spending in Sweden has an institutional basis in the strong management role of the PES. At least before recent increases in unemployment, PES officers managed unemployment spells individual by individual and, in the case of continued failure to find a market job, could eventually decide that a placement in an ALMP was needed. The national administration of the PES uses rules which are intended to ensure a supply of ALMP places adequate for this purpose, adjusting to unemployment rates which vary across regions and through time.

Other countries have some entitlement or semi-entitlement programmes, for example, subsidies to employers hiring a long-term unemployed person, which introduce a countercyclical element into ALMP spending. However, many programmes have budgets preset at the beginning of the year, or are managed without a direct link to what is going on in PES offices, factors which weaken the countercyclicality of spending.

PROGRAMME SIZE

The impact of labour market programmes may vary through time. In the case of the United Kingdom's programme of Restart interviews of unemployed people, some initial participants may have seen calls to interview as a sign that the Employment Service had detected or suspected something wrong, and reacted strongly. In later rounds, interviews probably had a lesser psychological impact. Early rounds probably assisted the people most easy to help, so that later rounds find it more difficult to achieve the same results. From other points of view, though, programme stability may be a benefit, as staff develop more effective routines and experience leads to refinements in programme design.

Experimental evaluations have often been made for programmes that are in size terms a drop in the labour market ocean, and the results may not be a good guide to performance of a programme that is expanded to become a major and permanent component of a country's labour market strategy. Declining returns to scale may come into play. Thus, vocational training may be successful at a certain level, but difficult to expand because specific training is valued by employers only for a limited range of occupations. In the case of a job-creation programme, expansion may make it increasingly difficult to identify meaningful activities for participants at the same time as satisfying 'additionality' aims (see above). Take-up of a small subsidy for new hires may be low. In general, programmes can be expanded by making conditions more generous (training for a wider range of occupations, increasing the hiring subsidy, paying the organisers of job creation projects better), but this increases the cost per hire or per place created and can lead to self-defeating distortions in the regular labour market.

At the aggregate level, once an employment strategy has a significant impact in reducing total unemployment it may suffer declining returns as the remaining stock of unemployed are less easily 'employable', and further reductions in unemployment may generate increasing wage pressures.

However, at the aggregate level, there are also mechanisms of increasing returns to a package of ALMPs that has a significant impact on total unemployment. A decline in numbers unemployed leads directly to an increase in the flow of job vacancies per unemployed person. This facilitates further falls in unemployment, since benefit administration and programmes such as interviews of the long-term unemployed are inherently more effective when 'real jobs' can be offered to the unemployed more frequently. Programmes of a relatively moderate size are naturally presented as options and are taken up by only some unemployed people, and this reduces the (average) opportunity cost of entering unemployment. Further expansion of programmes begins to eliminate the possibility of long-term passive benefit receipt, thus increasing the (average) opportunity cost of entering unemployment.

It may also be noted (see above) that when countries experience a 10 per cent reduction in unemployment, on average they cut ALMP spending by a smaller percentage, that is, ALMP spending per unemployed person rises as unemployment falls. Thus, as unemployment falls it may become possible to effectively train people who would be almost unemployable with a higher unemployment rate.

The power of positive feedbacks, by which low unemployment makes active labour market policy measures more effective, is one of the main reasons that many countries were for many years able to maintain low unemployment, and yet after a deep recession moved seemingly permanently to a higher unemployment rate, long after the recession passed.

Some national experiences

With inevitable oversimplification, this section briefly describes some aspects of how ALMPs have affected the labour market in particular countries, illustrating in a more concrete way some of the points made above.

Finland and Norway were both for many years models of Scandinavian labour market policy. More recently, both have experienced sharp rises in unemployment, starting in 1988 in Norway and 1991 in Finland, taking the unemployment rates to 6 or 7 per cent in Norway, and over 15 per cent in Finland. So labour market analysts need to ask whether the rise in unemployment — above its previously sustained low levels — can plausibly be explained in terms of the unprecedented strength of recent macroeconomic shocks, whether it will be persistent, and if so is it because these countries have abandoned active labour market policy or because active labour market policy has ceased to be effective at historically high unemployment rates?

Looking back about twenty years, unemployment benefits entitlements were significantly lower. In Finland in 1970, 57 per cent of wage earners had insurance coverage and this gave benefits for a maximum 150 days (twenty-five weeks) a year; in Norway in 1970, insurance cover was universal, but benefits had a maximum duration of twenty weeks in any year. Municipalities bore the immediate cost of assistance benefits in Norway, although there was a system of central government help for muncipalities in financial difficulties. Overall, social assistance in 1972 was 78 per cent financed by municipalities in Finland and 86 per cent in Norway (NOSOSCO, 1976). So all unemployed were a potential burden on the finances of their municipalities, which took an active interest in keeping benefit administration tight. In Norway in 1972 a programme rationalising local PES offices into a national structure was under way, but this had not been completed, and the PES remained profoundly marked by the former system of municipal responsibility for the employment exchanges. In some regions, the local PES office strictly applied the principle that benefits could only be paid as a last resort, benefits being refused to candidates who had refused jobs that local employment commissions had judged appropriate for them. There is some statistical evidence that this kind of tough administration of benefits dwindled away during the 1980s (OECD, 1992, table 3.6). Public works had been the main form of active labour market policy in the 1958-9 recession, but were run down after the early 1960s (OECD, 1972, p.87).

In Finland, as late as the early 1960s, state or municipal public works were the major options offered to the unemployed. The volume of public works was varied countercyclically in the 1960s, although in the 1970s and 1980s the countercyclical nature of this spending was less evident and labour administration influence over the content of public works fell greatly (Lilja et al., 1990, p.145). Another element in labour market policy in these times is that unemployed workers were expected to be geographically mobile if necessary in order to find a new job. Although the central government provided mobility subsidies to back up this policy, it was unpopular with municipalities themselves.

Pressure from the municipalities, and not (only) pressure from unions or voters, may have been a principal factor pushing the financing of benefits increasingly onto central government. Both Finland and Norway, in one or two stages, later made their benefits more generous — the maximum duration of a single spell rising in 1985 to eighty weeks in Norway (in 1992, the potential duration rose still further to 186 weeks) and 500 days (two years) in Finland. In 1985 Finland also introduced a system of universal means-tested unemployment assistance benefit, financed at the national level. Responsibility for the unemployed remains at the municipal level only in Norway, and there only for those who have never worked, mainly youths.

Although recent rises in unemployment in both countries have been widely attributed to macroeconomic, financial and terms-of-trade problems, from a labour market policy point of view, the changes to benefit entitlements and financing could explain why current disturbances have been less well resisted (in terms of the size of the rise in unemployment and subsequent persistence at a high level) than earlier ones. Although 'passive' spending on unemployment benefits has risen sharply, political commitment to the 'active' part of labour market policy was maintained in the 1980s. Finland in the 1987 Employment Act guaranteed a job to all long-term unemployed and in Norway, total 'active' spending more than doubled, as a percentage of GDP, between 1988 and 1991. However, there are some signs that ALMP spending at current levels may be less effective than in the past, or even counterproductive.

High rates of subsidy (about 50 per cent of labour costs) need to be paid to municipalities and private sector employers to get them to create temporary jobs. In Norway, many private sector employers want to hire only for the duration of the subsidy (this has led to attempts at restricting the subsidies to permanent jobs). In Finland, private sector employers have even begun to advertise vacancies requiring applications only from the long-term unemployed (who qualify for the subsidy). In the more depressed areas, municipalities are said to be increasingly relying on PES subsidies to finance their own staffing except for higher-level jobs. This pattern is also emerging in some state jobs — thus, university lecturers' contracts are said to be systematically not renewed, in order to permit hiring of an unemployed person.

Subsidies for hiring the long-term unemployed have therefore, in some subsections of the labour market, been increasing separations from employment and making it more difficult for the short-term unemployed to find work. The training element of ALMPs is also coming under strain. In Norway there is a shortage of schoolteachers, due to the expansion of training courses for the unemployed which use school premises and local schoolteachers. Such training courses are popular but they may not be making a great deal of difference to job-finding chances, or providing much of a work test for the administration of unemployment benefit.

At least in a partial way, current experiences illustrate the problem that ALMP spending is a flow of money towards the unemployed. It can be difficult to keep spending effective or prevent the creation of a direct or indirect financial incentive (for the individual, the employer, or the municipality) that induces activity that raises unemployment. Certainly, today's ALMP spending differs in content from the spending of many years ago, when unemployed people who asked for help from public authorities could only expect to be offered places on public works projects, with no period of passive benefit receipt. It may be premature to conclude that Scandinavian labour market policy no longer works better than its counterparts in many EC countries, but the system is clearly at risk.[7]

Denmark has to some extent modelled its labour market policy on that of its Northern neighbours, and like Finland and Sweden it has a voluntary system of unemployment insurance benefit with less than 100 per cent coverage. However, in 1970 it already had a generous system of insurance benefit paid for up to 2½ years. The 'job offer', the main form of ALMP, provides slightly more than six months of employment to people without benefit or approaching termination, thus (re)qualifying them for benefit. For many years critics have said that, since the unemployed person never needs to make a job-search effort even when benefit termination is approaching, these arrangements make wage-related benefits effectively indefinite.

A more recent form of the 'job offer', the 'education offer' scheme, 'has been widely judged among the unemployed to serve as a stepping-stone for benefit renewal rather than as enhancing job prospects. Education offers appear to have had negligible effects on the probability of participants being hired, and this holds for work-oriented courses as well as the courses aimed at giving practical work experience' (OECD, 1993a). As this kind of case shows, ALMPs may be aimed largely at reducing the hardship that would otherwise arise from the cessation of passive benefits. It may not mean much to ask whether the ALMP-related job offer in isolation reduces unemployment. As compared to the alternative of truly indefinite unemployment benefits, the job offer in Denmark provides an institutional basis for ensuring that unemployment spells are broken after 2½ years. As compared with the alternative of having no 'job offer' and allowing insurance benefits to terminate (until market work is found) after 2½ years, it may raise unemployment.

In Belgium labour market policy spending, as shown in table 6.1, is high and its role is different again. Whereas Scandinavian countries have traditionally had short benefit durations, temporary ALMP places, and a philosophy of 'activism', Belgium has long had an indefinite benefit duration and a tendency for ALMP places to be indefinite. Perhaps more than in any other country, Belgian policy has been based upon what might be called a 'mechanistic' model of unemployment in which the presumption of the policymakers is that any new job created or split into two part-time jobs, and any unemployed person hired or removed from the labour force, reduces aggregate unemployment. In the 1980s this found expression particularly in schemes which allow older workers to take early retirement conditional on an unemployed person being hired as a replacement (*prépension de retraite*), or place the very-long-term unemployed into permanent subsidised jobs (*Troisième Circuit de Travail*).

In 1982 Belgium also liberalised a preexisting provision in the benefit system which allows benefit claimants who find (only) part-time work to claim benefit for all normal hours not worked (previously, the provision applied only to wholly unemployed days). As in Norway, the 1980s saw an explosion in this type of benefit claim (there are now about two part-time beneficiaries for every three full-time beneficiaries in both countries). Policy thinking has at times reasoned that each entry into part-time work reduces unemployment (the worker concerned goes from unemployment to employment status). If this is correct, payment of unemployment benefit to part-time workers could be counted as Belgium's most significant form of ALMP (over 200 000 people). However, with so many part-time claims now arising, from the behavioural perspective it seems clear that these provisions are drawing some people into unemployment so as to qualify for later benefit payment while working part-time.

In the United Kingdom, the Restart programme has been extensively examined and no more will be said here. Less attention has been given (at least abroad) to Youth Training (formerly Youth Opportunities Programme and Youth Training Scheme), in many ways a spectacular success of labour market policy in the 1980s. Under YT, employers are subsidised to train young people and the trainees are paid a small weekly allowance. According to some critics, trainees were used as cheap labour by employers, and by 1988 or so there was more emphasis on ensuring that YT participation led to formal qualifications.

Aided by demographic trends, most countries achieved some reduction in youth unemployment over this period, but the fall in the United Kingdom was very large — the unemployment rate of 16–19-year-old males fell from 35 per cent in 1982 to 6.5 per cent in 1989 (OECD Labour Force Statistics, Part III).

According to regression-based estimates controlling for various personal and labour market factors, based on the Scottish Young People's Survey in 1985 and 1986, participation in YT raised expected employment probabilities at the latter date from 0.60 to 0.77 for a typical 'advantaged' school-leaver (with good educational attainment and related characteristics) and from 0.11 to 0.22 for a 'disadvantaged' school-leaver (Main and Shelly, 1990). Such results, though clearly positive, probably cannot fully account for the size of the fall in youth unemployment rates. However, the availability of YT places also facilitated changes in the benefit environment. In 1983 rules were changed so that refusal of a place on YT could lead to benefit sanctions (in general, acceptance of training is not a condition for receipt of benefits in the UK), and in 1987 the Youth Training Scheme had been expanded sufficiently that (together with some improvement in the general employment situation and perhaps demographic trends) it was possible to guarantee a place to any unemployed young person (16–19-year-old male unemployment rate was still 21 per cent in 1987). In 1988, the government abolished Income Support (assistance benefit) for 16–17-year-olds; some other benefits were created but of limited duration and paid to parents, or only for 'severe hardship' cases. That year, of the 1.67 million 16–17-year-olds in Britain 39 per cent were in education, 30 per cent in employment, 24 per cent in YT, and 9 per cent unemployed (Brown, 1990, p.180).

The changes in benefits with associated expansion of YT were part of a long-term strategy: at the end of 1984, the then minister for job creation matters (Lord Young) stated the intention of making schooling, training or employment the only options for 16 and 17-year-olds (see Brown, 1990, for a description). In a sense, this was an application of a Scandinavian-style active labour market policy to a small segment of the labour market — a proof that this was possible even in a high-unemployment country and in the middle of the 1980s.

Such an improvement in unemployment rates could have been illusory if it indicated nothing more than, in effect, a postponement of unemployment at entry into the labour market from age 16 to age 18. This must have happened for many individuals, but statistics do nevertheless suggest a sharp overall improvement. The fall in male unemployment rates from 35 to 6.5 per cent refers to 16–19-year-olds — not only to the 16–17-year-olds affected by the benefit changes — and was accompanied by an increase in the labour force participation rate of the whole age group.

In the current deep recession, the reduction in youth unemployment has come under severe strain since regular hirings have fallen and employers have reduced their offers of YT places. Thus, it has been necessary to make up the gap in one of two ways: relaxing the administration of 'severe hardship' benefits (which remain available to 16–17-year-olds, but are meant to be very strictly administered), or putting increased resources into YT so as to maintain the guarantee of a place for every person who needs it. Thus, maintaining an effective 'active' policy through a recession is not an easy option: it requires a confluence of favourable circumstances, notably a sound institutional background and persistent effort and determination on the part of the government and administration.

After excluding PES administration and measures for the disabled, Switzerland spends only 0.01 per cent of GDP on active labour market measures (training, youth measures, subsidised employment/job creation), much the lowest of any OECD country, yet most of the time it has probably had something close to the lowest unemployment rate (on a standardised basis).

There was no compulsory national unemployment benefit prior to 1977 and, as late as 1974, coverage under insurance funds was only about 20 per cent. From its inception, the compulsory benefit system was tightly administered with visits to employment offices required two or three times a week and the unemployed required to prove that they had made efforts to find work, for example, in the form of written statements from firms. People are (or perhaps were, since unemployment is now rising) expected to accept even low-level jobs (such as waiter in a restaurant), with little sympathy for those who refused such jobs. Thus, Switzerland is the best example of the fact that an active market policy can consist of spending on nothing more than placement and benefit administration.

With such problems as the collapse and transformation of the watch industry, Switzerland has faced problems of 'structural adjustment' as severe as most OECD countries. However, in 1973-6 (though not to any great extent after this) Switzerland had a unique safety-valve through its ability to send back foreign ('guest') workers: the labour force declined 7 per cent over this period, preventing the appearance of significant unemployment. This clearly made it easier to keep the 'active' model of placement and benefit administration operating for the next fifteen years or so, substituting for the role which countercyclical ALMPs have played in Sweden.

Japan also spends little on active labour market policy. The job creation programme has no current intake; the jobs created (for example, for miners affected by closures) were permanent, and the scheme is now considered not to have been an effective tool of labour market adjustment. In contrast to the large amounts spent on training in general in Japan, labour market training programmes are small. They focus on providing specific vocational skills for unemployed persons with significant labour market difficulties (such as returning war orphans, who have had to insert themselves into Japanese society, starting by learning Japanese). Thus, ALMPs are highly targeted and are not an instrument for tackling unemployment in general. In fact, the most significant ALMP is probably the re-employment bonus, which is shown as the 'unemployment compensation' line in the OECD spending figures. Under this system, workers who find a job before they have exhausted more than half their total entitlement to insurance benefit receive a proportion (only one third to one half) of the remaining entitlement as a lump sum.

This scheme was actually in force from 1960 to 1975 when it was abolished (perhaps because, in the extreme boom conditions of 1973, this payment had accounted for more than half the total expenditure on unemployment benefits in some regions), but it was reinstated with some minor changes as from 1984. Japan also illustrates the principle that unemployment compensation can be a partly 'active' programme just as employment subsidies or training can be a partly 'passive' programme.

In Spain and Italy, the role of ALMP spending is different again. Labour market policy has above all to tackle the consequences of some well-known rigidities. Best known of these is that firms find it difficult to close plants or dismiss individual workers without paying heavy compensation. Given that hiring a worker can approximate to a lifetime commitment to pay a monthly salary even if the work involved becomes unprofitable or the worker performs poorly, firms have, especially since 1973, become cautious about hiring, leading to a heavy concentration of unemployment on youths (meaning roughly, people under 30 years old). For youths in Spain, unemployment benefits have become an important element in the picture recently, but many youths have no benefits and live with their families, perhaps with some earnings from black-market work or a family enterprise, for years.

In this context, labour market policy is largely oriented towards 'contractation' (as defined above). One important measure common to both Spain and Italy is the training contract. Laws passed in 1984 allow firms to sign contracts of limited duration (up to two or three years) when hiring workers who are unemployed and below a certain age, conditional on there being a training element in the work. These contracts benefit from a subsidy in the form of partial or total exemption from employer social security contributions. About half of the workers with such fixed-term contracts are later hired by the same employer on a permanent basis. About 300 000 or more such contracts each year have been signed in both Italy and Spain in recent years. Although the subsidies involved are important components of total labour market spending, it would be misleading to attribute the success of the programme to the subsidy. The main attraction of the 'training contract' is its fixed-term nature which gives the employer some chance to screen young workers before making a permanent hire.

The strategy of creating employment by allowing employers to use fixed-term contracts (which were previously illegal except in certain specific circumstances) has, in Spain, run into problems in relation to unemployment benefits. Until recently, dismissal of redundant workers involved in most cases prior permission (from the Labour Inspectorate) or a court case. Workers who left a job without having appealed to these procedures to resist dismissal were assumed to have quit, and thus have no right to unemployment benefit. But by signing a fixed-term contract, employers and employees often generate a benefit claim one or two years later, without any complex administrative procedures or controls. The rise in the unemployment benefit cost of fixed-term contracts, and a suspicion that the labour market was being distorted by deliberate rotation between fixed-term contract work and unemployment spells with benefit, was probably among the factors behind restrictive changes in both fixed-term contract legislation and benefit entitlements in 1992.

Conclusions

Once the basic parameters of an active labour market programme (ALMP) such as the level of remuneration for participants and the duration of participation have been set, it is probably reasonable to identify a successful programme design as one which gives a high post-programme employment rate for participants. A minimum aim for ALMP management strategy should be to keep track of performance in these terms and be aware of problems that may be developing, and modify, expand or cut back schemes as needed in an orderly way.

A more ambitious and difficult aim is to get ALMPs working together with benefit administration, placement work, and incomes and macroeconomic policies as part of an overall strategy that attenuates the rise in unemployment during a recession, and during the expansionary phase of the cycle rapidly re- establishes frequent applications for jobs and intensive PES efforts at placement as the norm. Various strategic considerations need to be taken into account when assessing how ALMPs have affected the unemployment rate of one country relative to another or anticipating how effective a policy initiative in a particular country may be. These considerations include incentives for workers, incentives for programme providers, benefit financing, and size-of-programme effects.

ALMPs can have positive or negative effects on workers' incentive to enter or remain in unemployment.[8] So long as entry to ALMPs is voluntary on the part of the unemployed person, the availability of an ALMP as an alternative to passive receipt of unemployment benefit is utility-equivalent to an increase in benefit level (or perhaps duration). Thus, the guarantee of a relief job when unemployment (insurance) benefit ends in some countries has reduced the incentive to find work that the ending of benefit would otherwise require. The payment of a subsistence allowance (or continued unemployment benefit) during quite long education and training courses, especially if these are chosen by the unemployed person, may encourage a 'training through unemployment' strategy. In some countries, the possibility of receiving benefit while working part-time has recently become widely known (part-time workers without the benefit learn about it from co-workers), and this has probably encouraged entries to unemployment. By contrast, when entry to ALMPs is managed by officers of the public employment service (PES), this might discourage entries to or continuation in unemployment, since the unemployed person may fear being put into an ALMP not of their choice or at an inconvenient moment.

Incentives for programme providers should be for them to manage the programmes so as reduce unemployment. But since payments to providers of ALMP places go where the unemployment is, there is a risk that indirect incentives to increase unemployment may arise. This is especially a problem for job creation schemes and hiring subsidies. A typical scheme might pay private employers and local authorities 50 per cent of wage costs, during the first year of employment, when they hire a long-term unemployed person. In the worst case this could generate micro labour markets where employers hire only long-term unemployed people and only temporarily, so as to maximise the proportion of the wage bill being subsidised. Workers in such micro labour markets can only alternate between one-year spells of unemployment and short-term employment with a subsidy, so that they are unemployed half the time.

The allocation of responsibility for financing the benefits of people who remain unemployed can affect the cost and effectiveness of ALMPs. If local government is financing benefits and managing ALMPs, it has an incentive to employ unemployed people whose output falls slightly short of the wage that has to be paid in employment (since this is cheaper than paying them benefit) and also an incentive to stop benefits for people who refuse such job offers.

Expansion of programmes may lead to declining or increasing returns to scale. In the case of training programmes, expansion may increasingly involve taking in people for whom training is not such an important barrier to employment, or may saturate the market for specific skills on which training can productively be targeted.[9] In the case of job creation programmes, as programmes expand it becomes increasingly difficult to find suitable activities that meet 'additionality' criteria. Increasing returns to scale arise as regards the rate of job (or ALMP place) offers to unemployed people; if ALMPs reduce unemployment to low levels, the frequency of job offers for people not in ALMPs is kept high, and this makes job-broking and benefit administration more effective.

In its heyday, active labour market policy in Scandinavian countries came close to an ideal labour market and social policy; it was an essential component (together with factors such as wage restraint and Keynesian economic management) of a strategy which came close to eliminating unemployment while providing a safety net against misfortune and poverty. This strategy depended on keeping unemployment benefit entitlements limited, ensuring an adequate supply of places on ALMPs, and never allowing the unemployment rate to rise to levels where truly 'passive' unemployment could emerge. The model was fragile and it may have broken down recently. But it would be wrong to exaggerate its fragility, for it resisted relatively well the two oil shocks of the 1970s which pushed many other countries into permanently higher unemployment rates. It deserves to remain a vision of success for labour market specialists, even if these countries now experience prolonged difficulty in trying to climb out of their current recessions.

Unemployment — at least that part of it due to redundancies — indicates that workers have not been producing enough of the right form of output to justify their wages. Since the problem is real, only real adjustments — possibly real wage reductions, but perhaps more often the learning of new skills or a change of workplace or residence — can solve it. Adjustments take place most rapidly if efforts are made on every side — the former employer, the unemployed person, and local government and other potential managers of ALMPs. Since the adjustments are microeconomic, central government cannot directly implement them. Its task is, rather, to create an institutional setting whereby the money it spends really promotes and encourages the necessary microeconomic adjustments, and does not become a transfer or get deflected from the adjustment aim. This paper has tried to illustrate what this generalisation means, more concretely, for active labour market policy.

Notes

1 The opinions expressed and arguments employed here are the responsibility of the author and do not necessarily represent those of the OECD.
2 The regressions with unemployment benefit given in the main text can be run another way round using the variable RP (replacement rate), defined as

$$RP = UB/U$$

that is, RP is the ratio of the share of unemployment compensation in GDP to the unemployment rate. This gives

$$\log(RP85) = c + 0.48(1.3)\log(U85)$$

or

$$\log(U85) = c + 0.13(1.3)\log(RP85)$$

that is, unemployment rates are slightly higher in countries with higher replacement rates. Since there are some 'errors' in the unemployment variable (due to the fact that, since not all countries have standardised data, the standardised data are still not perfect, and that unobserved factors cause the number of uncompensated unemployed to vary, etc.) the coefficient on *RP* has a negative bias. Thus the underlying relationship between replacement rates and unemployment rates is in principle stronger, but we cannot say by how much. Reverse causality may be present here too (that is, it could be that higher unemployment causes governments to increase the replacement ratio, rather than that a higher replacement ratio causes higher unemployment) but is perhaps not such a significant factor.

3   'Contractation' is relevant because, in the countries concerned, hirings using newly created forms of employment contract in some cases carry subsidies to the employer and in any case are viewed as jobs created by labour market policy. Wider questions of labour market regulation and deregulation are not considered here, however. Also not separately analysed here are programmes of rehabilitation and job creation for the disabled. Rehabilitation increases employability, similar to training for the unemployed. Job creation for the disabled should reduce unemployment if the people concerned are considered unemployed when out of work and yet would not be able to find market work. A further category deserving mention involves schemes helping the unemployed to set up businesses, which are useful but only for a limited proportion of the unemployed.

4   Total social assistance spending in the latter groups of countries is sometimes less, sometimes more, than total UI spending but there is not always an official breakdown of this spending between the unemployed and the non-employable. In Canada, social assistance spending exceeds UI spending and some localities assessed two thirds of their caseload of new claims as employables in 1985 (MSSC, 1986, pp.100–3).

5   A multiplication of the options available to unemployed people seems to have been quite frequent during the 1970s and 1980s, doing something to make unemployment a less unpleasant situation than it was in the past but with possibly perverse incentive effects.

6   Under a system of obligatory participation in ALMPs, a government official implicitly or explicitly says to an unemployed person 'enter this ALMP or you will lose your benefit'; with fixed benefit durations, the same official can say 'in one month you are going to lose your benefit but we are prepared to offer you a place in an ALMP which will maintain your income'. The two cases may be functionally equivalent, but the latter may be easier to implement effectively since the official concerned appears more generous!

7   It might be better to say that the Scandinavian systems are at risk, since the nature and functions of ALMPs vary considerably between Finland, Norway and Sweden. For instance the 1987 Employment Act in Finland was vigorously implemented but, nevertheless, led to certain problems and became increasingly difficult to operate meaningfully as unemployment rose during 1991 and 1992.

8   An 'incentive to enter unemployment' may operate through the aggregate wage level; the guaranteed availability of ALMP places reduces the costs of unemployment, leading unions to press for higher wages although they know that this increases the risk of unemployment. Calmfors and Nymoen (1990) and Calmfors and

Forslund (1991) give econometric evidence of this effect in Sweden.
9   Programmes may need to be run at a certain scale so as to amortise the costs of development, staff training, documentation, technical support, advertising and so on.

References

Björklund, A. (1991), *Labour Market Policy and Unemployment Insurance*, Oxford, Clarendon Press.

Brown, J. (1990), *Victims or Villains? Social Security Benefits in Unemployment*, London, Joseph Rowntree Memorial Trust and Policy Studies Insitute.

Calmfors, L. and Forslund, A. (1991), 'Real wage adjustment and labour market policies: the Swedish experience', *Economic Journal,* 101.

Calmfors, L. and Nymoen, R. (1990), 'Real wage adjustment and employment policies in the Nordic countries', *Economic Policy,* 11.

CEC (Commission of the European Communities) (1988), *MISEP Basic Information Report: Denmark,* Maastricht, European Centre for Work and Society.

De Koning, J., Koss, M. and Verkalk, A. (1990), 'A quasi-experimental evaluation of the Vocational Training Centre for adults', paper for the 1990 EALE conference, Lund, 20–23 September.

Lilja, R., Santamaki-Vuori, T. and Standing, G. (1990), *Unemployment and Labour Market Flexibility: Finland,* Geneva, ILO.

Main, B.G.M. and Shelly, M.A. (1990), 'The effectiveness of the youth training scheme as a manpower policy', *Economica,* 57, 495–514.

MSSC (Ministry of Supply and Services, Canada) (1986), *Report of the Commission of Inquiry on Unemployment Insurance* (chairman C. Forget), Ottawa, Canadian Government Publishing Centre.

NOSOSCO (1976), *Social Security in the Nordic Countries 1972,* Copenhagen.

OECD (1972), *Manpower Policy in Norway,* Paris.

OECD (1988), *Employment Outlook,* Paris.

OECD (1990), *Employment Outlook,* Paris.

OECD (1991), *Evaluating Labour Market and Social Programmes: the state of a complex art,* Paris.

OECD (1992), *Employment Outlook,* Paris.

OECD (1993a), *Economic Survey: Denmark,* Paris.

OECD (1993b), *Taxation in OECD Countries,* Paris.

OECD (1993c), *Employment Outlook,* Paris.

Schmid, G., Reissert, B. and Bruche, G. (1991), *Unemployment Insurance and Active Labor Market Policy,* Detroit, Wayne State University Press.

7   Structural differences in European labour markets

RAY BARRELL, NIGEL PAIN AND GARRY YOUNG[1]

Introduction

Macroeconomic performance is strongly dependent on the performance of the labour market, with the response of output to policy changes being largely dependent on its speed of adjustment. It has been common to ana- lyse differences in labour markets by looking at the determinants of unemployment. This can be particularly illuminating, as can be seen from the work of Layard, Nickell and Jackman (1991), hereafter LNJ, and the papers collected in Drèze and Bean (1991). These authors all accept that an explanation of unemployment requires a relationship which depends on the profit-making decisions of firms, and hence on labour demand, the labour supply decisions of individuals and institutional factors such as the bargain- ing power of trade unions and the structure of unemployment benefits. This chapter first discusses the demand for labour in a European context, and then proceeds to look at the determination of real wages and the supply of labour. In particular, we compare structures in three major European economies, Germany, France and the UK.

We would not expect to observe major differences between these three countries in the structure of the underlying production technology. All three have similar levels of productivity (although Prais, 1989, amongst others, demonstrates that significant differences remain) and they have access to common technology. There will be differences that derive from differing industrial structures and the more immutable aspects of comparative advantage that depend upon immobile factors of production. Differences in the product market may also show up in the demand for labour. There may also be differences that result from different patterns of relative factor prices, but these represent a movement around a production frontier, rather than a difference in structure. We would not, however, expect the paths of dynamic responses to be the same. These will depend both on the adjustment costs faced by firms, and factors such as redundancy legislation.

There is no reason to expect that the supply of labour and the formation of wages should be the same in these three countries. They have different histories and different institutional structures. The UK has moved towards a very decentralised wage bargaining system in the last fourteen years although union density has remained relatively high. Calmfors and Driffill (1988) argue that the move towards a more decentralised system of bargaining may moderate wage inflation. However, the evidence in favour of this proposition remains weak. Developments in France appear, at least on the surface, to have been similar, and trade unions have become moribund, especially since the collapse of communism. However, the French government has maintained its interventionist role in wage bargaining, partly through the effects of the minimum wage, and partly through its role as a major employer, both in the public sector and in the nationalised industries. Soskice (1990) argues that the German bargaining structure remains very centralised. We would expect these, and other differences, to show up in estimated wage equations.

Our previous work has suggested that there are observable differences between the three economies that we are studying. Such results are in line with those produced by other researchers. Barrell (1990) reports on a study of wage and price formation in France, Germany, Italy and the UK, and argues that the behaviour of the labour market depends in part on history. In an environment where there have been few severe shocks, and where the authorities are known to be able to deliver low and stable inflation, labour market institutions will develop to reflect these facts. Contracting intervals in Germany, and to a lesser extent in France, reflect the anti-inflation credibility of the authorities. As a result the labour market produces real wage flexibility and a slow feedthrough to wages from shocks to prices. In an environment where the authorities have had little anti-inflation success, such as in Italy, contract intervals will be short, indexation will be prevalent and price shocks will feed through rapidly into wages. Supporters of the ERM have argued that there are considerable advantages in demonstrating anti-inflation resolve by tying the exchange rate to the DM. However, the evidence suggests that credibility has to be won by hard work and by success. Anderton, Barrell, in't Veld and Pittis (1992) argue that there is little evidence of structural change in European labour markets. Only in Italy is there any evidence that labour market institutions have changed, and the process of dismantling the indexation mechanism has been slow and painful.

The objective of this chapter is to take the three labour markets where there is no evidence of structural change (France, Germany, the UK) and test whether there are any statistically significant structural differences. The first section sets out a framework for the analysis of labour demand in an open economy. The second section presents our estimates of the labour demand relationship in the three countries and presents tests of the differences in these relationships across countries. The third section describes the historical development of some key variables influencing the supply of labour and wage bargaining. An outline of the framework used for the analysis of wage bargaining then follows in which we describe how this may be used to develop two different specifications of the aggregate wage relationship: that used by LNJ and an alternative suggested by Manning (1993). The next section presents our estimates of the aggregate wage relationship for the three countries using both the LNJ and Manning specifications. These are tested for cross-country differences in wage setting under both types of specification and in the following section we use these various estimates to calculate sustainable levels of unemployment for these countries under a variety of different assumptions. Finally we summarise our main findings and draw some conclusions.

The demand for labour

The imperfectly competitive profit maximising firm (or the cost minimising organisation) has to take decisions about the price it sets for its outputs and the quantity of factors of production that it requires. The solution to the maximisation problem produces factor demands and a pricing relationship, each dependent on factor prices, the firms' technology and conditions in the product market. If we know the demands for the factors of production then we can determine the price of the product, and hence we do not need a separate relationship for the price. Conversely, knowledge of the pricing relationship enables us to infer factor demands. In order to understand and analyse the behaviour of the firm we need to estimate either a labour demand curve or a price equation. In this chapter we have chosen to depart from the approach adopted by LNJ, in that we have decided to estimate labour demand curves. However our results should be comparable to studies that have chosen the alternative route.

Analysis of the demand for labour usually starts from the individual firm and aggregates up to a relationship covering the demand for labour by all firms. This is the way we proceed, and it allows us to draw a distinction between 'individual experiments' and 'market experiments' (see Patinkin, 1968). Appendix 1 sets out a formal description of the derivation of our results. In an imperfectly competitive world the individual firm will face a downward sloping demand curve for its products:

$$Y_i = \left(\frac{P_i}{P}\right)^{-\eta} \frac{Y}{F} \tag{1}$$

where Y_i is the output of the firm, Y is total demand for the class of products and P_i/P is the price set by firm i relative to the average price for the class of products. The (absolute) elasticity of demand is assumed to be constant and is given by η and there are F identical firms.

The individual firm will maximise its profits subject to the cost of production which is determined by the prices of factors of production and by the production technology. Profit maximisation is achieved when marginal revenue equals marginal cost. The price equation and the labour demand for the individual firm can then be written as (2) and (3) (corresponding to (A5a) and (A6) in appendix 1)

Price equation

$$P_i\left[1 - \frac{1}{\eta}\right] = (1 - \alpha)W \cdot \frac{N_i}{Y_i} \tag{2}$$

Labour demand equation

$$N_i = \left(\frac{W\alpha}{rT(1-\alpha)}\right)^{-\alpha} \frac{Y_i}{AT} \cdot \tag{3}$$

Here α is the capital share parameter in the Cobb-Douglas production function, W is the wage, r is the nominal user cost of capital, N_i is the quantity of labour used by the firm and AT depends upon technical progress.

The price and labour demand equations are obviously similar, but before we can go on to aggregate across firms we have to acknowledge that the output of the firm is a choice variable, and if we wish to understand the factors that determine the demand for labour we have to substitute out for this variable. If we do so (see (A7) in appendix 1) we find that the demand for labour by the individual firm should depend separately upon relative factor prices (W/r), the price of factors relative to the market price of output, (W/P) and (r/P), as well as on the overall level of demand, Y. There are two factor price effects for the firm (or for any subset of firms). There is a substitution effect from relative factor prices and an output effect from real factor prices. This output effect arises because a fall in factor prices will reduce marginal cost and allow the firm to cut its prices relative to other firms in the market. It will therefore increase its market share.

When we move from the 'individual experiment' to the 'market experiment' it is possible that output will no longer be an endogenous variable. When we aggregate across all firms in the market then market share effects will drop out. If all firms face the same fall in factor prices then all will cut their marginal costs and attempt to increase output. However, because all firms cut their prices none gains an advantage. If this is the case then aggregate employment will be given by (3), but with N_i and Y_i replaced by total employment, N, and output, Y, respectively. Hence the aggregate demand for labour will depend on relative factor prices, the production technology and the level of demand.

However, the world does not consist of just one market and one set of firms, and we have to decide upon the appropriate level of aggregation for the problem we are considering. Our study concerns the demand for labour in a number of countries in a 'common' market. Firms may be operating in this or the wider world market or they may be operating only in the domestic market. Aggregate employment in a particular country will be determined by summing up the employment in all firms located in the country. If some are competing in the wider common market then aggregate employment will depend upon their costs relative to those of their competitors abroad.

There are two ways that we can proceed. We can aggregate employment and output in an individual country and produce a country specific demand for labour. We would then have to accept that the total level of national output is dependent on cost competitiveness. Alternatively and, we would argue, more consistently, we could aggregate the individual labour demand equations, acknowledging that they depend upon community wide output. Our aggregate demand for labour for the UK, say, will then depend upon relative factor prices (reflecting substitution effects), factor prices in the UK relative to product prices in the common market (or equivalently relative cost competitiveness) and on a wider measure of output such as total EC output. This gives an aggregate labour demand equation for each of the countries of the form

$$N_i = \tau_i \left(\frac{W_i}{r_i} \frac{\alpha}{T(1-\alpha)} \right)^{\alpha} \left(\frac{W_i}{TP} \right)^{-\eta(1-\alpha)} \left(\frac{r_i}{P} \right)^{-\alpha\eta} Y_{EC} \qquad (4)$$

i = France, Germany, UK

where N_i is employment in country i, τ_i is a country specific constant, the first term involves relative factor prices, the second and third will pick up competitiveness effects through costs relative to community-wide prices, and Y_{EC} is total output in the EC.

Estimating labour demand equations

There have been a number of attempts to estimate aggregate single country demand curves for labour (and equivalently demand curves for capital and hence for investment). Symons and Layard (1984) study the demand for labour in the UK. They start with a general error correction form with a rich dynamic specification, and they find significant factor price effects, especially when they include the price of raw materials. Our approach is similar, although more explicit account is taken of both the production process and issues of aggregation across firms. We start from (4) above, and in order to ensure comparability with other studies we also include relative material costs.

Our main interests are in the similarities between countries as well as as in the structure of the demand for labour in each of the economies. Our research strategy is therefore determined by these objectives. We have to use an estimation technique that allows us to test for differences between the long-run structural parameters across countries.[2] We specified a general dynamic model for each country and then sequentially eliminated insignificant variables.[3] Once a separate parsimonious form had been obtained for each country the equations were re-estimated jointly by three-stage least squares in order that we could test for differences in long-run structure between countries. The long-run solution for each country has the general form (see equation (A9) in appendix 1):

$$\ln N_t = a_0 + a_1 \ln Y_t + a_2 \ln(W/P)_t + a_3 \ln(W/r)_t + a_4 \ln(W/M)_t + a_5 \ln(T)_t + \varepsilon_t \text{ (5)}$$

The basic variable definitions are (the data appendix contains more detail):

N:	employees in employment (in person hours)
Y:	European output
W/r:	wages relative to cost of capital
W/M:	wages relative to materials input prices
W/P:	wages relative to output prices in the EC
T:	Technical progress

In each case European-wide output was used as the output scale variable. The choice of European-wide measures is supported by findings in recent studies of foreign direct investment, with Pain (1993) showing that investment within the UK is driven by European demand and Barrell and Pain (1993) finding that relative labour costs within the EC are an important determinant of the location of Japanese foreign direct investments.

The results are reported in table 7.1. Our equations are in general well specified. We have tested the validity of the instruments we have used (the Sargan test) and in all cases this test is passed. There is no evidence of serial correlation or of non-standard error structures. Tests for cointegration suggest that the long-run structure is coherent.[4,5] In summarising the results shown in table 7.1 it is important to recognise that, in principle, the underlying parameters are over-identified (there are two parameters, α and η, and three esti-

Table 7.1 *European labour demand equations, single country estimates*
Dependent variable: $\Delta \ln(N)$ Sample period: 1972Q2–1991Q4

	United Kingdom		France		Germany	
Constant	0.2018	(2.6)	-0.1096	(1.3)	-0.2614	(2.0)
T	-0.0004	(2.1)	-0.0003	(2.4)	-0.0012	(7.3)
$\ln(N - Y)_{-1}$	-0.0877	(2.6)	-0.1077	(4.5)	-0.2695	(7.3)
$\Delta \ln(N)_{-1}$	0.5510	(9.3)				
$\Delta\Delta \ln(N)_{-1}$			0.1278	(1.5)		
$\Delta \ln(N)_{-4}$					0.2594	(3.4)
$\Delta \ln(Y)$	0.2867	(4.4)	0.1792	(4.9)	0.2368	(4.6)
$\Delta \ln(W - M)\ddagger$	-0.0363	(2.1)				
$\Delta \ln(W - r)\ddagger$					-0.0876	(1.8)
$\Delta_2\Delta \ln(W - r)\ddagger$			-0.1799	(4.6)		
$\Delta \ln(W - r)_{-2}$	-0.0043	(2.8)				
$\ln(W - r)\ddagger$	-0.0002	(0.1)				
$\ln(W - r)_{-1}$			-0.0362	(4.7)	-0.0744	(4.4)
$\ln(W - P^*)_{-1}$	-0.0134	(2.4)			-0.0234	(2.1)
$\bar{R}^2$	0.8315		0.8089		0.6839	
SE	0.0033		0.0021		0.0029	
LM(4)	4.76		7.22		4.32	
NORM(2)	0.40		3.80		0.22	
HET(1)	0.04		1.65		1.19	
SARGAN	$\chi^2(7) = 8.65$		$\chi^2(5) = 6.39$		$\chi^2(4) = 2.46$	
t^1_{ECM}	-4.83 (5)		-4.39 (5)		-5.73 (5)	
t^2_{ECM}	-5.05 (3)		-8.02 (2)		-8.40 (3)	
OLS final vs. general	F(23,45) = 1.10		F(24,43) = 1.64		F(25,44) = 1.03	

Notes:

t-statistics in brackets. Δ indicates first difference. $\ddagger$ indicates a variable has been instrumented. The SARGAN test is a variable addition LM test of the exogeneity of the instrument set. LM(4) is a $\chi^2(4)$ test for serial correlation. NORM(2) is a Bera-Jarque χ^2 variable addition test for higher order moments in the errors. HET(1) is a version of the Breusch Pagan test for heteroskedasticity. t^1_{ECM} is a Kremers *et al.* (1992) χ^2 test for the cointegrability of the set of variables in the long run of the general form. (This may contain redundant variables and may hence have lower power.) t^2_{ECM} is a Kremers *et al.* (1992) χ^2 test for the cointegrability of the set of variables in the long run of the final form. Final vs general is a variable addition test on the set of variables excluded from the final form.

Table 7.2 *Characteristics of labour demand equations*

	Germany	France	UK	France/UK		
Long-run elasticities						
Global output	1.0	1.0	1.0	1.0		
Factor substitution (labour/capital)	-0.2762	-0.3359	-0.002	-0.011		
Competitiveness	-0.0868	-	-0.1525	-0.196		
Technical progress	-0.0046	-0.0030	-0.0049	-0.0046		
Dynamic median lags in quarters					France	UK
Output	(2-3)	(5-6)	(2-3)	(5-6)		(2-3)
Factor substitution (labour/capital)	(2-3)	(7-8)				
Competitiveness	(2-3)	-	(5-6)	(7-8)		(4-5)

mated combinations of them, a_2, a_3 and a_5). But given that technical progress is proxied by a linear time trend which may be a poor indicator, it is better to infer estimates of α and η from the estimated coefficients on relative labour to capital costs and competitiveness. A summary of the results is shown in table 7.2.

In each country, it is possible to impose the restriction of a long-run unit elasticity with respect to global output, but the relative factor price and competitiveness effects appear to be substantially different. In particular, the long-run elasticity of labour demand with respect to relative labour/capital prices in Germany and France is of a similar order to the share of capital in output.[6] However, in the UK no significant relative factor price effect could be found. By contrast, significant long-run competitiveness elasticities can be observed in Germany and the UK, but not in France. In addition, the dynamics of adjustment to changes in prices appears to be slower in the UK and France than in Germany.

In order to test whether these apparent differences in the structure of labour demand are statistically significant, the three equations were estimated simultaneously, adding back in the long-run effect of competitiveness found to be insignificant in the French equation reported in table 7.1. The results are affected slightly by adopting a simultaneous equation method

Table 7.3 *Tests of cross-country restrictions*

		Germany SE	France SE	UK SE	Test statistic
Unrestricted		0.0027	0.0018	0.0030	
Long-run effects the same in all 3 countries	(1)	0.0033	0.0019	0.0031	$\chi^2_8 = 48.3**$
	(2)	0.0030	0.0018	0.0031	$\chi^2_6 = 19.9**$
Long-run effects the same in UK and France	(1)	0.0027	0.0018	0.0030	$\chi^2_4 = 5.3$
	(2)	0.0027	0.0018	0.0030	$\chi^2_3 = 2.8$
Long-run effects the same in UK and Germany	(1)	0.0033	0.0018	0.0031	$\chi^2_4 = 44**$
	(2)	0.0028	0.0018	0.0032	$\chi^2_3 = 14.5**$
Long-run effects the same in France and Germany	(1)	0.0031	0.0019	0.0030	$\chi^2_4 = 26.7**$
	(2)	0.0029	0.0019	0.0030	$\chi^2_3 = 14.6**$

Notes: ** indicates significant at 1 per cent level

(1) tests that the coefficients on the levels terms on relative wage to capital costs, competitiveness, the time trend and the error correction term are the same across countries, (2) tests the non-linear restriction that the long-run elasticities are the same across countries.

The table shows for each country the value of the equation standard error (SE). The validity of any restriction on the equation can be informally assessed by examining the extent to which this worsens. A formal test of the validity of the restriction is given by the χ^2 statistic.

but the differences were small and they are not reported here. They are available in Barrell, Pain and Young (1993). The hypothesis that the long-run elasticities are the same in subsets of the three countries was then tested. The results are shown in table 7.3.

These formal statistical tests indicate that it is not possible to reject the hypothesis that the structure of labour demand in France and the UK is the same. However, it is possible to reject the hypothesis that German labour demand is the same as in the other two countries. The structure of the labour demand curve applying to the UK and France is summarised in the final two columns of table 7.2. The long-run elasticities with respect to relative factor prices, reported in table 7.2, are small and insignificantly different from zero. This is consistent with the UK single-equation evidence but substantially different from the French single-equation evidence. The competitiveness elasticity is about –0.2, which is larger than in either of the single equation studies.

These results indicate some of the benefits gained from using pooled cross-country, time-series evidence. If it is possible to impose the same structural relationships across countries, then the extra information available makes it possible to give more precise parameter estimates. Thus the single-equation estimates reported in table 7.1 suggest that employment in France responds to relative factor prices rather than competitiveness. Inspection of equations including competitiveness rather than relative factor prices suggests that this works almost, but not quite, as well. It is difficult to discriminate between the two terms, but the UK evidence suggests clearly that it is competitiveness that matters. If labour demand in the two countries has the same structure then it must be competitiveness that works in both countries. Further, the greater variability in this when considered across, as well as within, countries provides better evidence as to its effects.

It remains to explain the different results obtained for Germany, both in terms of the speed of adjustment and the effects of relative factor prices and competitiveness. Table 7.2 suggests that the dynamic speed of response is faster in Germany than in either the UK (for competitiveness) or France (for output and relative factor prices). When we estimate these equations together these dynamic differences remain and this could cause a test failure. Adjustment speeds to changes in demand in France may well have been reduced over our sample period by the stringent redundancy regulations that were only partially relaxed in 1986. An explanation of the lack of factor substitutability observed in the UK and France is that, because of adjustment costs, firms only respond to permanent changes in relative factor prices. The greater variability in factor prices in these countries, especially in the cost of capital, might explain why firms appear to respond less to what might prove to be only temporary changes in relative costs. The more stable macroeconomic environment in Germany over the sample period may also explain why firms appear to react more quickly there to changes in relative factor prices and competitiveness.

There may also be significant differences in product markets. The evidence suggests that German labour demand conforms almost exactly to the structure set out in (3) above. This type of structure occurs when domestic firms dominate the product market in which they operate so that changes in the level of domestic factor prices do not lead to gains in competitiveness. One circumstance where this arises is when domestic employment is determined mainly by domestic output, but tests of whether German employment is determined solely by German output and relative factor prices rejected this hypothesis.[7] An alternative possibility, which has a certain amount of plausibility, is that German firms dominate the global market in which they operate as far as price setting is concerned. If German firms act as price leaders in global markets then changes in German factor prices will be matched by changes in world prices which moderate the initial gain in competitiveness. In this case the influence of factor price changes on factor demands will be felt mainly through factor substitution rather than changes in competitiveness.

The supply of labour and the real wage

It has become common to analyse the determination of wages in a bargaining context. European countries generally do exhibit quite centralised bargaining, although over the 1980s there have been forces at work that have reduced the role of unions. These are not only the consequence of the actions of the state, as in the UK, but also the result of largely exogenous processes. There has been a move away from the production of standardised goods and greater reliance on part-time working. This has reduced the scope for collective bargaining, and individualised wage packages have become more common. However, union density has remained high in much of Europe.

The evolution of trade unions in the three countries under study has been quite divergent. Figure 7.1 plots density data for the UK, Germany and France.[8] Density in the UK peaked in the early 1980s and since then it has been falling, whilst it has been relatively constant in Germany. Union membership in France has never been as high. It is hard to find data on unionisation in France in part because the unions themselves have not kept records. Since the mid-1980s the trade union movement has been collapsing, with the socialist unions discouraged by the Mitterrand U-turn in 1982/3, and the communist CGT being dragged down by the decline of the Communist party and the collapse of the USSR. The socialist and communist union federations never covered more than a quarter of the workforce, and density had dropped to 10 per cent by 1990.

These changes reflect, in part, the differing histories of these economies in the 1980s. The appreciation of the real exchange rate in the UK in the early 1980s accelerated the decline in manufacturing, where unionisation has always been strong. The subsequent recovery was not associated with an equivalent period of undervaluation, and hence manufacturing employment did not recover. Figure 7.2 plots the share of employees in manufacturing. This has been declining in all three countries, but the decline has been much more marked in the UK. The boom of the late 1980s in the UK was driven

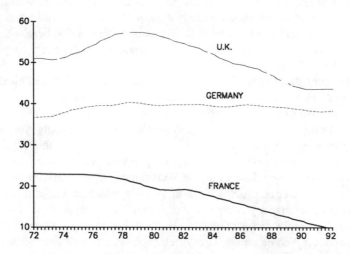

Figure 7.1 Trade union density in Germany, France and the UK
See appendix for sources.

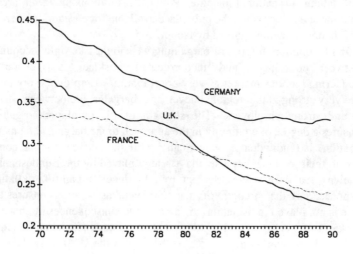

Figure 7.2 Manufacturing share in employment
See appendix for sources

by consumer spending and the effects of financial liberalisation, with many new jobs created in the traditionally low union density service sector. The 1980s were probably less volatile in France and Germany. There was no significant appreciation in the exchange rate, and hence manufacturing only declined from 36 to 30 per cent of output in France and by 3.5 per cent in Germany over the 1980s. This has been a major factor behind continued union strength in Germany. The same cannot be said for France.

These diverse trends suggest that it might be difficult to formulate and estimate a common model of wage determination or labour supply for these three economies. However, we would argue that a common bargaining approach is still a testable proposition. Bargains between unions and employers are about many things, but one of them must be the mark-up of union over non-union wages. Such a mark-up is only possible either if product markets are not perfectly competitive or if employers ubiquitously face upward-sloping supply curves of labour. In either case there is a rent available to the producer. Trade unions have often been set up with the objective of gaining some share of the rents for the employees. The bargain is therefore in part about the share of labour in the product of the firm, and hence over the share of labour in national income. Political institutions, however, are diverse and the shop floor is not the only place available for bargaining over the share of national income gained by labour.

The first distinction in types of bargaining we should take into account is that between coordinated and uncoordinated. Soskice (1990) characterises the German labour market as very coordinated.[9] Employers' organisations are very strong at the regional level and bargains are between strong unions and strong employers. The strength of the employers' organisations ensures a degree of continuity in the approach to the bargain and ensures coordination. No individual bargainer can ignore the macroeconomic consequences of their actions because the strategy played by the Bundesbank is well known. An excessive settlement round induces a painful, deflationary response and the strength of the employers' associations ensures that the game is not played in isolation. As a result the consequences of an action feed back onto the actor. This high degree of coordination is in contradistinction to the labour market in the UK. At the start of the 1990s it is clear that the UK has much less coordination than Germany. The authorities stand back from bargains and collective bargaining is largely conducted at plant and company level. This has not always been the case. The current government has gradually rolled back the corporatist structures established in the 1960s. The abolition of NEDO in the summer of 1992 can be seen as the last in a sequence of moves that changed the UK from being coordinated to uncoordinated. However, bargaining does still take place.

We would argue that a bargaining approach to wage determination is still useful when analysing French experience, despite the moribund state of French trade unions. Individuals bargain with their employers in order to capture a share of the rents. It is also the case that throughout the 1980s the French state has played a central role in wage determination and it can be seen as bargaining on behalf of (but not always to the advantage of) labour. The determination of the government to hold down wage inflation in the 1980s has been central to the process. The public sector and the nationalised industries are very important in setting the going rate for settlements. Nationalisation increased in the early 1980s and nationalised firms occupy crucial areas in French industry. Employers organisations have been the bargaining partners for the government in many wage deals and the nationalised industries have been a major tool in the process of determining wages. The other element in the construction of the bargain over the share of labour has been the minimum wage system. The minimum wage system has changed over the 1980s and has become less formal, but Bazen and Martin (1991) argue that its coverage and effect has increased. Our conclusion is that a bargaining framework is probably more applicable to France than to many other countries, in part because there are fewer players in the game.

The nature of the bargain

Most empirical work on wages in the UK has been based on the bargaining framework developed by LNJ. It is usually assumed that there are two partners to the bargain, the union and the firm. Unions are seen as wishing to maximise the welfare of their members whilst firms maximise profits. Firms also retain the 'right to manage' in that they are free to determine the level of employment. Union members may either work in the firm, work elsewhere, or spend time searching for a job whilst unemployed. There is a difference between the real reward to working obtained by workers (the real consumer wage) and the real costs of employing them (the real producer wage) paid by firms. These are linked by a multiplicative identity of the following form:

$$w = wc \left(\frac{PC}{P} \right) \left(\frac{1+et}{1-dt} \right) \tag{6}$$

or $w = wc *$ wedge where w is the real producer wage, wc is the real consumer wage, PC is the consumer price index, P is the output price index, et is the rate of employers tax and dt is the direct tax rate. The wedge is always present in our analysis. If we estimate a consumer wage equation, this can be converted directly to a producer wage equation by dividing both sides by (subtracting the log of) the wedge.

There has been much debate over the role of wedge effects and real wage resistance. If unions offer real wage resistance to increases in, say, taxes, then the bargain may be affected by elements of the wedge. This would mean that the real producer wage and hence the level of employment (and unemployment) would depend upon the wedge. LNJ argue that there are good reasons to believe that wedge effects do not affect the bargain in the long run, although they may be present in the short run. In all cases we allow for the potential existence of long-run wedge effects in the producer wage equations. If the supply of labour is perfectly inelastic there will be no wedge effects on the producer wage and workers will 'bear' the whole wedge. In addition it is clear that as long as the tax system is homogeneous in its effects there should be no effect from the wedge on the bargained mark-up. However, the progressivity of the tax system should, in principle, affect the mark-up (see Lockwood and Manning, 1992).

The solution to the bargaining problem gives the mark-up of the wage over the returns to not working in the unionised firm (equation (A16) in appendix 2). This will depend upon union bargaining power, union attitudes to jobs and the elasticity of demand for labour and profits with respect to wages. Most recent empirical research into the behaviour of aggregate wages, at least in the UK, has been based on this framework. However, it is now widely recognised that there is a problem with the conventional implementation of this approach where wages are related to factors such as productivity from the labour demand side and benefit levels from the labour supply side. The problem arises because the 'structural' wage equation excludes nothing that is included in the labour demand or price equation and is therefore not identified. This has led Manning (1993) to propose an alternative specification to be used in estimating aggregate wage equations that is based on the same framework but does not suffer from any lack of identification. It turns out that his preferred specification is that of a Phillips curve. Manning proceeds by assuming (in contrast to LNJ) that the elasticity of profits and labour demand with respect to the wage are constant. As is demonstrated in appendix 2, this exclusion restriction is sufficient to identify the parameters of the wage equation. However, it is not necessarily enough to establish that the resulting equation is the supply curve of labour.

The LNJ bargained real wage will depend positively upon real benefits, on union power, and on the probability of re-employment for redundant workers. If those at work have a lower chance of being unemployed next period than do those currently unemployed, then the discount rate will have a positive effect on wages (see equation (A17) in appendix 2). All labour market transition probabilities will depend on unemployment, and we would expect that higher unemployment will reduce the mark-up of union wages over the alternatives. We can write the wage equation in either the LNJ style (equation (A20) in appendix 2):

$$\log \left(\frac{W_t}{P_t} \right) = \log \left(\frac{Y_t}{N_t} \right) + \lambda_0 - \lambda_1 u_t + \lambda_2 \frac{B_t}{P_t} + \lambda_3 \chi_t \tag{7}$$

or after Manning (equation (A19) in appendix 2):

$$\Delta \ln(W/P)_{t+1} = \lambda_0 - \lambda_1(L) E_t u_{t+1} + \lambda_2 \frac{B_t}{P_t} + \lambda_{31} E_t \Delta \mu_{t+1} - \lambda_{32} \mu_t - \lambda_4 \delta_t \tag{8}$$

where W/P is the real producer wage, u is the rate of unemployment, B/P are real benefits, and χ and μ reflect union power, δ is the discount factor, Y/N is average productivity and E_t is the expectations operator. The latter equation is 'dynamic', in that the rate of change of the real wage will depend upon expected unemployment, the discount rate, the replacement rate and other factors that affect labour market transitions. The Manning equation is 'identified' because it excludes output per person, which is included in the demand for labour/price equation. The LNJ approach includes the level of productivity as a determinant of the level of real wages, and as such it is not identified. However, it may still represent an adequate description of history.

Estimating wage equations

Since our purpose is to discuss the similarities in wage setting across countries it is not necessary for us to make a stand on the issue of the appropriate specification of the wage equation. Instead we are able to present cross-country evidence on wage setting across countries using *both* modelling approaches. In doing this we use generalisations of the types of specifications used by Manning and LNJ themselves. Our estimation strategy is the same as for labour demand, and our main focus remains the comparison of results across countries.

It should be noted that LNJ invariably use the real producer wage as the dependent variable in the wage equation. An implication is that this might well be independent of the wedge between the real producer wage and real consumer wage, and that the costs of different taxes affecting this wedge are borne by labour. By contrast, the equations estimated by Manning use the growth in the real consumer wage as the dependent variable. However the bargaining framework determines the real producer wage, and consequently

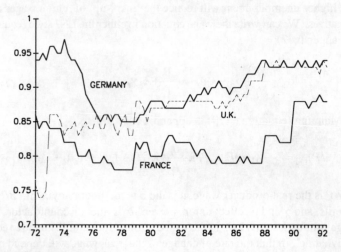

Figure 7.3 Tax progressivity
See appendix for sources

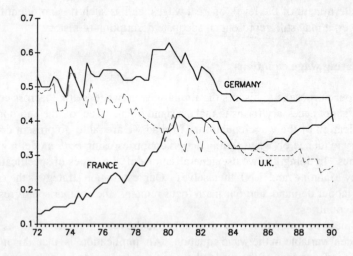

Figure 7.4 Replacement ratios
See appendix for sources

we would expect the wedge to enter the long-run solution of the consumer wage equation possibly with a coefficient of minus unity (see equation (6) above). To test this we have added a growth term in the wedge to the general specification of our equation. We also include additional terms in the growth of productivity in order to pick up further expectational effects.

The Manning-style equations also contain terms in the progressivity of the tax system. This is based on the analysis of Lockwood and Manning (1992) who claim that the progressivity of the tax system influences the wage bargain with some evidence of 'over-shifting' whereby a more progressive tax system reduces wage pressure. Our measure of the progressivity of the tax system (defined as (1–marginal tax)/(1–average tax)), is plotted in figure 7.3. Before undertaking the cross-country comparison it is useful to look at figure 7.4, which plots the replacement ratio for the stock of unemployed people ((total benefits/unemployment)/(Personal disposable income per worker)). This ratio has fallen in the UK, risen in France and remained consistently high in Germany. This across-country variation should be a great aid to testing hypotheses about the effects of benefit levels.

Manning

The dependent variable in our Manning-style wage equations is the change in the real consumer wage. There are a number of simultaneously determined contemporaneous variables ($\Delta PROD$, ΔU and U) in our equation as well as a number of expected variables such as the current real interest rate and the change in the wedge. All these variables are instrumented. The notation is as follows: ($W^1 - PC$) is the real consumer wage, U is the unemployment rate,[10] RR is the real interest rate, REP is the replacement rate, $DENS$ is union density, $PROG$ is progressivity, $PROD$ is productivity. A ‡ indicates that a variable has been instrumented. The results are presented in table 7.4.

As with labour demand, these equations have been derived as the result of general-to-specific modelling strategy. The main interest lies in the estimated coefficients on the levels of unemployment, the real interest rate, the replacement ratio, union density and progressivity. Where these have dropped out in the sequential testing procedure, tests are reported as to whether it is valid to add them to the final equation.

The results suggest that the rate of unemployment is a significant restraining influence on real wage growth in each country. Higher real interest rates add to real wage pressure. The effects from the other variables appear to be more diverse. The level of the replacement ratio is significant in the UK but only changes in it matter in France and Germany. Similarly the level of union density is significant in France, whereas changes matter in Germany

Table 7.4 *Final Manning equations including wedge terms, single country estimates*
Dependent Variable: $\Delta \ln(W^1 - PC)$ *Sample Period:1972Q1–1991Q4*

	UK	France	Germany
Constant	0.0050 (0.3)	-0.0002 (0.0)	0.0110 (5.4)
$\Delta \ln(W^1 - PC)_{-1}$		-0.2918 (3.8)	-0.4085 (5.8)
$\Delta \ln(W^1 - PC)_{-2}$			-0.1208 (1.7)
$\Delta U(\ddagger)$			-0.0155 (4.4)
$U(\ddagger)$	-0.0013 (2.0)		-0.0015 (4.3)
U_{-3}		-0.0019 (4.4)	
$RR(\ddagger)$	0.0019 (3.6)	0.0019 (2.7)	
$(RR_{-2} + RR_{-3})$			0.0008 (3.7)
REP_{-1}	0.0675 (2.5)		
$\Delta_2 REP_{-1}$		0.1042 (3.3)	
$\Delta_2 REP_{-2}$			0.0654 (3.0)
$DENS_{-2}$		0.0705 (2.1)	
$\Delta\Delta DENS$	1.2323 (2.0)		
$\Delta DENS_{-2}$			1.7968 (2.5)
$\Delta PROG$	-0.2441 (2.3)	-0.3679 (2.5)	
$\Delta PROG_{-3}$			-0.1230 (2.1)
$\Delta \ln(PROD)(\ddagger)$	0.5497 (2.2)	0.3778 (2.1)	
$\Delta_2 \Delta \ln(PROD)(\ddagger)$			0.2901 (3.4)
$\Delta \ln(WEDGE)(\ddagger)$	-0.4852 (1.8)	-0.3813 (2.5)	-0.7298 (4.1)
$\Delta\Delta \ln(WEDGE)_{-1}$			-0.3650 (5.4)
$\overline{R}^2$	0.675	0.823	0.711
SE	0.0095	0.0039	0.0058
LM(4)	3.24	6.60	3.69
NORM(2)	2.51	0.25	0.73
HET(1)	3.14	0.08	0.09
SARGAN	$\chi^2(11) = 13.4$	$\chi^2(11) = 12.26$	$\chi^2(10) = 12.29$
Variable addition tests on variables excluded from the long run			
1) Progressivity	$\chi^2(1) = 0.02$	$\chi^2(1) = 0.38$	$\chi^2(1) = 0.06$
2) Density	$\chi^2(1) = 0.97$		$\chi^2(1) = 3.01$
3) Replacement ratio		$\chi^2(1) = 0.66$	$\chi^2(1) = 2.34$
OLS final vs general	$F(30,39) = 1.33$	$F(30,39) = 0.75$	$F(26,41) = 0.89$

Notes: t-statistics in brackets. Δ indicates first difference. $\ddagger$ indicates a variable has been instrumented. The SARGAN test is a variable addition LM test of the exogeneity of the instrument set. LM(4) is a $\chi^2(4)$ test for serial correlation. NORM(2) is a Bera-Jarque χ^2 variable addition test for higher order moments in the errors. HET(1) is a version of the Breusch Pagan test for heteroskedasticity. Final vs general is a variable addition test on the set of variables excluded from the final form.

Table 7.5 *Tests of differences in Manning-style wage equations*

		Germany	France	UK	Test Stat
		SE	SE	SE	
Unrestricted		0.0049	0.0035	0.0076	
All countries	(1)	0.0051	0.0036	0.0082	χ^2_{10} = 28.1**
the same	(2)	0.0050	0.0036	0.0079	χ^2_8 = 17.5**
UK and France	(1)	0.0049	0.0036	0.0081	χ^2_5 = 15.2**
the same	(2)	0.0049	0.0035	0.0079	χ^2_4 = 7.4
UK and Germany	(1)	0.0051	0.0035	0.0081	χ^2_5 = 20.3**
the same	(2)	0.0049	0.0035	0.0079	χ^2_4 = 8.2
France and Ger.	(1)	0.0050	0.0036	0.0076	χ^2_5 = 10.0
the same	(2)	0.0050	0.0036	0.0076	χ^2_4 = 9.8*

Notes:
(1) tests that the coefficients on the level terms on unemployment, progressivity, union density and the replacement ratio are the same in all countries, (2) tests whether the ratio of the coefficients on progressivity, union density and the replacement ratio to that on unemployment are the same in all countries.
** indicates significant at 1 per cent level, * indicates significant at 5 per cent level.
The table shows for each country the value of the equation standard error (SE). The validity of any restriction on the equation can be informally assessed by examining the extent to which this worsens. A formal test of the validity of the restriction is given by the χ^2 statistic.

and acceleration is important in the UK. In all countries the growth in the wedge is seen to reduce the growth in the real consumer wage although the coefficient is less than unity suggesting that growth in the wedge leads to growth in the real producer wage. Growth in productivity is seen to add to real wage growth in the UK and France whereas only the change (second difference) in its growth is significant in Germany.

As with the case of labour demand, it is possible to test whether these apparent differences between countries are significant. The results are shown in table 7.5. We have added back omitted terms in progressivity, density and the replacement ratio where required in order to allow for the possibility that this statistically more powerful approach will uncover similarities in structure. The equations with these terms added in are shown as the unrestricted result in table 7.5. More details are reported in Barrell, Pain and Young (1993).

The results indicate clearly that it is not statistically acceptable to impose the same Manning-style wage equation in all three countries. This is true whether interest is focused only on the long-run solution (the tests in rows marked (2) of table 7.5) to the wage equations or whether some account is taken of similarities in the speed of adjustment to disequilibrium (the tests in rows marked (1) of table 7.5).

The pairwise comparisons throw up some interesting results. Ignoring the speed of adjustment, it is not possible to reject the hypothesis that the parameters of the UK wage equation are the same as in France or in Germany. But it is possible to reject the hypothesis that the parameters are the same in France and Germany. When the speed of adjustment is taken into account, the UK wage equation is different from that in France and Germany, but the French and German wage equations are not different.

The impact effect on real wages of a rise in unemployment in the UK is considerably smaller than elsewhere, and this suggests that the speed of adjustment of the real wage over the short to medium term is significantly slower than that in the other countries. However, the long-run equilibrium is difficult to distinguish from those pertaining in either France or Germany. Inspection of the long-run solution suggests that when the same parameters are imposed in the UK and German wage equations, the replacement ratio has an economically implausible sign. When the same parameters are imposed in the UK and French wage equations, the effect of union density and the replacement ratio have the right sign but are insignificant. If we discriminate between equations on the plausibility of the results then it appears that, as with labour demand, Germany is the outlier.

Layard Nickell Jackman

Table 7.6 shows the LNJ wage equations for the three countries. The dependent variable here is the growth in the real producer wage. All equations are estimated over the same sample period as table 7.4. One novel feature of our empirical work is the inclusion of terms in expected inflation and expected productivity to take account of the possibility that the wage bargain will reflect expected developments over the period of the contract. These variables were initially included separately and instrumented but, as might be expected, they had virtually identical coefficients, suggesting that ex-

Table 7.6 *Final Layard-Nickell equations, single country estimates*
Dependent variable: Δ ln(W)   Sample period: 1972Q1–1991Q4

	UK	France	Germany
Constant	0.2054 (3.2)	-0.4344 (2.1)	-0.3277 (2.9)
$[\ln(W/P) - \ln(PROD)]_{-1}$	-0.1121 (2.8)	-0.1215 (2.1)	-0.0920 (3.0)
$\Delta \ln(W)_{-1}$			-0.2132 (2.6)
$\Delta \ln(W)_{-2}$	0.4845 (7.8)		
$\Delta \ln(W)_{-4}$	-0.1807 (2.9)		
$\Delta \ln(WEDGE)_{-1}$	0.1317 (2.3)		
$\Delta \ln(WEDGE)_{-2}$			0.2277 (2.2)
ΔU_{-1}		0.0125 (3.3)	
U_{-1}	-0.0009 (2.2)		
U_{-2}		-0.0013 (1.8)	-0.0021 (3.9)
$[\Delta\ln(P) + \Delta\ln(PROD)]\ddagger_{+1}$	0.2506 (2.1)		
$[\Delta\ln(P) + \Delta\ln(PROD)]\ddagger$	0.3641 (3.1)	0.6716 (4.1)	0.7317 (4.0)
REP_{-2}		0.0801 (4.1)	
ΔREP_{-1}		0.3399 (4.8)	
$DENS_{-2}$		0.2700 (2.9)	
$\bar{R}^2$	0.86	0.86	0.62
SE	0.0064	0.0048	0.0078
LM(4)	6.45	1.23	0.23
NORM(2)	0.59	3.75	0.14
HET(1)	0.58	0.15	0.08
SARGAN	$\chi^2 (12) = 15.07$	$\chi^2 (12) = 14.9$	$\chi^2 (6) = 5.14$
t^1_{ECM}	-4.29 (6)	-6.48 (6)	-4.39 (6)
t^2_{ECM}	-3.80 (2)	-5.48 (3)	-4.15 (2)
Variable addition tests for excluded variables			
1) Replacement Ratio	$\chi^2 (1) = 3.15$		$\chi^2 (1) = 0.54$
2) Density	$\chi^2 (1) = 1.61$		$\chi^2 (1) = 0.05$
3) Real Interest Rate	$\chi^2 (5) = 3.88$	$\chi^2 (5) = 6.52$	$\chi^2 (5) = 3.67$
4) Progressivity	$\chi^2 (5) = 5.40$	$\chi^2 (5) = 4.15$	$\chi^2 (5) = 8.06$
5) Error-Correction	$\chi^2 (2) = 5.05$	$\chi^2 (2) = 0.68$	$\chi^2 (2) = 1.42$
OLS Final vs general	F(32,39) = 1.36	F(31,38) = 1.72	F(33,39) = 1.69

Notes: See table 7.1.

pected inflation and expected productivity growth enter the wage equation symmetrically.[11]

Before proceeding to joint estimation we undertook a number of variable addition tests. We added back the long-run effects of union density and the replacement ratio in equations that did not contain them. They were not sig-

Table 7.7 *Tests of differences in the LNJ wage equation*

	Germany	France	UK	Test Stat
	SE	SE	SE	
Unrestricted	0.0070	0.0044	0.0058	
All countries the same	0.0074	0.0050	0.0060	$\chi^2_8 = 38.6^{**}$
UK and France the same	0.0070	0.0048	0.0061	$\chi^2_4 = 22.4^{**}$
UK and Germany the same	0.0071	0.0044	0.0059	$\chi^2_4 = 5.3$
France and Ger. (1) the same (2)	0.0076	0.0048	0.0058	$\chi^2_4 = 29.1^{**}$

Notes: ** denotes significant at the 1% level. The table shows for each country the value of the equation standard error (SE). The validity of any restriction on the equation can be informally assessed by examining the extent to which this statistic worsens. A formal test of the validity of the restriction is given by the χ^2 statistic.

nificant. We also considered the proposition that nominal wages do not fully reflect movements in producer prices and productivity by testing the significance of the restrictions required to obtain the error correction term in table 7.6. The restriction was accepted. Finally, in order to test comparability with our Manning-style results, we added the real interest rate and the tax progressivity variables to the equations. They were not significant. Results from the Kremers *et al.* test for the coherency of the long run in the final equation (t^2_{ECM}) suggest that the variables in table 7.6 form a cointegrating set.

There is considerable variation in the levels of benefits and union density between countries, and it should therefore prove possible to enhance our understanding by estimating these three equations together, and then test them to see if the explanation changes when coefficients are restricted to be the same across countries. Our general form for each country in the 3SLS procedure included all previously omitted levels terms in the replacement ratio and union density. The resulting equations are described as the unrestricted estimates in table 7.7. A summary of our results is given in table 7.7. Full details are in Barrell, Pain and Young (1993).

These results suggest that there are no significant differences in the LNJ wage equations in the UK and Germany, but that both have different wage equations from that in France.

Summary of results

The results indicate significant effects of unemployment on wages in all three countries in both approaches. The results on replacement ratios are more diverse. Although they are significant in the UK Manning equation (but not elsewhere), when we estimate all three countries together they are not significant anywhere. Replacement ratios are also significant in our French LNJ equation but not elsewhere. Cross-section evidence should help us ascertain the importance of replacement ratios, as they have varied significantly between countries and over time. It is important to note that Germany has constantly had the highest replacement rate along with the lowest unemployment rate. This suggests that the connection between the level of the replacement ratio and the level of unemployment is not strong. Both Grubb (this volume) and LNJ have argued that the administration of benefits matters at least as much as the level, and our results may be consistent with this conclusion.

Union density effects are also rather sparse, especially given the large cross-country variation in both levels and trends (see figure 7.1). Our Manning-style equations contain density effects only in France, and these become insignificant in pooled analysis. Our LNJ-style equations for France have strong density (and replacement rate) effects, but they are not present elsewhere. This suggests either that France differs from other countries, or that the results are somehow anomalous. We consider the joint significance of these two effects to be in part a statistical artefact as one has trended strongly upwards whilst the other has declined, and they offset each other.

The two sets of results on wage setting suggest that there are a number of statistically significant differences in the process of wage formation between the three major European countries. There is some evidence that the dynamics of adjustment of nominal wages are slower in Germany and that real wages are least flexible in the UK. The results reported in table 7.4 suggest that the usual measure of real wage flexibility (the long-run coefficient on unemployment) is largest in Germany, and smallest in the UK. The UK also has the shortest lag between price changes and wage changes in these equations.[12]

We should judge our results in terms of both their statistical plausibility and their implications for equilibrium unemployment. Our equations contain a diverse set of factors, many of them significant, but their impact may still be so small that they are not important. The next section of this chapter attempts to evaluate our results by calculating the NAIRUs implied by our equations.

Accounting for changes in unemployment rates

Our empirical analysis has indicated the type of factors influencing the pressure for higher real wages in the three countries we are studying. However, the actual level of real wages is strongly influenced by what firms in aggregate are willing to pay. The role of unemployment may be seen as bringing about a balance between the demand for real wage growth coming from the bargaining process with the feasibility of real wage growth determined by the production process. The purpose of this section is to attempt to quantify the level of unemployment that brings about equilibrium in each country and the importance of the various factors that influence it. In order to do this we need the basic structure of the estimated wage equations and a price equation for each country.

The sustainable level of unemployment (or NAIRU) is an equilibrium concept. It is the level of unemployment that would be attained if the endogenous variables in the wage (and price) system were at their equilibrium, or steady state, values. The factors that we consider as endogenous will depend upon the time frame of our analysis. In the short to medium term the real interest rate can be seen as subject to policy choice, and hence it is not endogenous. It is therefore possible for us to calculate a NAIRU that depends on current values of unionisation, benefits and the real interest rate. However, we have to acknowledge that in the longer term the real interest rate is an endogenous variable whose equilibrium is conditional on the rest of the macroeconomy. This should change our calculations of the NAIRU for long-term analysis. There are other variables, such as the mark-up of prices over costs, that may be subject to the vagaries of the world market in the short to medium term, but do have a long-term equilibrium. We think it useful to distinguish between the benchmark level of the NAIRU that affects the current behaviour of the labour market, and the longer-term equilibrium level of the NAIRU. The calculation of the former should take variables such as the real interest rate as given, while the latter should take them at their equilibrium values.

Our estimates of the NAIRU, presented below, distinguish between these medium and longer-term estimates. The calculation of the NAIRU differs between the LNJ and Manning approaches. The former requires that we solve for unemployment using both the price and wage equations, whereas the Manning approach to wage determination produces a simpler derivation of the NAIRU, by directly inverting the wage equation. The resulting expressions are shown as equations (A24) and (A25) in appendix 3.

Table 7.8 *NAIRU estimates for Manning-style equations*

	UK (a)			Germany			France		
	U	NAIRU	NAIRU2	U	NAIRU	NAIRU2	U	NAIRU	NAIRU2
72Q1-91Q4	6.7	7.7	7.7	6.0	5.5	5.5	7.1	5.8	5.8
75Q1-79Q4	4.1	7.9	3.9	4.4	3.8	1.2	5.0	5.3	3.0
80Q1-84Q4	9.0	7.9	9.4	7.1	7.2	8.4	8.1	6.8	7.1
85Q1-89Q4	9.5	7.6	10.3	8.7	6.5	7.3	10.1	5.4	7.5
90Q1-91Q4	7.1	7.8	10.9	6.7	7.1	9.3	9.3	6.3	9.4

(a) Although our empirical estimates for the UK use the population not working rate, we have translated our implied estimates of the NAIRU back to claimant unemployment in order to ensure comparability with France and Germany. In making this adjustment we have to allow for an additional registration effect (see Gregg, 1990) which accounts for the different behaviour of the two series.

These equations can be used to generate estimates of the NAIRU. Table 7.8 reports two estimates of the NAIRU for the UK, Germany and France on the basis of the Manning-style wage equations reported earlier with the cross-country restrictions imposed for the UK and France.[13] Two estimates are presented because the size of the effect of the real interest rate on the NAIRU might be thought implausibly large. Hence we show an estimated NAIRU that takes account of movements in the real interest rate (NAIRU2) and one that fixed the contribution of the real interest rate at its period average (NAIRU)). These equilibrium unemployment rates seem relatively stable over time, especially if we assume that real interest rates are constant.

It is possible to account for the changes in equilibrium unemployment in each country using the estimated wage equation coefficients. The results are shown in table 7.9. The sub-sample estimates in this table indicate the changes in the NAIRU that result from the differences between the average values of the explanatory variables in each sub-sample and their average in the complete sample. For example, the estimated value of NAIRU2 for Germany in 1975Q1–1979Q4 is 4.3 percentage points below that for the full sample. Of this difference some 2.5 percentage points is accounted for by the real interest rate and some 1.8 percentage points by productivity growth. The variation caused by changes in replacement rates is very small, and this is of some importance because they have fallen sharply in the UK and risen rapidly in France. Although replacement rates in the UK in 1990–91 were 40 per cent below the period average they produced only a 0.08 per cent decrease in the

Table 7.9 *Accounting for differences in the NAIRU from its period average (72Q1–91Q4) (Manning estimates)*

	Real interest rate			Replacement ratio		
	UK	GE	FR	UK	GE	FR
75Q1-79Q4	-3.9	-2.5	-2.3	0.02	-	-0.04
80Q1-81Q4	1.4	1.2	0.3	-0.01	-	0.04
85Q1-89Q4	2.7	0.9	2.1	-0.05	-	0.03
90Q1-91Q4	3.1	2.3	3.1	-0.08	-	0.08
	Productivity growth			Union density		
75Q1-79Q4	-0.5	-1.8	-1.2	0.6	-	0.5
80Q1-81Q4	..	1.7	0.8	0.4	-	0.1
85Q1-89Q4	-0.3	0.9	0.2	-0.5	-	-0.5
90Q1-91Q4	1.0	1.5	1.6	-1.0	-	-1.0
	Progressivity			Registration effect		
75Q1-79Q4	0.2	-	0.3	-0.1		
80Q1-81Q4	..	-	0.1	0.0		
85Q1-89Q4	-0.2	-	0.1	1.0		
90Q1-91Q4	-0.4	-	-0.2	0.7		

NAIRU for that period when compared to the whole period. We can draw similar conclusions for the effects of unionisation. We estimate that French union membership in 1990–91 was 40 per cent below its whole period average, but this only reduced the NAIRU by 1 per cent when compared to its whole period average.

Table 7.9 allows us to decompose the 'causes' of the change in the NAIRU. If we undertake calculations with sub-period variation in real interest rates then in the UK the NAIRU is 3.2 points higher in the early 1990s than the average for the whole period. However, this is almost entirely accounted for by the high level of real interest rates. The replacement ratio is lower, as is unionisation, but they reduce the NAIRU by 0.08 and 1 points respectively, whilst the reduced progressivity of the tax system helped reduce the NAIRU by 0.4 points. If we abstract from the effects of real interest rates, then these estimates suggest that the NAIRU has been roughly constant in

Table 7.10 *Estimates of the NAIRU derived from the LNJ wage equation*

	UK (a)			Germany			France		
	U	NAIRU	NAIRU2	U	NAIRU	NAIRU2	U	NAIRU	NAIRU2
72Q1-91Q4	6.7	6.1	6.1	6.0	5.6	5.6	7.1	6.0	6.0
75Q1-79Q4	4.1	6.0	5.5	4.4	5.6	4.4	5.0	9.9	7.8
80Q1-84Q4	9.0	6.0	5.9	7.1	5.6	5.1	8.1	10.9	7.1
85Q1-89Q4	9.5	7.1	7.9	8.7	5.5	7.0	10.1	0.6	3.4
90Q1-91Q4	7.1	7.0	6.1	6.7	5.4	8.0	9.3	-2.1	3.2

(a) Although our empirical estimates for the UK use the population not working rate, we have translated our implied estimates of the NAIRU back to claimant unemployment in order to ensure comparability with France and Germany. In making this adjustment we have to allow for an additional registration effect (see Gregg, 1990) which accounts for the different behaviour of the two series.

the UK over the last twenty years, and that 'supply side' factors such as union density and replacement rates have little effect on it.

Estimates of the NAIRU derived from the LNJ-style wage equations with the same structure imposed in the UK and Germany are presented in table 7.10. Two methods have been used to calculate the influence of product market pressures. The first of these assumes that the mark-up of prices over unit labour costs desired by firms is given by its whole period average. The second assumes that the desired mark-up changes exogenously over time and is given by its average value in each sub-period (NAIRU2). As can be seen, these assumptions have a crucial influence on estimates of the NAIRU.

The calculated NAIRUs in the UK and Germany do not vary very much over time, especially if we assume the mark-up over unit labour costs is constant. Changes in the product market and hence in the mark-up can change the NAIRU. A lower mark-up helps to reduce the NAIRU, and we might therefore conclude that more competition in the product market will help to reduce sustainable unemployment.

As before it is possible to explain the change in the NAIRUs in terms of the exogenous factors in the wage equation and the change in the price-cost mark-up desired by firms. This decomposition is shown in table 7.11. It is clear from this table that the French results are somewhat anomalous, showing particularly large responses to changes in the replacement ratio, union density and the price-cost mark-up. This is perhaps an example of

Table 7.11 *Accounting for differences in the NAIRU from its period average (LNJ estimates)*

	Percentage mark-up			Replacement ratio		
	UK	GE	FR	UK	GE	FR
75Q1-79Q4	-0.5	-1.3	-2.0	0.1	0.1	-3.7
80Q1-81Q4	-0.0	-0.5	-3.8	..	0.1	4.1
85Q1-89Q4	0.8	1.5	2.8	-0.1	-0.1	2.8
90Q1-91Q4	-0.9	2.6	5.3	-0.2	-0.3	7.2
	Union density			Registration effect		
75Q1-79Q4	-0.2	0.0	7.5	-0.1		
80Q1-81Q4	-0.1	0.0	0.8	0.0		
85Q1-89Q4	0.2	0.0	-8.1	1.0		
90Q1-91Q4	0.4	0.0	-15.3	0.7		

where the cross-country evidence may be used in a negative sense to question whether the effects of density and the replacement rate can really be so large in France but not the other countries. Union density has the 'wrong' sign in the UK and Germany, suggesting that the higher is union density the lower is the NAIRU. This is not consistent with the simple LNJ analysis nor with our results from the Manning equations, but is in line with the arguments in Soskice (1990) that suggest more cooperative bargaining can reduce wage pressures.

Our pooled results for both sets of wage equations suggest considerable similarities in structure, and this implies that similar changes in the exogenous variables have similar effects. The major influences on the NAIRU come from changes in demand-related variables such as the real interest rate or the desired price-cost mark-up. The other factors have trivial effects, suggesting that the NAIRU is largely independent of those supply side factors. Abstracting from movements in the price-cost mark-up or the real interest rate suggests a virtually constant NAIRU throughout the period in all countries.

Conclusions

Macroeconomic performance has varied considerably between the three countries we have studied, and some of the differences are likely to stem from the different operation of their labour markets. This chapter has looked at both the demand for labour and the determination of wages, and we have detected both significant differences and important similarities.

Although the underlying production technology is similar in the three countries, their differing macroeconomic environments and product market structures do produce interesting differences in the demand for labour. German labour demand reacts more rapidly to changes in factor prices than does labour demand in either the UK or France. This may reflect a perception that the macroeconomic environment in Germany is more stable, and that changes in relative factor prices or in demand contain more information about the future of these variables than is the case in the UK or France. The major path for the effect of factor prices in Germany comes through their relative effect, whereas in France and the UK the major path for their effect comes through competitiveness. This in part reflects the considerably noisier nature of relative factor prices in the UK and France. More significantly, we feel, it reflects the market leadership role taken by many German producers. If they change their prices then competitors follow, and there is no (significant) change in their already large market share. This distinction in market roles may be a factor behind the different approaches (at least over the past) to the use of the exchange rate as an instrument of macroeconomic policy in these countries. Both the UK and France can, at least temporarily, increase output and employment after a devaluation. It is not so clear that this option is as beneficial for Germany, because German manufacturing acts as a market leader, and the followers would tend to cut their prices in response to a German devaluation.

The process of wage formation and the associated determination of the level of sustainable unemployment are in many ways even more interesting. All three countries display significant, long-run negative effects from unemployment onto real wages. This result holds up in both the approaches to bargaining that we investigate. The more commonly used specification advocated by Layard *et al.* allows us to look directly at real wage flexibility as indicated by the long-run coefficient on unemployment. The UK and France are again similar, but real wages appear to be considerably more flexible in Germany. This may again reflect the response of institutions and customs to a more stable economic environment, or it may be the result of a different and more cooperative bargaining structure. More flexible real wages, along with a more rapid response to changes in factor prices, suggest that the problem of macroeconomic management in Germany has, at least over our sample period, been somewhat easier than in the rest of Europe.

We do find some role for supply-side factors such as the level of benefits and the role of trade unions. However the evidence is somewhat mixed, and when we pool information across countries there is little support for a strong role for either factor. This is particularly surprising because at most points in our sample period the across-country difference in union density has exceeded the change over the whole sample period in any one country. Replacement ratios have also varied significantly over time (and across countries) and yet we find it hard to discover a large role for them in determining real wages and equilibrium unemployment.

Our analysis of bargaining contains two 'demand side' factors in the determination of the wage and the NAIRU. The real interest rate and the mark-up of prices over costs enter our two approaches to the NAIRU and they both have large effects, in part because they have varied considerably over time. If we factor out these demand variables by setting them at their period averages then it appears that the NAIRU has been remarkably stable, especially in the UK and to a lesser extent in Germany (and France). The equilibrium level of unemployment appears to be between 7 and 8 per cent for the UK, 5.5–7 per cent for Germany and probably in the same range for France. These levels are all well below the actual rate of unemployment we currently observe in these three countries.

The 'supply side' policies adopted in the 1980s seem to have had little effect on the macroeconomic functioning of the labour market. The reduction in benefits in the UK cut the replacement ratio from 43 per cent to 25 per cent of average earnings between the late 1970s and the early 1990s. This is clearly a major factor in the increase in poverty in the UK and it will have been one of the reasons why the relative pay of the bottom decile of the workforce has deteriorated so much (see Blanchflower and Freeman, and Gregg and Machin, in this volume). This significant reduction in the real incomes of the unemployed has produced a fall of less than half a per cent in sustainable unemployment. The reduction of union density in the UK between the late 1970s and the early 1990s has probably reduced sustainable unemployment by 1½ points at most.

What, then, can be done about unemployment in the medium term? First, it is noticeable that Germany has the lowest NAIRU and the highest level of skills in our sample. Increased training may raise productivity and help fulfil real wage aspirations. However, the differences between the NAIRU in the UK and Germany are not great, and we cannot expect quick results from an increased flow of trained labour into the workforce. There are, however, demand policies that can be used. A cut in real interest rates would, we suspect, raise demand and reduce unemployment. We know that macroeconomies exhibit a considerable degree of nominal inertia and employment gains could be sustained for some time. In the long run the authorities cannot determine the real interest rate (at least not with monetary policy) because it is driven by the forces of productivity and thrift, but they can affect it in the short term. The monetary expansion associated with the initial cut in real rates will eventually raise the price level, but output and employment will increase for several years.[14] If we are to believe the effects of real interest rates in the Manning-style wage equations then the temporarily lower real interest rate will also temporarily lower the NAIRU and hence will help to moderate wage pressure.

There are a whole range of other policies that can be adopted, and they are discussed in Britton (1993) and Barrell, Caporale and Sefton (1993). Active labour market policies might help, although the macroeconomic evidence on these is mixed. Expansionary fiscal policies can also be of use in pushing the economy towards the NAIRU. Sustaining 7.5 per cent unemployment in the UK for a period of years with stable inflation would be considered a great success.

Appendix 1   The demand for labour

In order to investigate the existence of differences across countries in the demand side of the labour market it is necessary to set up a model of employment determination. We follow the general LNJ approach except that we work with a labour demand relationship rather than a price equation. Also we assume that firms consider all factors to be variable rather than treating capital as fixed.

It is assumed that firms operate in imperfectly competitive markets and choose factors of production to maximise profits. Suppose further that there are F identical firms indexed i who each face a demand curve for their product of the following type:

$$Y_i = \left(\frac{P_i}{P}\right)^{-\eta} \frac{Y}{F} \tag{A1}$$

where P_i/P is the price set by firm i relative to the average market price, Y is the market demand and η is the absolute price elasticity of demand ($\eta > 1$).

Profits are given by:

$$\Pi_i = P_i Y_i - C(Y_i, W, r) \tag{A2}$$

where $C(Y_i, W, r)$ is the cost function conditioned on output and the nominal price of labour (W) and capital (r). For expositional purposes it is assumed that the technology is Cobb-Douglas so that:

$$Y_i = AK_i^\alpha (TN_i)^{1-\alpha} \tag{A3}$$

where T is the rate of labour augmenting technical progress. It is assumed that the production function is the same for all firms. The cost function can therefore be written as (see Varian, 1984, p.28):

$$C(Y_i, W, r) = \frac{Y_i}{A}\left(\frac{W}{T}\right)^{1-\alpha} r^\alpha \left(\left(\frac{1-\alpha}{\alpha}\right)^\alpha + \left(\frac{\alpha}{1-\alpha}\right)^{1-\alpha}\right) \tag{A4}$$

Profit maximisation is achieved when marginal revenue equals marginal cost. That is:

$$P_i\left(1 - \frac{1}{\eta}\right) = \frac{1}{A}\left(\frac{W}{T}\right)^{1-\alpha} r^\alpha \left(\left(\frac{1-\alpha}{\alpha}\right)^\alpha + \left(\frac{\alpha}{1-\alpha}\right)^{1-\alpha}\right) \tag{A5}$$

Note, for future reference, that the firm's price can also be written as:

$$P_i\left[1 - \frac{1}{\eta}\right] = \frac{(1-\alpha)WN_i}{Y_i}. \tag{A5a}$$

By substituting the firm's optimum price P_i (from (A5)) into (A1) it is possible to find its output, Y_i. The level of employment can be found by differentiating the cost function with respect to the wage (by Shephard's lemma). Written as a function of (endogenous) output this is:

$$N_i = \left(\frac{W\alpha}{rT(1-\alpha)}\right)^{-\alpha} \frac{Y_i}{AT}. \tag{A6}$$

Substituting for Y_i in (A6) gives:

$$N_i = \left(\frac{W\alpha}{rT(1-\alpha)}\right)^{-\alpha} \left(\frac{W}{TP}\right)^{-\eta(1-\alpha)} \left(\frac{r}{P}\right)^{-\alpha\eta} \frac{\theta Y}{FT} \tag{A7}$$

$$\text{where } \theta = \left[\left[\left(\frac{1-\alpha}{\alpha}\right)^{\alpha}+\left(\frac{\alpha}{1-\alpha}\right)^{1-\alpha}\right]\frac{1}{A(1-\frac{1}{\eta})}\right]^{-\eta}\cdot\frac{1}{A}$$

This employment function illustrates that employment in firm i is related to relative factor prices (W/rT), the price of factors relative to the average price of output (W/TP and r/P) and the overall level of demand (Y). The first of these is the substitution effect due to changes in factor prices and the second is the output effect. This comes about because reductions in factor prices in the firm reduce its marginal cost and allow it to cut prices relative to other firms in the market and expand output.

In aggregating across firms it is important to recognise that the latter effect will tend to disappear at the market level. For example, if it is assumed, as in LNJ, that all firms are identical then the aggregate price is given by (A5) and output in each firm is given by Y/F. Aggregate employment is then given by

$$N = \left(\frac{W\alpha}{rT(1-\alpha)}\right)^{-\alpha}\frac{Y}{AT} \tag{A8}$$

so that aggregate employment depends on relative factor prices and the (exogenous to the firm) level of demand.

But suppose that firms operate in a global market. Aggregate employment in a particular country will then be determined by summing over the employment levels of firms located in that country. If firms located within that country are small relative to the global market then (A7) is likely to be a reasonable representation of its aggregate employment equation. Because the various firms in the market are located in several different countries where factor prices are different it is not necessarily the case that they will choose the same price. Rather, the average price will reflect desired mark-ups and factor prices in these different countries.

There are two caveats to this and both relate to the longer-term comparative advantage of producing particular goods in one country rather than in another. First, differences in costs across countries will be reflected in relative prices and the more perfect is the product market the less will be produced in the high cost countries. Second, firms themselves can choose where they locate production and will tend to gravitate towards the country where the cost of producing this product is lowest. Thus, in the limit, goods produced in different countries will be sold at the same price or be produced in only one country.

In the case where the global market is dominated by producers from one country it is likely that employment in those firms will be determined by (A8). Wage costs will affect employment through the substitution effect rather than the output effect. This is because changes in wage costs will be common to most firms in the market who therefore do not benefit from a demand expansion arising from greater competitiveness.

This discussion suggests two types of employment equations depending on whether domestic firms compete in competitive global or domestic markets. For firms operating in competitive global markets the relevant equation is (A7) and may be written in log-linear form as:

$$\ln N = \text{constant} - \alpha(1-\eta)\ln(W/r) - \eta\ln(W/P) \qquad (A9)$$
$$+ \ln Y - (1 - \alpha - \eta(1-\alpha))\ln T$$

where Y is global demand and P is the global price level (expressed in domestic currency). Bradley and Fitzgerald (1988) argue that firms in small open economies are in this situation with domestic output determined by world demand and competitiveness.

When firms from one country compete mainly with domestically based firms the relevant aggregate equation is:

$$\ln N = \text{constant} - \alpha\ln(W/r) + \ln Y - (1-\alpha)\ln T. \qquad (A10)$$

The distinction between (A9) and (A10) is that (A9) allows for international competitiveness effects. This does not arise in (A10) because all firms are assumed to operate in the same product and factor markets. This may be because they operate in the domestic non-traded sector, or because firms operating in the domestic factor market dominate the global product market. In the former case the relevant output variable is domestic output, in the latter it is global output.

Appendix 2 The nature of the bargain

The bargaining framework is used in what follows to develop specifications of the wage equation that conform to both the conventional approach and that suggested by Manning. It is assumed that firms and unions bargain over the wage in each particular firm. The utility of the union associated with firm i at date t is given by:

$$U_{it} = N_{it}^{\Psi}(V_{it} - V_t^a)$$
(A11)

where N_{it} is employment in the i'th firm at date t, v_{it} is the value to workers of employment in this firm, V_t^a is the value of the alternatives available at date t. The parameter ψ indicates the extent to which the union cares about employment in bargaining over wages.

The value of employment in the firm is

$$V_{it} = \frac{W_{it}}{P_t} + \delta_t E_t[q_{t+1}V_{t+1}^u + (1 - q_{t+1})V_{t+1}]$$
(A12)

where W_{it} / P_t is the real consumer wage which for current purposes is assumed equal to the real producer wage, δ_t is a discount factor, q_{t+1} is the probability that a worker employed this period will be unemployed in the next period and V_{t+1}^u is the value of being unemployed. This is given by

$$V_t^u = \left(\frac{B}{P}\right)_t + \delta_t E_t[s_{t+1}V_{t+1}^u + (1 - s_{t+1})V_{t+1}]$$
(A13)

where B/P is the real benefit level and s_{t+1} is the probability of an unemployed worker being unemployed next period.

The value of the alternatives to employment in the firm at t is

$$V_t^a = \eta_t V_t + (1 - \eta_t)V_t^u$$
(A14)

where η_t is the probability of obtaining another job at t.

The Nash bargaining solution indicates that the chosen wage maximises

$$\Omega_{it} = U_{it}^{\chi_t} \Pi_{it}^{1-\chi_t}$$
(A15)

where Π_{it} is the profit of firm i and χ_i is the bargaining power of the union. The first order conditions imply that:

$$\frac{W_{it}}{P_t} = \mu_t(V_{it} - V_t^a)$$
(A16)

where $\mu_t = \psi \varepsilon_{\pi t} + \dfrac{1-\chi_t}{\chi_t}$

where ε_{Nt} and $\varepsilon_{\pi t}$ are the absolute elasticities of labour demand and profits with respect to wages.

There are a number of different ways of deriving an aggregate wage equation from (A16). The approach favoured by Manning is to treat μ_t in (A16) as exogenous depending only on union power (χ_t) and union attitudes to jobs (ψ). By using the definitions of the value functions, V_{it}, V_t^a, V_t^u and V_t, it is possible to show that in the steady state where $(V_t - V_t^u) = (V_{t+1} - V_{t+1}^u)$, the bargained real wage is given by:

$$\frac{W_t}{P_t} = \frac{\mu_t(1 - \eta_t)}{\mu_t(1 - \eta_t) - [1 - \delta_t(s_t - q_t)]}\left(\frac{B_t}{P_t}\right). \tag{A17}$$

This indicates that the bargained real wage depends positively on real benefits, the probability of re-employment of redundant workers in the current period (η_t), union power (which has a negative effect on μ) and negatively on the degree to which unions care about jobs (which has a positive effect on μ). If those who are currently unemployed have a greater chance of being unemployed next period than those who are currently in work $(s_t > q_t)$ then the discount rate (δ_t is the discount factor) also has a positive effect on wages. One of the benefits of being in work today is that it improves the chances of having a job tomorrow, but the higher the discount rate the less beneficial this is. As a consequence a higher discount rate raises wage pressure.

The transition probabilities (n_t, s_t, q_t) in (A17) will depend upon the rate of unemployment. In fact (A17) may be interpreted as a (non-linear) relationship between the desired wage benefit mark-up and the rate of unemployment: the higher the rate of unemployment the lower the wage benefit mark-up. If it turns out that public policy determines the actual wage benefit mark-up through choice of the replacement ratio, then the equation will determine the rate of unemployment that makes unions choose that particular wage benefit mark-up. As Manning points out, in these circumstances it is possible to estimate the parameters of the wage setting relationship by estimating an unemployment equation which depends on the replacement ratio and the other variables in (A17).

As an alternative it is possible to derive a dynamic aggregate wage equation from (A16) by not imposing the assumption of a steady state. This is given in the following solution for current real wages:

$$\frac{W_t}{P_t} = \frac{\mu_t(1 - \eta_t)}{\mu_t(1 - \eta_t) - 1}\left(\frac{B_t}{P_t}\right) - \frac{\mu_t(1 - \eta_t)}{\mu_t(1 - \eta_t) - 1} \cdot \delta_t E_t\left(\frac{(s_{t+1} - q_{t+1})W_{t+1} / P_{t+1}}{\mu_{t+1}(1 - \eta_{t+1})}\right). \tag{A18}$$

This reduces to (A17) in the steady state. Note that future real wages have a *negative* effect on current real wages. This is because higher expected real wages increase the reward to being in employment in the next period and the best way to achieve that is by being in employment today. Manning indicates that by relating the transition probabilities to the rate of unemployment and by taking a log linear approximation this can be written as:

$$\Delta \ln(W/P)_{t+1} = \lambda_0 - \lambda_1(L)E_t u_{t+1} + \lambda_2 \frac{B_t}{P_t} + \lambda_{31} E_t \Delta \mu_{t+1} - \lambda_{32} \mu_t - \lambda_4 \delta_t . \quad (A19)$$

This suffers from none of the identification problems referred to in the text as it excludes the variables that appear in the labour demand curve. Equation (A19) represents one of the specifications of the aggregate wage equation that is estimated in the text (see (8)).

It is important to recognise that the identifiability of the wage equation has come about because of an exclusion restriction. Manning's point of departure from the LNJ approach is in treating the variable μ_t as exogenous. This depends on the elasticities of profits and labour demand with respect to wages. LNJ-type wage equations can be derived by solving out for these in terms of the parameters of the production function and the product demand curve. Manning indicates that if this is done, the following LNJ-type wage equation may be derived

$$\log\left(\frac{W_t}{P_t}\right) = \log\left(\frac{Y_t}{N_t}\right) + \lambda_0 - \lambda_1 u_t + \lambda_2 \frac{B_t}{P_t} + \lambda_3 \chi_t. \quad (A20)$$

The choice between the two formulations of the aggregate wage equation depends largely on whether it is appropriate to treat as exogenous the elasticities of labour demand and profits with respect to wages. If this is considered appropriate, the Manning-style wage equations can be estimated. If not, the LNJ-type equations are better descriptions of the structural process determining wages. However they are not necessarily identified.

Appendix 3 Deriving the NAIRU

The basic structure of the wage equations can be written:
LNJ:

$$\ln\left(\frac{W}{P}\right) = a_0 + \ln\left(\frac{Y}{N}\right)_t - a_1 U_t + a_2 \frac{B_t}{P_t} + a_3 \chi_t + a_4 \Delta \ln WEDGE + a_5 \Delta \ln W_t \quad (A21)$$

Manning:

$$
\Delta \ln\left(\frac{W}{P}\right)^c_t = b_0 - b_1 U_t + b_2 \frac{B_t}{P_t} + b_3 \chi_t - b_4 \Delta \ln WEDGE
$$
$$
- b_5 PROG + b_6 \Delta \ln PROD_t + b_7 RR_t
$$

(A22)

(all variables are defined as in the text).

The aggregate producer price equation may be written as:

$$
\ln\left(\frac{P}{W}\right)_t = c_0 - \ln\left(\frac{Y}{N}\right)_t
$$

(A23)

where c_0 is related to firms' desired mark-up of prices over costs. The left-hand side is the inverse of the real producer wage and may be substituted directly into (A21) to derive a solution for the rate of unemployment consistent with the LNJ analysis. To do the same for the Manning wage equation note that the growth in the real consumer wage is equal to the growth in the real producer wage less the growth in the wedge (see (6) in text). Substituting into the left-hand side of (A22) and re-arranging gives a solution for the rate of unemployment generated by the Manning-style wage equations. Hence stylised solutions for the equilibrium rate of unemployment are:

LNJ:

$$
U_t^* = \frac{a_0 + c_0}{a_1} + \frac{a_2}{a_1}\frac{B_t}{P_t} + \frac{a_3}{a_1}\chi_t + \frac{a_4}{a_1}\Delta \ln WEDGE_t + \frac{a_5}{a_1}\Delta \ln W_t
$$

(A24)

Manning:

$$
U_t^* = \frac{b_0}{b_1} + \frac{b_2}{b_1}\frac{B_t}{P_t} + \frac{b_3}{b_1}\chi_t + \frac{1 - b_4}{b_5}\Delta \ln WEDGE_t
$$
$$
+ \frac{b_5}{b_1}PROG_t - \frac{(1 - b)_0}{b_1}\Delta \ln PROD_t + \frac{b_7}{b_1}RR_t
$$

(A25)

We use versions of (A24) and (A25) to generate estimates of the equilibrium rate of unemployment. In doing so we do not take account of dynamic terms in the wedge and in inflation, as we would expect these to be constant in the steady state.

Data appendix

Labour demand

1. The quantity of work is defined as:

	WORK =	(EE*HRS*MANSH+EE*(1–MANSH))
where	EE:	Employees in employment
	HRS:	Hours index in manufacturing
	MANSH:	Share of total employees in manufacturing
Source:	Germany:	Federal Labour Office
	France:	OECD *Labour force Statistics* and *Main Economic Indicators*
	UK:	*Department of Employment* Gazette

2.

	Output:	GDP at Factor Cost
Source:	UK:	CSO, non-oil GDP
	Germany:	OECD *Quarterly National Accounts*
	France:	OECD *Quarterly National Accounts*
	EEC:	OECD *Quarterly National Accounts*

3.

	Output Deflator:	GDP deflator at factor cost
Source:	UK:	CSO, non-oil GDP
	Germany:	OECD *Quarterly National Accounts*
	France:	OECD *Quarterly National Accounts*
	EEC:	OECD *Quarterly National Accounts*

4.

	Wage:	Total compensation of employees including employers' taxes
Source:	UK:	CSO
	Germany:	Deutsches Bundesbank
	France:	INSEE National Accounts

5.

	Cost of Capital:	Non Residential Private Sector Investment deflator
Source:	UK:	User cost of capital, See Young (1992) and NIESR database
	Germany:	OECD *Quarterly National Accounts*
	France:	OECD *Quarterly National Accounts*

6.

	Materials Costs:	Materials inputs price for manufacturing
Source:		*Economic Trends* and NIESR database

Wages

7. The producer wage is ((Wage/Work)/Output deflator)

8. The consumer wage is $(((Wage*(1-dt)/Work)/CED)$

    where *dt* is the average direct tax rate including employees' national insurance contributions, and CED is the consumers expenditure deflator
    Source: CSO, INSEE and Deutsches Bundesbank

9. Unemployment: Registered unemployed for France and Germany
    Source: Bundesbank and OECD L.F.S.
                               Population not working rate for UK. Source: *An nual Abstract of Statistics* and NIESR database

10. Real Interest Rates: short-term forward looking real consumer interest rates
    Source: NIESR database — short-term forward looking real consumer interest rates

11. Replacement Ratio
    Total Benefits Paid (including income supplement) divided by the number of unemployed, as a proportion of post-tax earnings per employee
    Source: UK: *Social Security Statistics*
            France: INSEE *Comptes et Indicateurs Economiques*
            Germany: Statistisches Bundesamt *Statistisches Jahrbuch*

14. Union Density
            UK: Department of Employment *Gazette*
            Germany: Statistisches Bundesamt *Statistisches Jahrbuch*
            France: Bean (1989) and ILO (1993)

15. Marginal tax rates
            UK: *Annual Abstract of Statistics*
            Germany: Finance Ministry mimeo
            France: INSEE, mimeo

We would like to thank Catherine Dargent and Dirk Faltin for their hard work in constructing this data set.

Notes

1 We would like to thank Andrew Britton, Stephen Nickell, Andrew Oswald, Peter Westaway, David Worswick and other conference participants for useful comments. All errors remain ours. This research was financed by grants from the ESRC Macroeconomic Modelling Consortium and from the Leverhulme Foundation.

2 We are therefore constrained from using two (or three) stage Granger/Engle (Engle and Granger, 1987) cointegration techniques. Our alternatives are the Johansen style system cointegration approach or the more traditional least squares based estimation of the error correction mechanism. Johansen (1988) techniques require the prior imposition of overidentifying restrictions on a set of eigenvectors in order to extract the structural equations. Although these restrictions can be tested the results are not as transparent as those available in the (asymptotically equivalent) least squares based approach.

3 With around 40 regressors being included in the initial unrestricted general dynamic model, degrees of freedom were limited, prohibiting the use of instrumental variables at this stage. Thus the procedure adopted was to derive a data-based specification from the initial model by means of OLS and to then re-estimate this using instrumental variables to instrument contemporaneous endogenous variables.

4 An important issue in any empirical study is whether a long-run equilibrium relationship exists between the variables of interest, that is whether these variables are cointegrated. The most frequently applied tests for cointegration are the 'two-step' approach of Engle and Granger (1987) and the multivariate approach of Johanson (1988). In a recent paper Kremers et al. (1992) argue that cointegration tests based on an estimated error-correction coefficient in a general dynamic model may have greater power than the conventional Dickey-Fuller statistics used to test for cointegration in the 'two-step' approach as the latter impose a potentially invalid common factor restriction. Their suggested alternative is to re-estimate either the general or the final dynamic model with the long-run numerical solution imposed in an error-correction term and to compare the value of the t-statistic on this term with the critical values reported in MacKinnon (1991) for the Dickey-Fuller test. Results from this procedure are reported in table 7.1 denoted t^1_{ECM} and t^2_{ECM}.

5 For the purposes of this chapter we assume that any cointegrating vector is unique, although the test procedure we use merely requires that all cointegrating vectors appear in the conditional model alone, that is that weak exogeneity is satisfied.

6 The relative material-labour cost term is of little consequence. It never has a significant long-run effect and has a short-run effect only in the UK.

7 The test statistic is $\chi^2_4 = 16.34$.

8 Source: Handbook of Labour Statistics and Department of Employment *Gazette*, various issues, and German Statistical Yearbook. Registration of members in France has been intermittent, and our graph includes some interpolation based on ILO (1993). High density in the UK, along with the industrial composition of unions, may lead to bias in our estimates. A number of registered union members may be unemployed, and hence exerting no bargaining pressure. Metcalf (in this volume) suggests that this bias could be as high as 10 per cent in 1990.

9   This is in contrast to Calmfors and Driffill (1988) who, according to Soskice, look at the form of the bargain rather than the substance.
10 We have used registered unemployment in France and Germany, but continual changes in registration rules in the UK make this less than adequate. We have therefore used the Institute measure of population not working (see Gregg, 1990).
11 The effect of this restriction is that productivity growth does not affect the NAIRU calculations reported below.
12 The long-run coefficients on unemployment in these equations are -0.0027 for the UK, -0.004 for France and -0.0044 for Germany, whilst the mean lags on past prices are 2.96 quarters, 2.70 quarters and 5.23 quarters respectively. This underestimates the speed of response of wages to prices in the UK because the equation also includes a lead term in prices.
13 We used our single equation estimates for Germany and parameters from a joint estimate of our French and UK equations.
14 This is the argument in the recent OECD study on unemployment (see OECD, 1993).

References

Anderton, R., Barrell, R., in't Veld, J.W. and Pittas, N. (1992), 'Forward-looking wages and nominal inertia in the ERM', *National Institute Economic Review*, 141, August 1992.

Barrell, R. (1990), 'Has the EMS changed wage and price behaviour in Europe?' *National Institute Economic Review*, 134, November 1990.

Barrell, R., Caporale, G. and Sefton, J. (1993), 'Prospects for European unemployment' in Grieve-Smith, J. and Michie, J. (ed.), *Unemployment in Europe — Policies for Growth*, London, Academic Press.

Barrell, R. and Pain, N. (1993), 'Trade restraints and Japanese direct investment flows', paper presented at the Econometric Society European Meetings, Uppsala, August 1993.

Barrell, R., Pain, N. and Young, G. (1993), 'Structural differences in European labour markets', National Institute Discussion Paper.

Bazen S. and Martin, J. (1991), 'The effect of the minimum wage on employment and earnings in France, 1963–85', *OECD Economic Studies*, 16, Spring.

Bean, R. (1989), *International Labour Statistics, A Handbook*, London, Routledge.

Bradley, J. and Fitzgerald, J. (1988), 'Industrial output and factor input, determination in an econometric model of a small open economy', *European Economic Review*, 32, 1227–41.

Britton, A. (1993), 'Two routes to full employment', *National Institute Economic Review*, 144, May.

Calmfors, L. and Driffill, J. (1988), 'Centralisation of wage bargaining and macroeconomic performance', *Economic Policy*, 6 13–61.

Drèze, J. and Bean, C. (1991), *Europe's Unemployment Problem*, Cambridge, Mass., MIT Press.

Engle, R.F. and Granger, C.W. (1987), 'Cointegration and error correction: representation, estimation and testing', *Econometrica*, 55, 251–76.

Gregg, P. (1990), 'Out for the count', National Institute Discussion Paper no. 167.

International Labour Office (ILO) (1993), *World Labour Report*, Geneva.

Johansen, S. (1988), 'Statistical analysis of cointegration vectors', *Journal of Economic Dynamics and Control*, 12, 231–54.

Kremers, J.N., Ericsson, N. and Dolado, J. (1992), 'The power of cointegration tests', *Oxford Bulletin of Economics and Statistics*, 54, 3, August.

Layard, R., Nickell, S. and Jackman, R. (1991), *Unemployment: Macroeconomic Performance and the Labour Market*, Oxford University Press.

Lockwood, B. and Manning, A. (1992), 'Wage setting and the tax system: theory and evidence for the UK', Centre for Economic Performance, Discussion Paper no. 115.

Mackinnon, J. (1991), 'Critical values for cointegration tests' in Engle, R. and Granger, C. (eds), *Long Run Economic Relationships*, Oxford University Press.

Manning, A. (1993), 'Wage bargaining and the Phillips Curve: the identification and specification of aggregate wage equations', *Economic Journal*, 103, 98–118.

OECD (1993), *Interim Report on Unemployment,* Paris, June.

Pain, N. (1993), 'An econometric analysis of foreign direct investment in the United Kingdom', *Scottish Journal of Political Economy*, 40.

Patinkin, D. (1968), *Money, Income and Prices*, New York, Harper & Row.

Prais, S. (1989), *Productivity, Education and Training, Britain and Other Countries Compared*, London, National Institute of Economic and Social Research.

Soskice, D. (1990), 'Wage determination: the changing role of institutions in advanced industrialised countries', *Oxford Review of Economic Policy*, 6, 4.

Symons, J. and Layard, R. (1984), 'Neoclassical demand for labour functions for six major economies', *Economic Journal*, 94, 788–800.

Varian, H.R. (1984), *Microeconomic Analysis*, London, Norton.

Young, G. (1992), 'Industrial investment and economic policy' in Britton, A. (ed.), *Industrial Investment as a Policy Objective*, NIESR Report Series no. 2.

8 The UK labour market: micro rigidities and macro obstructions

PATRICK MINFORD AND JONATHAN RILEY[1]

In recent months UK unemployment has again approached three million. A number of economists have suggested that it will not fall much below three million in the foreseeable future. The implication of such a view is that the UK 'equilibrium' or natural rate is of this order. In this chapter we set out an alternative view based on our work in Liverpool and embodied in the Liverpool model of the UK.

This model (a full account of it in its early annual form is Minford *et al.*, 1984; and in its latest quarterly version in Minford *et al.*, 1990) is new classical in approach, though it includes a unionised sector which strikes collective wage bargains. These bargains generate a fairly slow rate of real wage adjustment, which underlies the model's slow rate of adjustment of real variables. By contrast there is little nominal rigidity in the model (notably in its current quarterly version) so that inflation rapidly reaches its equilibrium (apart from some modest adjustment element contributed by real variables such as real balances). Nominal disturbances have their effect through interest rates and wealth effects. Real disturbances come from changes in 'supply-side' variables such as the tax rate, unemployment benefits and union power.

In what follows we discuss first the model estimate of the natural rate, U^*, and the contribution to it of different exogenous variables. Secondly we look at the deviation from U^* of the actual unemployment rate and the elements contributing to this. Finally we discuss the contrast between this set of findings and the more pessimistic claims referred to at the start.

The natural rate

This is calculated in the model from the equilibrium version of four behavioural equations:

— a wage equation, treated as the supply price of labour. Real wages are a function of unemployment, real benefits grossed up for direct taxes, the unionisation rate, and (with only a small impact) surprise movements in prices. Because there is assumed to be a non-negligible non-union sector this is not a 'bargaining' equation as for example in Layard and Nickell (1985) and their many followers. It is identified by the exclusion of current influences on labour demand, as noted by Manning (1993). The non-union wage depends on benefits and unemployment (the proxy for labour supply); but the average wage also includes the union wage, whose mark-up depends on unionisation, and unanticipated inflation, and is subject to lagged adjustment.
— a price-cost relation (with a cyclical mark-up which drops out in equilibrium), derived from the implicit (constant returns) production function.
— a wage=marginal product relation for (un)employment where marginal product is conditioned on expected output. This too comes from the implicit production function. (Given that prices are set mainly in relation to long-run average costs, this set-up implies that output and labour demand respond in the short run to aggregate demand, with a capacity utilisation variable in the production function.)
— the previous three equations give rise to an 'open economy supply curve' of output, with the real exchange rate as its principal argument (an increase, or decline in competitiveness, causes more supply because this lowers import prices enabling home suppliers to pay higher real consumer wages while still maintaining their producer price to cost margin). As our supply curve of labour is not vertical more labour is supplied at a higher real consumer wage and hence more output is produced.

The fourth equation is for the current (external) balance, a function of home and foreign output, and the real exchange rate: the effect of net interest, profits and dividends related to accumulated net foreign assets is neglected as second order (inclusion of it would produce a small hysteretic influence on the equilibrium). We assume that in equilibrium stocks of net foreign assets cannot be changing: this is an approximation to the stock-flow equilibrium condition that all asset holdings increase at the steady state growth rate — effectively assuming net foreign assets to be close to zero. Also we should realise that for a fast-growing economy (for example an LDC) this condition is too stringent, as one would expect large capital inflows in this case for long periods. However this is not relevant for a mature economy with a moderate steady growth rate. On our assumption we can turn this equation into a long-run demand relation, where output is related to the real exchange rate (negatively) and to world output (or trade).

Of course in the long run capacity utilisation must be normal and so we can illustrate the system by a four-quadrant diagram adapted from Parkin and

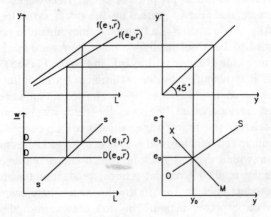

Figure 8.1 The open economy under imperfect competition in the long run

Bade (1990) and for a detailed derivation see Minford (1992, chapter 8, appendix). Notice that capital is completely endogenous in this solution: capital flows in from abroad or from domestic savings until normal profit is restored. It is the (world) cost of capital that is exogenous here.

Figure 8.2 shows the overall natural rate we obtain over the last two decades from the resulting long-run equations (in the appendix we set out the equations used). It rose to a peak of three million in 1981–3 and since then has fallen to below one million today (1993).

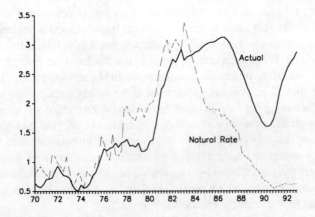

Figure 8.2 Actual and natural rate of unemployment (thousands)

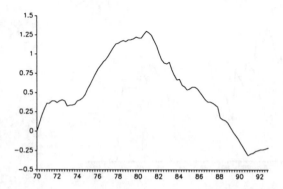

Figure 8.3 Effect (on log U^*) of unionisation

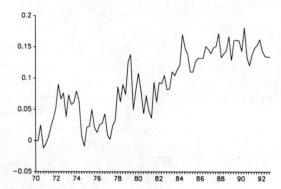

Figure 8.4 Effect (on log U^*) of VAT

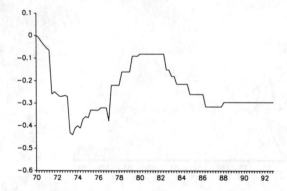

Figure 8.5 Effect (on log U^*) of employers' labour tax

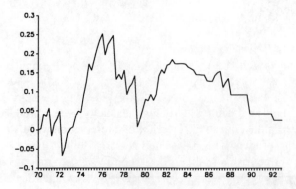

Figure 8.6 Effect (on log U^*) of employees' labour tax

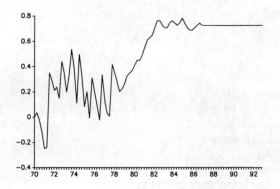

Figure 8.7 Effect (on log U^*) of unemployment benefit

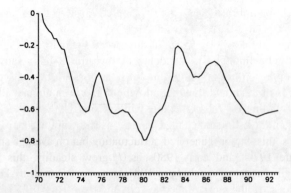

Figure 8.8 Effect (on log U^*) of productivity and world trade

We now proceed to decompose this rather striking pattern of change in the natural rate into its constituent determinants. Figures 8.3–8.8 show the results.

Interestingly the flat profile of benefits during the 1970s rules them out as having contributed to U^* changes in that decade. However in the 1980s the sharp rises in council house rents, fully compensated in unemployment benefits, but only partially in in-work benefits, substantially raised the benefit package. Besides this contributory role, the key role of benefits is in giving the labour supply schedule a fairly high elasticity, which produces a degree of real wage rigidity, due to the presence of a reservation wage.

The main elements producing change are unionisation, followed by taxes of various sorts. The former rises steadily to 1980 before steadily falling back. The tax rates move in largely offsetting ways until 1983 when their net effect is to lower unemployment, led by falling employer taxes on labour.

Besides these we can see that the trend elements (productivity and world trade trends) produce a tendency to improvement which is reversed by the serious world recession of the early 1980s. Thereafter the ground is gradually recaptured over the 1980s.

One way to summarise this story is to say that trends in productivity and world markets managed after the world recession of 1982 to dominate (just) the effect of rising benefits, while 1980s supply-side influences reducing union power and lowering taxes had further reduced equilibrium unemployment by 1991 to below the level of 1970, restoring it (at 0.6 million) well towards the natural rate of the 1950s (put by the annual model at about 0.3 million).

$U–U^*$ — the story of 'temporary' unemployment

We put temporary in quotes because it can take a long time before unemployment reaches its natural rate. There are two sources of $U–U^*$, the 'unemployment gap'.

First as U^* changes it takes time — about three years — before U is fully affected. This lag can be thought of as the delay in investment taking advantage of new profit opportunities or being run down as losses are realised. It follows that changes in U^* affect the unemployment gap in a manner illustrated in figure 8.9: falling U^* raises the gap while rising U^* lowers it. The net effect on $U–U^*$ of the estimated changes in U^* is shown in figure 8.10. In the early 1970s this factor generated a fluctuating but on average small gap. But by the late 1970s and early 1980s, as U^* grew steadily, this had become substantially negative, peaking in 1981 at minus 0.7 million. From 1981, as U^* levelled off, the gap dropped to zero and then from 1983 as U^* has fallen the unemployment gap has risen, to a peak of 0.7 million in 1984. It then fluctuates before falling away as U^* levels off in the late 1980s.

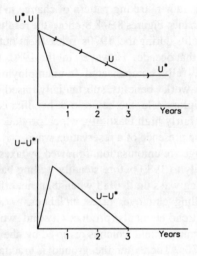

Figure 8.9 Effect of U^* on $U–U^*$

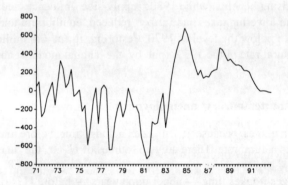

Figure 8.10 Effect of U^* on $U–U^*$

The second element is the effect of shocks to demand. We do not attempt to decompose this element here. In Matthews and Minford (1987) we did attempt it (using the earlier annual Liverpool model) for a purely floating period from 1980-86. On this occasion we are faced with a much longer period and a regime change — the shadow ERM 1987-8 and the ERM proper 1990-92 — which upset this floating transmission in a manner that is not easy to model. Instead of formal decomposition we make some informal comments about the demand pressures revealed by this second (residual) element.

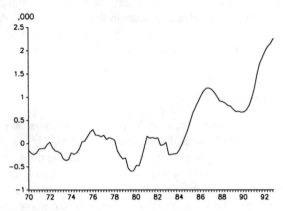

Figure 8.11 Demand-induced effect for $U-U^*$

The most significant residual factor has, we believe, been the evolution of the real long-term interest rate. Figure 8.11 shows the demand-induced effect on $U-U^*$. During most of the 1970s fluctuations in it were fairly modest. There was a peak of demand-induced unemployment of 0.3 million in 1976, against a trough of –0.4 million in 1973, a not-implausible net swing of 0.7 from the Barber boom to the recession after the first oil price rise. Thereafter the swings become larger. In the 1979 expansion it falls to –0.6 in 1979 before emerging into the trauma of the 1980s.

During the early 1980s demand-led unemployment fluctuates between 0.2 and –0.2 million before the lagged effects of persistent deflation (see Matthews and Minford, 1987) come through from 1984 onwards. The peak of demand-induced unemployment is 1.2 million in 1986 (much in line with Matthews and Minford, 1987). From then the recovery begins to reduce the total, bringing it down to 0.7 million in 1990.

At this point we run into the phase of deflation associated with the aftermath of the 1988 boom and the entry into the ERM. According to these figures demand-led unemployment had reached no less than 2.3 million by the end of 1992. They clearly indicate that this deflation has been of an extraordinary magnitude.

Clearly these numbers must be treated with more than the usual caution. There are high standard errors around natural rate estimates. Nevertheless the direction and size of these movements in the natural rate and their broad decomposition into supply- and demand-driven components does in our view indicate four main things. First, that there was a large rise in the natural rate between the 1960s and the early 1980s. Second, that this rise was probably more than reversed by the somewhat draconian labour market reforms of the 1980s. Third that there have been two major deflationary episodes with sharp effects on unemployment in the 1980s. Fourth, that of these the second, associated with ERM entry, was the more deflationary and had the sharper unemployment effect, on a scale comparable with that of the 1930s.

Interpretation and contrast

The picture drawn in this chapter could not be in greater contrast with the generality of comment one reads about the UK economy today. This is as true of most forecasting houses as it is of economic commentators, business or academic. The general view seems to be that the UK has little excess capacity and that, in the labour market, wage pressures will restart at unemployment rates not much below three million, most of these unemployed being considered to exert little if any market pressure on wages because of the power of 'insiders'.

There is of course a natural human tendency to extrapolate current experience. This tendency is all the greater in a world of rapid change, today's *par excellence*; it is hard to rely on past regularities when these are being upset with equally alarming regularity.

But this tendency can be overdone. This chronic Lucas Critique condition does not imply that we should jettison all modelling relationships in favour of a know-nothing random walk model whose implication is that one should extrapolate the present endlessly into the future. We must try to separate out the shifting from the stable relations, adjust our models rather than throw them away. We have made some adjustments to our model here, notably for the ERM and the productivity shifts induced by the major tax reforms introduced by Nigel Lawson. But we can see no reason to abandon modelling: indeed, although we have not dwelt on this aspect here, what exercises we have done on the model's forecasting capacity have been reasonably encouraging (for example, Matthews and Minford, 1987; Matthews, Minford and Riley, 1986; and Andrews *et al.*, 1990).

What sort of evidence is adduced for the agnostic random walk position against our own? There are three main pieces of which we are aware.

First, it is argued that wage behaviour became aggressive again as unemployment fell below 2.5 million in 1988. Wages grew by 10 per cent by 1990, after averaging 8 per cent through the mid-1980s.

Second, unemployment itself is argued to be on a rising ratchet-like trend. In the latest boom it fell only to 1.6 million (in mid-1990), against 1.3 million in the last cyclical upturn of 1979. It is commonly forecast that unemployment will reach 3.4 million or more in the current contraction against 3.3 million in 1986, the last peak.

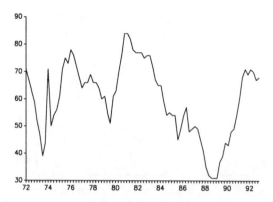

Figure 8.12 CBI survey: firms reporting below-capacity working (%)

Finally, on capacity it is said that there is limited excess capacity because of accelerated write-offs of plant during this recession. As evidence we are pointed to the latest CBI survey's answer to the below-capacity question — figure 8.12 (showing only 70 per cent below capacity as against 83 per cent in 1980)— and to the high import penetration figures and balance of payments deficits that emerged in 1988 and have continued even in the midst of severe recession.

This is a daunting charge sheet on the key trio of wages, unemployment and capacity; we may have left out some further charges but these are perhaps the major ones and certainly enough to be getting on with. We do not deny that one can fit a pessimistic story to these facts. Let us reply in two ways; first by 'encompassing' these facts within our story — that is, explaining them away in our own terms. Secondly by suggesting some stray inconsistencies and weaknesses within the pessimistic story itself. The first tactic is defensive, the second is offensive, in intellectual terms.

Why did the rate of increase in average earnings rise from 8 per cent to 10 per cent? According to our story this reflected rising inflationary expectations in the monetary context of 1987–90. It is actually remarkable how little wage settlements reacted to a sharp rise in inflation (from 5 per cent to 10 per cent on the RPI and around 8 per cent on 'underlying' measures); we explain this by our view that unemployment was above not below the natural rate. For all this period real wages were growing by substantially less than the 4.7 per cent 1980s average growth in manufacturing (let alone still higher general industrial) productivity.

Why did unemployment drop only to 1.6 million and why has it risen to around 3 million? Our answer is that owing to our tragic errors in monetary policy we had to hit on the head an economy which otherwise could

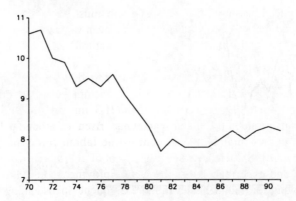

Figure 8.13 UK share of world trade in manufactures

have remained on a sustained growth path of some 3 per cent. After we had so hit it on the head we joined the ERM proper and continuing raining blows on its prostrate body. The resulting deep recession has produced an unemployment excess, $U-U^*$, of over two million. In short it is recession, not the trends of a poorly-performing labour market, that has delivered us this apparent ratchet.

Finally why the apparent lack of capacity? We explain the high import penetration partly by reference to the ERM overvaluation; we also note the fairly good export share performance (figure 8.13) in spite of this overvaluation, so a further explanation lies in the free trade orientation of the UK economy — we are specialising and dividing labour.

There is also little doubt that the sheer speed of the 1988 expansion overtook available capacity at that time. Nevertheless a distiction must be made between actual capacity and the potential output (or natural output rate) associated with the natural rate of unemployment. It takes time for the necessary capital to be installed, to exploit the profit opportunities linked with potential output: had growth been steady and controlled in 1988, we would argue that overheating would have been avoided and unemployment would have fallen without the interruption caused by the temporary inflationary pressure and the subsequent squeeze.

As for capacity, the CBI question is qualitative and must be treated with caution. Furthermore capacity, even when 'written off', does not thereby cease to exist, it is merely discounted by managers or even sold off; interestingly total private gross fixed investment has fallen only 20 per cent from its peak during this long and severe recession suggesting that apart from 'write-off' (that is, in physical terms) there is large-scale spare capacity.

Turning from encompassing to the offensive, we must stress that the behaviour of expected real wages remained moderate even when unemployment had fallen to 1.6 million; this is inconsistent with a natural rate of 2.5 million and above.

Then we must query the lack of pressure from 'outsiders', in the form of the long-term unemployed. The numbers of those unemployed more than a year had dropped by end-1990 to 0.5 million from 1.3 million in 1987. Furthermore the turnover rate in the labour market had risen to around 0.3 million per month, approximately 14 per cent of the labour force per year (against 9 per cent in 1988). Hence some 50 per cent of the labour force may have 'quit' jobs and experienced a spell of unemployment in the last four years; even allowing for double and even more frequent spells among these this high rate of activity suggests a wide experience of unemployment in the labour force. This is not a picture of supine labour market behaviour by the unemployed, not even those with the misfortune to become 'long-term' unemployed. Nor would supinity be consistent with other evidence we have on benefits (now exceedingly low relative to the wages of all but the lowest paid), on the greater vigour with which worktesting (plus job- and re-start programmes) is being applied, and finally the weakness of the traditionally militant unions.

A supposed lack of excess capacity is difficult to reconcile with the answers to the CBI's pricing question (virtually no respondents plan price rises), especially given the large rise in imported material costs since exit from the ERM. There is clear unwillingness to raise prices and margins, which can only be explained by an extreme desire to raise sales and use of capacity.

Conclusions

We bring together here the implications of our work at Liverpool for the issue of micro rigidities and macro obstructions in the UK labour market. Our view is that the micro problems have been substantially diminished by the supply-side reforms of the 1980s but that macro policy has been particularly savage during the past four years, as a by-product of the ERM experiment. Looking ahead, we see promising scope therefore for bringing unemployment down sharply without risks of re-igniting inflation. Ironically, we have a government which needs to be persuaded towards greater monetary ease — not a typical democratic experience!

Appendix   The natural rate equations

The equations estimated for the quarterly model used FIML, with expectations exogenised but iterated between FIML estimates. In a few cases parameters in the model itself are somewhat different from the final FIML estimates; this arose because the model's parameters were taken from a slightly earlier iteration than the final one shown below. The relevant ones are shown in square brackets.

$$D\log RW = 0.13 + 0.37\ UNR + 0.20\log(BEN[1 + TAXL])$$
$$\qquad\quad (0.12)\ (0.31) \qquad\quad (0.07)$$

$$\qquad -0.014\log(U) - 0.20\log(RW[-2]) - 0.06PUE + 0.19PUE[-1]$$
$$\qquad\ (0.027) \qquad\quad (0.07) \qquad\qquad\quad (0.22) \qquad\ (0.22)$$

$$RXR = -0.3 + 1.33\log(RW[1 + BOSS + VAT]) + 1.0\log(1 + VAT) - 0.034TIME$$
$$\quad (0.1)\ (0.55)\ [1.53] \qquad\qquad\qquad\qquad\quad (-) \qquad\qquad (0.017)$$

$$\log(U) = 22.7 - 2.04\log(Y) + 0.61\log(RW[1 + BOSS + VAT])$$
$$\qquad\quad (7.8)\ \ (0.72)\ [2.15]\ (0.55)\ [0.79]$$

$$\qquad + 0.011TIME + 0.79\log(U[-1]) + 0.31ERROR[-1]$$
$$\qquad\ (0.0052) \qquad (0.10) \qquad\qquad (0.09)$$

$$XVOL/0.32Y^* = 10.4 + 0.54Log(WT) - 1.2\log(Y) - 0.44(0.6RXR + 0.4RXR^*)$$
$$\qquad\qquad\quad (5.7) \quad (0.23) \qquad\qquad (0.62) \qquad\ (0.24)$$

The resulting coefficients of the reduced form, for the natural rate of unemployment, are as follows:

$$\log(U^*) = 11.2UNR + 5.3\log(1 + BOSS) + 5.0\log(BEN[1 + TAXL])$$
$$\qquad\quad (7.0) \qquad\ (4.0) \qquad\qquad\qquad (3.9)$$

$$\qquad + 0.0023TIME + 7.4\log(1 + VAT) - 2.72\log(WT)$$
$$\qquad\ (0.03) \qquad\quad (4.7) \qquad\qquad (2.13)$$

+ constant and dummies for productivity shifts (see below) (standard errors bracketed)

The terms used are:

$*$ = equilibrium ('natural')

U = unemployment

Y = output

RXR = real exchange rate (CPI-based)

RW = real wage (W/CPI)
$BOSS$ = employed tax rate on wages
VAT = indirect tax rate
UNR = unionisation rate
BEN = value (real) of unemployment package
$TAXL$ = employee tax rate on wages (including national insurance, net of in-work benefit rate)
WT = world trade
PUE = unanticipated price inflation

Productivity Shift Dummies

(1) One from 1983 picks up the effect of the rise in union sector productivity and associated wage rises (as poor practices were bought out) — this raises the log of U^* (as union workers are shaken out) by 0.12 in 1983, falling slowly with UNR to 0.10 in 1992.
(2) A second from 1987 picks up a further trend in productivity growth raising labour's marginal product generally and also wages — this on balance reduces unemployment, cumulating to a reduction of 0.02 in the log of the natural rate of unemployment.

Note

1 We are grateful for useful comments to Samuel Brittan, Andrew Britton, and other conference participants. This work has been partly supported by a grant from the Esmée Fairbairn Trust.

References

Andrews, M., Minford, P. and Riley, S. (1990), 'On comparing macroeconomic models using non-nested tests', Working Paper 90/03, Liverpool Research Group in Macroeconomics, University of Liverpool.
Layard, R. and Nickell, S. (1985), 'The causes of British unemployment', *National Institute Economic Review*, 111, February.
Manning, A. (1993), 'Wage bargaining and the Phillips Curve: the identification and specification of aggregate wage equations', *Economic Journal*, 103, 98–118.
Matthews, K.G.P. and Minford, P. (1987), 'Mrs. Thatcher's economic policies 1979–86', *Economic Policy* (The Conservative Revolution: a special report), Cambridge University Press.
Matthews, K.G.P., Minford, P. and Riley, J. (1986), 'The forecast performance of the

Liverpool Group: the record straightened', *Quarterly Economic Bulletin*, Liverpool Research Group in Macroeconomics, 7 (1).

Minford, P. (1992) *Rational expectations — an introductory handbook*, Oxford, Basil Blackwell.

Minford, P., Sprague, A., Matthews, K.G.P. and Marwaha, S. (1984), 'The Liverpool Macroeconomic model of the United Kingdom', *Economic Modelling*, 1, January.

Minford, P., Matthews, K.G.P. and Rastogi, A. (1990), 'A quarterly version of the Liverpool model of the UK', Working Paper 90/06, Liverpool research Group in Macroeconomics, University of Liverpool.

Parkin, M. and Bade, R. (1990), *Modern Macroeconomics*, Phillip Allan.